PETER PORKER, THE SPECTACULAR

SPIDER-HAM

IN

APORKALYPSE NOW

PETER PORKER, THE SPECTACULAR SPIDER-HAM

in

APORKALYPSE NOW

WRITER:
ZEB WELLS

ARTIST:
WILL ROBSON

COLOR ARTIST:
ERICK ARCINIEGA

LETTERER:
VC's JOE CARAMAGNA

COVER ART:
WENDELL DALIT (#1) AND **WILL ROBSON** & **ERICK ARCINIEGA** (#2-5)

ASSISTANT EDITOR:
DANNY KHAZEM

EDITOR:
DEVIN LEWIS

EXECUTIVE EDITOR:
NICK LOWE

PANELS FROM PETER PORKER, THE SPECTACULAR SPIDER-HAM #15
STEVE MELLOR, JOE ALBELO, PIERRE FOURNIER, JANICE CHIANG & **JULIANNA FERRITER**

COLLECTION EDITOR: **JENNIFER GRÜNWALD**
ASSISTANT MANAGING EDITOR: **MAIA LOY**
ASSISTANT MANAGING EDITOR: **LISA MONTALBANO**
EDITOR, SPECIAL PROJECTS: **MARK D. BEAZLEY**

VP PRODUCTION & SPECIAL PROJECTS: **JEFF YOUNGQUIST**
BOOK DESIGNER: **ADAM DEL RE**
SVP PRINT, SALES & MARKETING: **DAVID GABRIEL**
EDITOR IN CHIEF: **C.B. CEBULSKI**

SPIDER-MAN
CREATED BY
STAN LEE &
STEVE DITKO

SPIDER-HAM: APORKALYPSE NOW. Contains material originally published in magazine form as SPIDER-HAM (2019) #1-5. First printing 2020. ISBN 978-1-302-92162-0. Published by MARVEL WORLDWIDE, INC., a subsidiary of MARVEL ENTERTAINMENT, LLC. OFFICE OF PUBLICATION: 1290 Avenue of the Americas, New York, NY 10104. © 2020 MARVEL No similarity between any of the names, characters, persons, and/or institutions in this magazine with those of any living or dead person or institution is intended, and any such similarity which may exist is purely coincidental. **Printed in Canada.** KEVIN FEIGE, Chief Creative Officer; DAN BUCKLEY, President, Marvel Entertainment; JOHN NEE, Publisher; JOE QUESADA, EVP & Creative Director; TOM BREVOORT, SVP of Publishing; DAVID BOGART, Associate Publisher & SVP of Talent Affairs; Publishing & Partnership; DAVID GABRIEL, VP of Print & Digital Publishing; JEFF YOUNGQUIST, VP of Production & Special Projects; DAN CARR, Executive Director of Publishing Technology; ALEX MORALES, Director of Publishing Operations; DAN EDINGTON, Managing Editor; SUSAN CRESPI, Production Manager; STAN LEE, Chairman Emeritus. For information regarding advertising in Marvel Comics or on Marvel.com, please contact Vit DeBellis, Custom Solutions & Integrated Advertising Manager, at vdebellis@marvel.com. For Marvel subscription inquiries, please call 888-511-5480. **Manufactured between 6/19/2020 and 7/21/2020 by SOLISCO PRINTERS, SCOTT, QC, CANADA.**

10 9 8 7 6 5 4 3 2 1

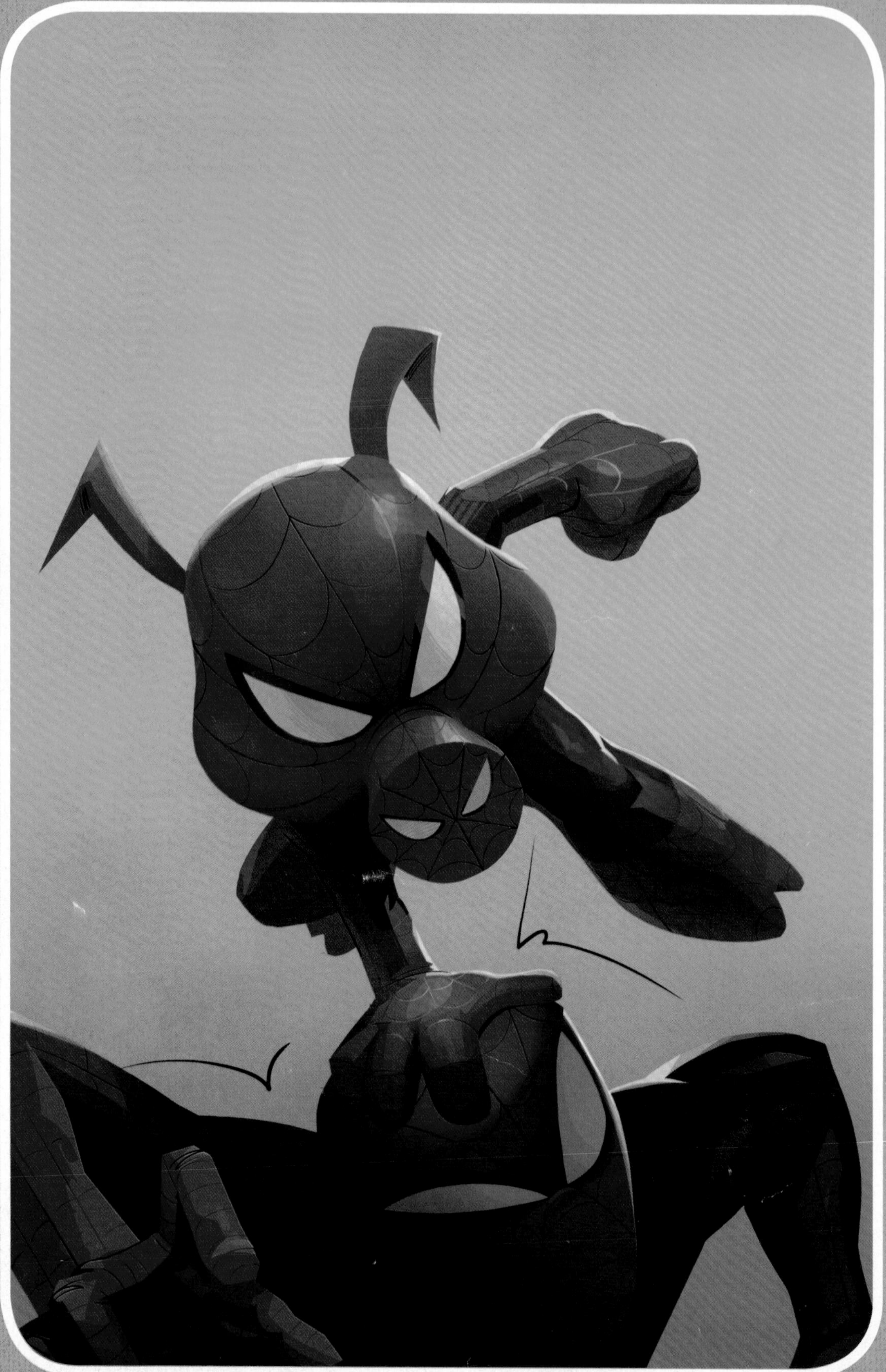

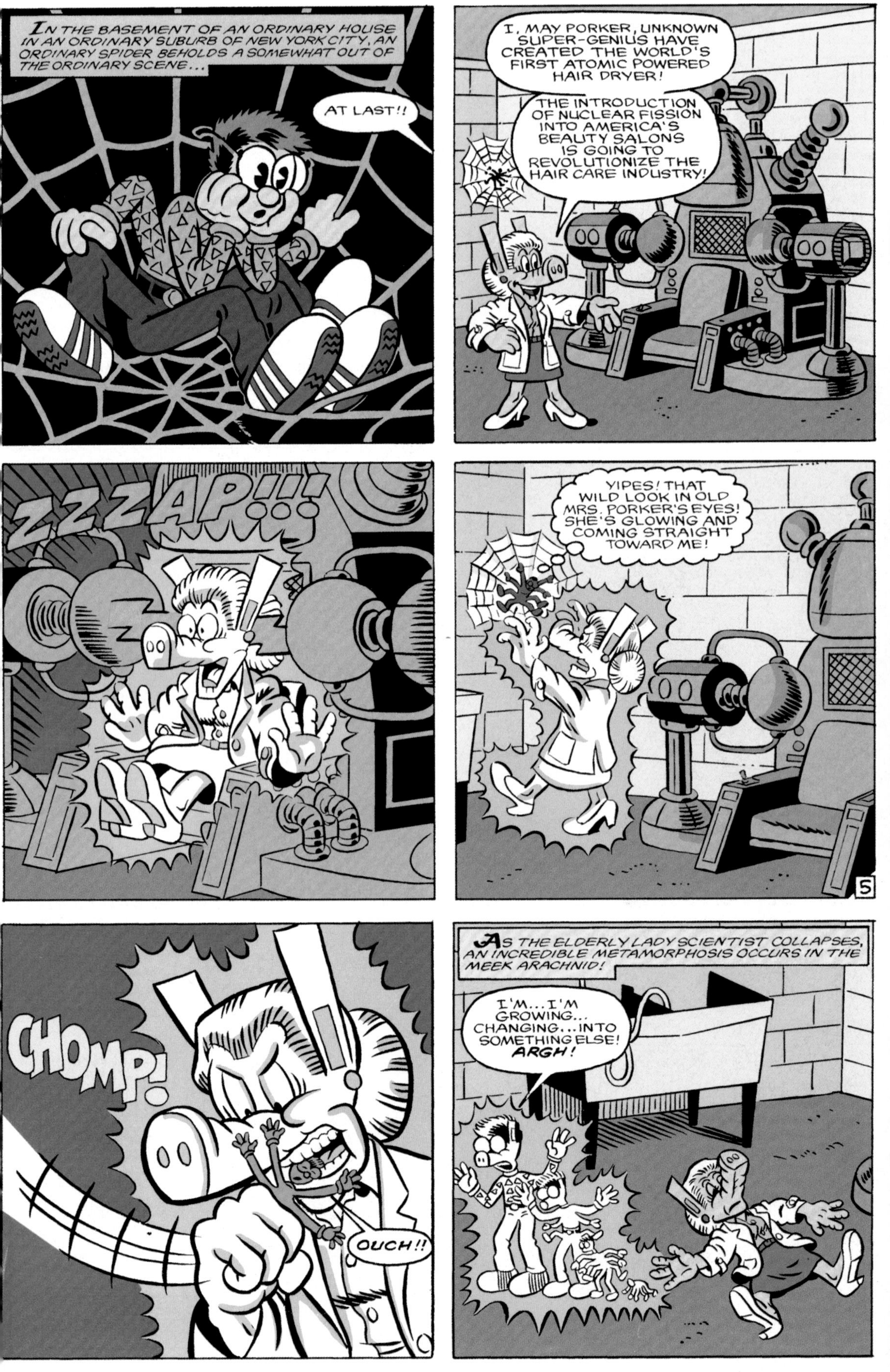
IN THE BASEMENT OF AN ORDINARY HOUSE IN AN ORDINARY SUBURB OF NEW YORK CITY, AN ORDINARY SPIDER BEHOLDS A SOMEWHAT OUT OF THE ORDINARY SCENE...
AT LAST!!
I, MAY PORKER, UNKNOWN SUPER-GENIUS HAVE CREATED THE WORLD'S FIRST ATOMIC POWERED HAIR DRYER!
THE INTRODUCTION OF NUCLEAR FISSION INTO AMERICA'S BEAUTY SALONS IS GOING TO REVOLUTIONIZE THE HAIR CARE INDUSTRY!
ZZZAP!!!
YIPES! THAT WILD LOOK IN OLD MRS. PORKER'S EYES! SHE'S GLOWING AND COMING STRAIGHT TOWARD ME!
5
CHOMP!
OUCH!!
AS THE ELDERLY LADY SCIENTIST COLLAPSES, AN INCREDIBLE METAMORPHOSIS OCCURS IN THE MEEK ARACHNID!
I'M... I'M GROWING... CHANGING... INTO SOMETHING ELSE! ARGH!

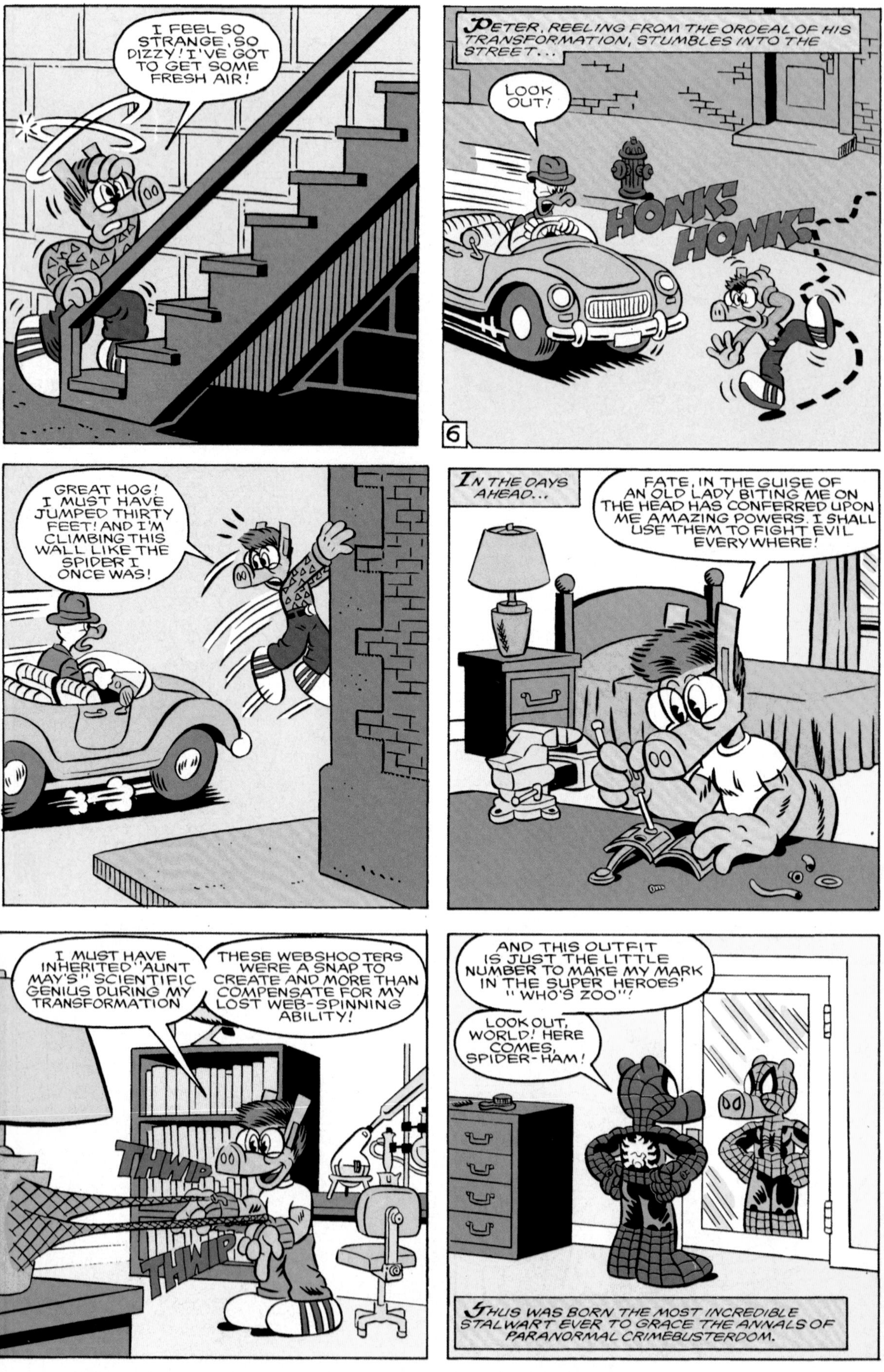
I FEEL SO STRANGE, SO DIZZY! I'VE GOT TO GET SOME FRESH AIR!
PETER, REELING FROM THE ORDEAL OF HIS TRANSFORMATION, STUMBLES INTO THE STREET...
LOOK OUT!
HONK! HONK!
6
GREAT HOG! I MUST HAVE JUMPED THIRTY FEET! AND I'M CLIMBING THIS WALL LIKE THE SPIDER I ONCE WAS!
IN THE DAYS AHEAD...
FATE, IN THE GUISE OF AN OLD LADY BITING ME ON THE HEAD HAS CONFERRED UPON ME AMAZING POWERS. I SHALL USE THEM TO FIGHT EVIL EVERYWHERE!
I MUST HAVE INHERITED "AUNT MAY'S" SCIENTIFIC GENIUS DURING MY TRANSFORMATION
THESE WEBSHOOTERS WERE A SNAP TO CREATE AND MORE THAN COMPENSATE FOR MY LOST WEB-SPINNING ABILITY!
THWIP
THWIP
AND THIS OUTFIT IS JUST THE LITTLE NUMBER TO MAKE MY MARK IN THE SUPER HEROES' "WHO'S ZOO"!
LOOK OUT, WORLD! HERE COMES, SPIDER-HAM!
THUS WAS BORN THE MOST INCREDIBLE STALWART EVER TO GRACE THE ANNALS OF PARANORMAL CRIMEBUSTERDOM.

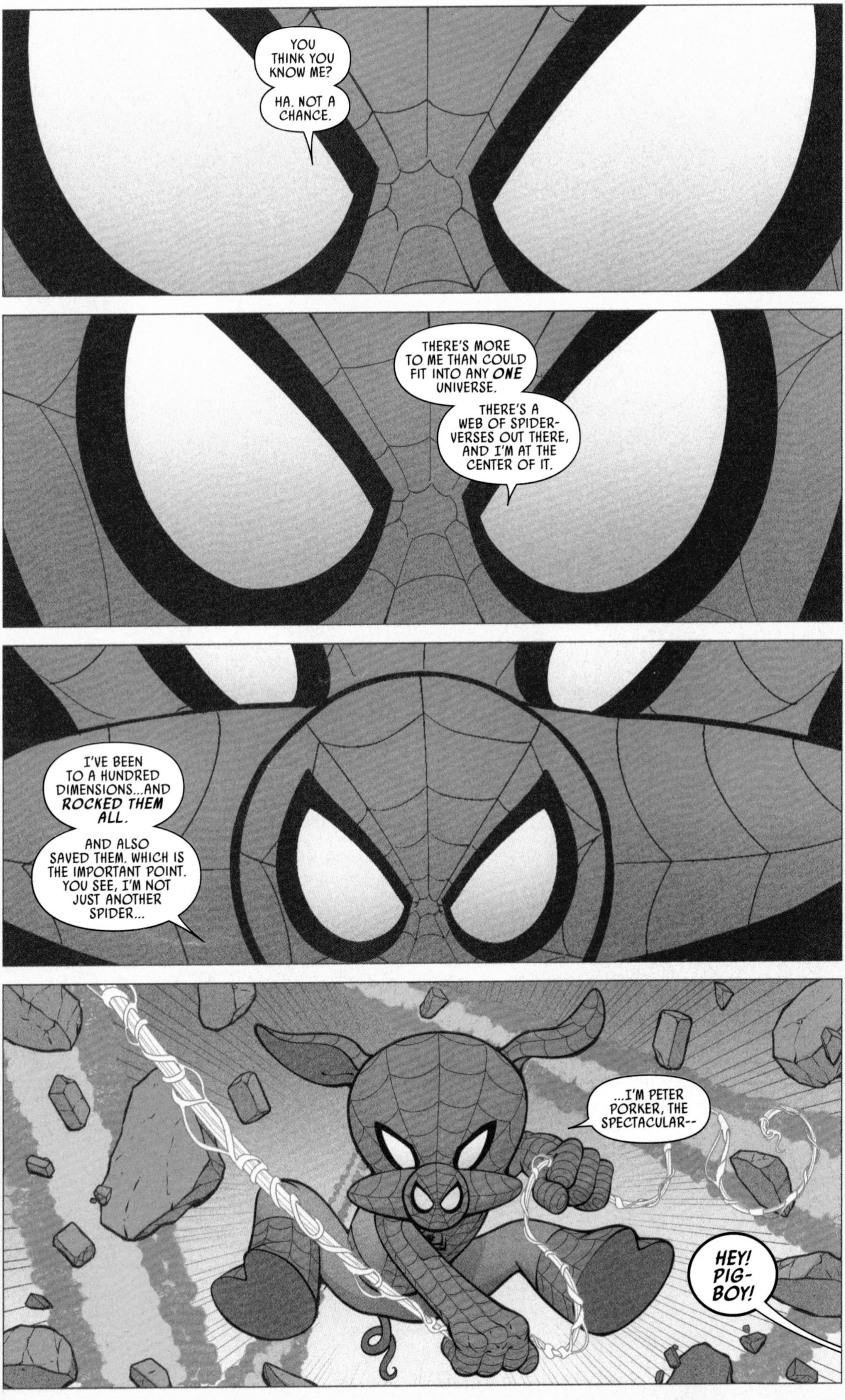
YOU THINK YOU KNOW ME?
HA. NOT A CHANCE.
THERE'S MORE TO ME THAN COULD FIT INTO ANY *ONE* UNIVERSE.
THERE'S A WEB OF SPIDER-VERSES OUT THERE, AND I'M AT THE CENTER OF IT.
I'VE BEEN TO A HUNDRED DIMENSIONS...AND *ROCKED THEM ALL.*
AND ALSO SAVED THEM. WHICH IS THE IMPORTANT POINT. YOU SEE, I'M NOT JUST ANOTHER SPIDER...
...I'M PETER PORKER, THE SPECTACULAR--
HEY! PIG-BOY!

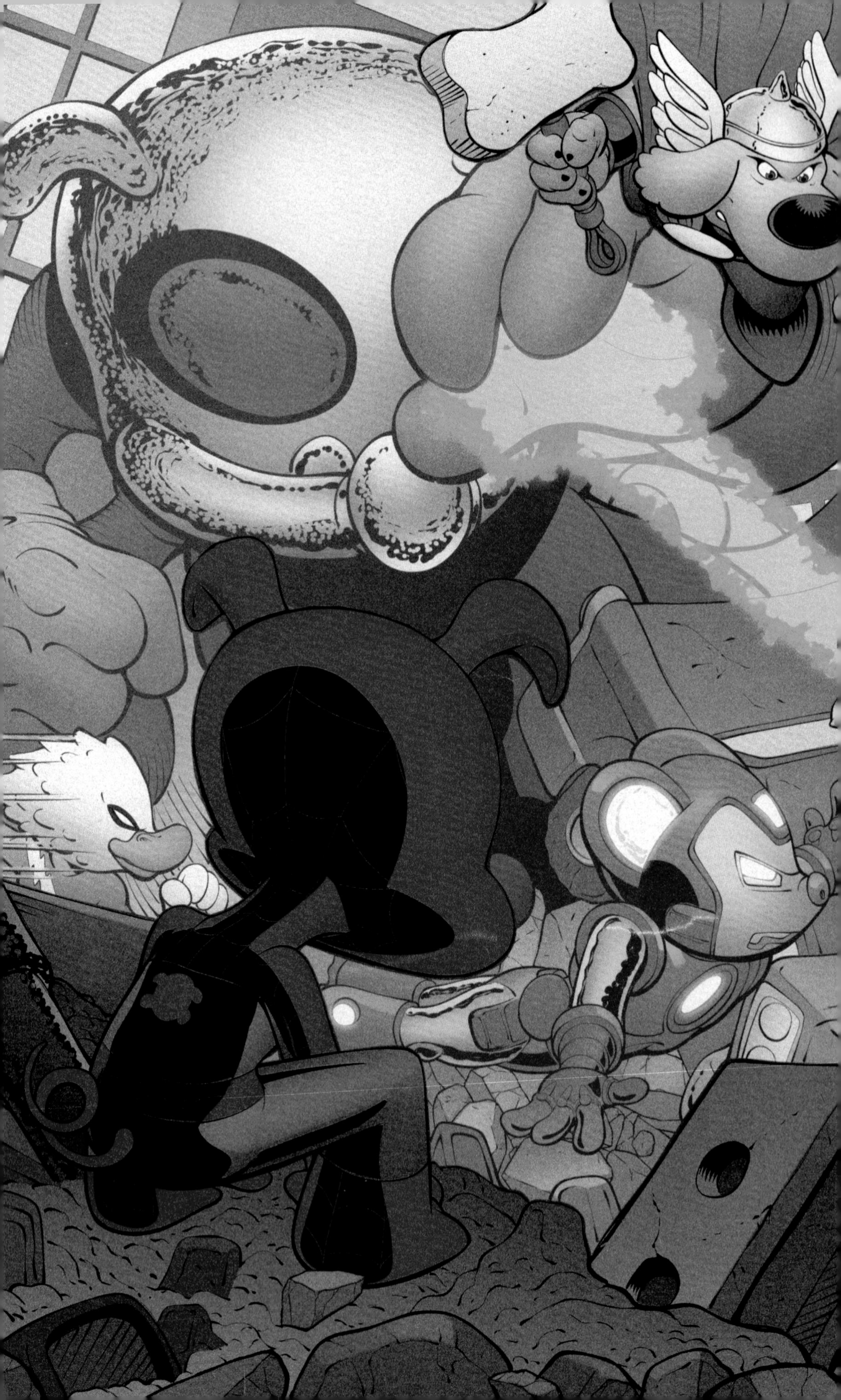

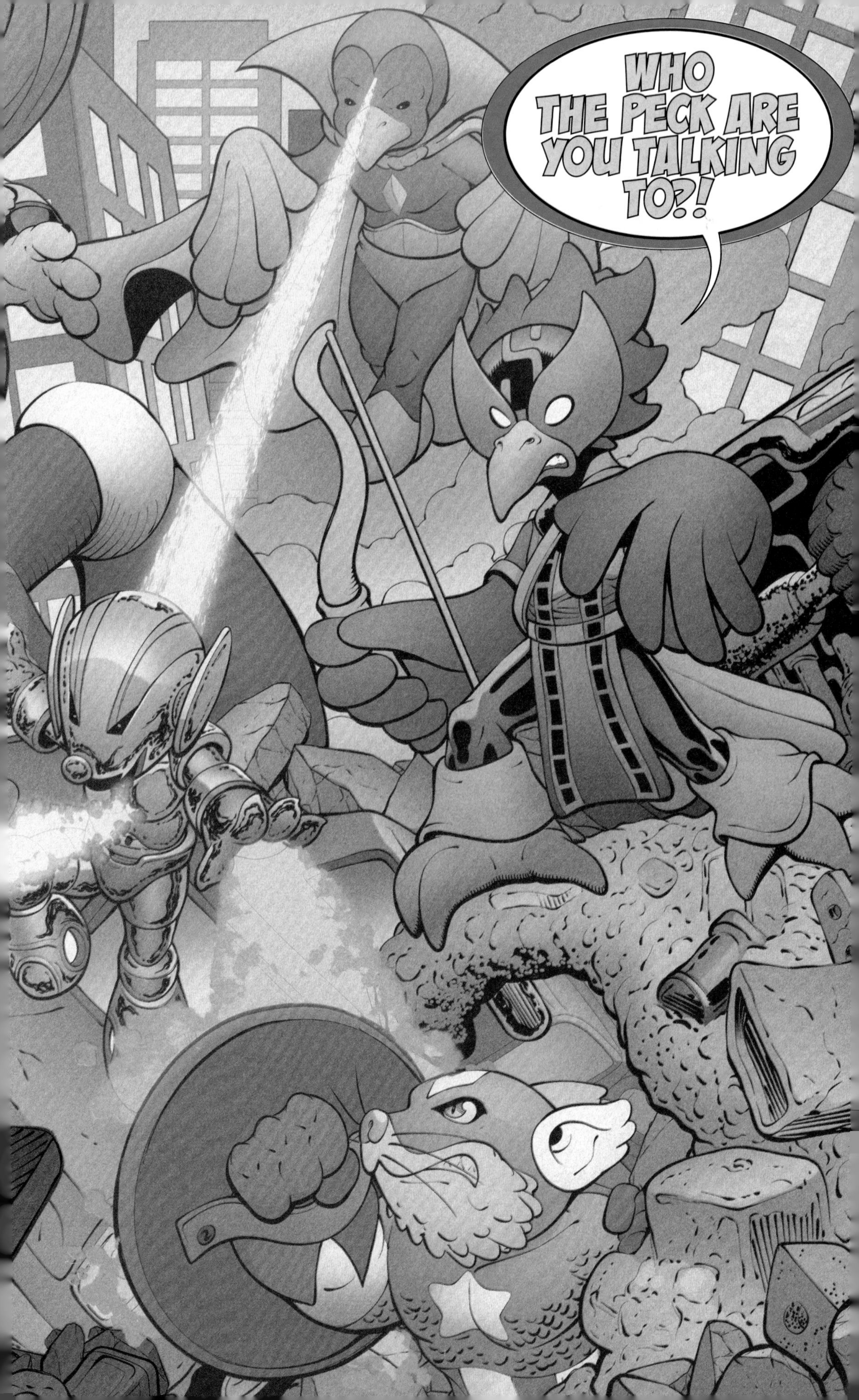
WHO THE PECK ARE YOU TALKING TO?!

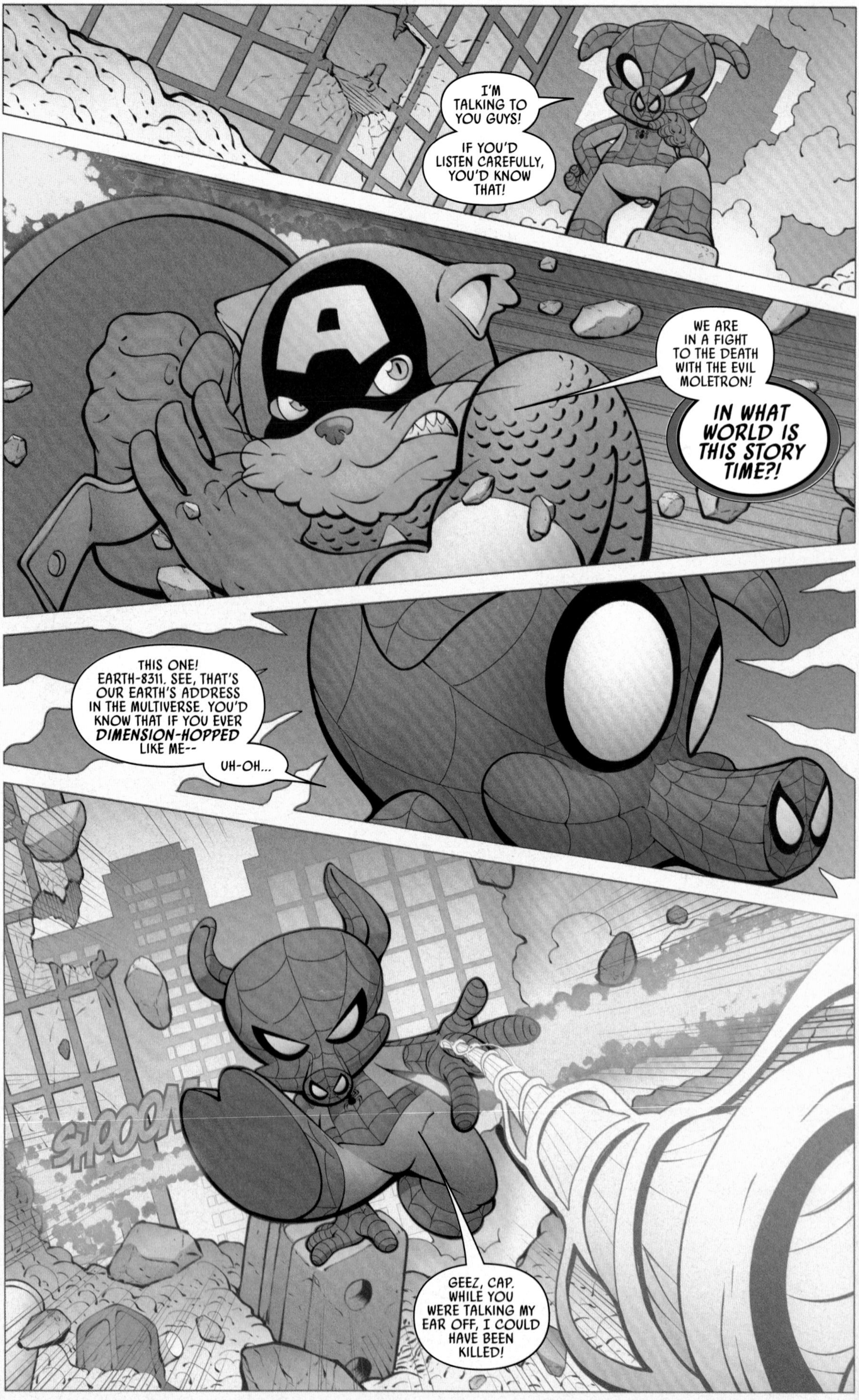

I'M TALKING TO YOU GUYS!
IF YOU'D LISTEN CAREFULLY, YOU'D KNOW THAT!
WE ARE IN A FIGHT TO THE DEATH WITH THE EVIL MOLETRON!
IN WHAT WORLD IS THIS STORY TIME?!
THIS ONE! EARTH-8311. SEE, THAT'S OUR EARTH'S ADDRESS IN THE MULTIVERSE. YOU'D KNOW THAT IF YOU EVER DIMENSION-HOPPED LIKE ME--
UH-OH...
SHOOOM
GEEZ, CAP. WHILE YOU WERE TALKING MY EAR OFF, I COULD HAVE BEEN KILLED!

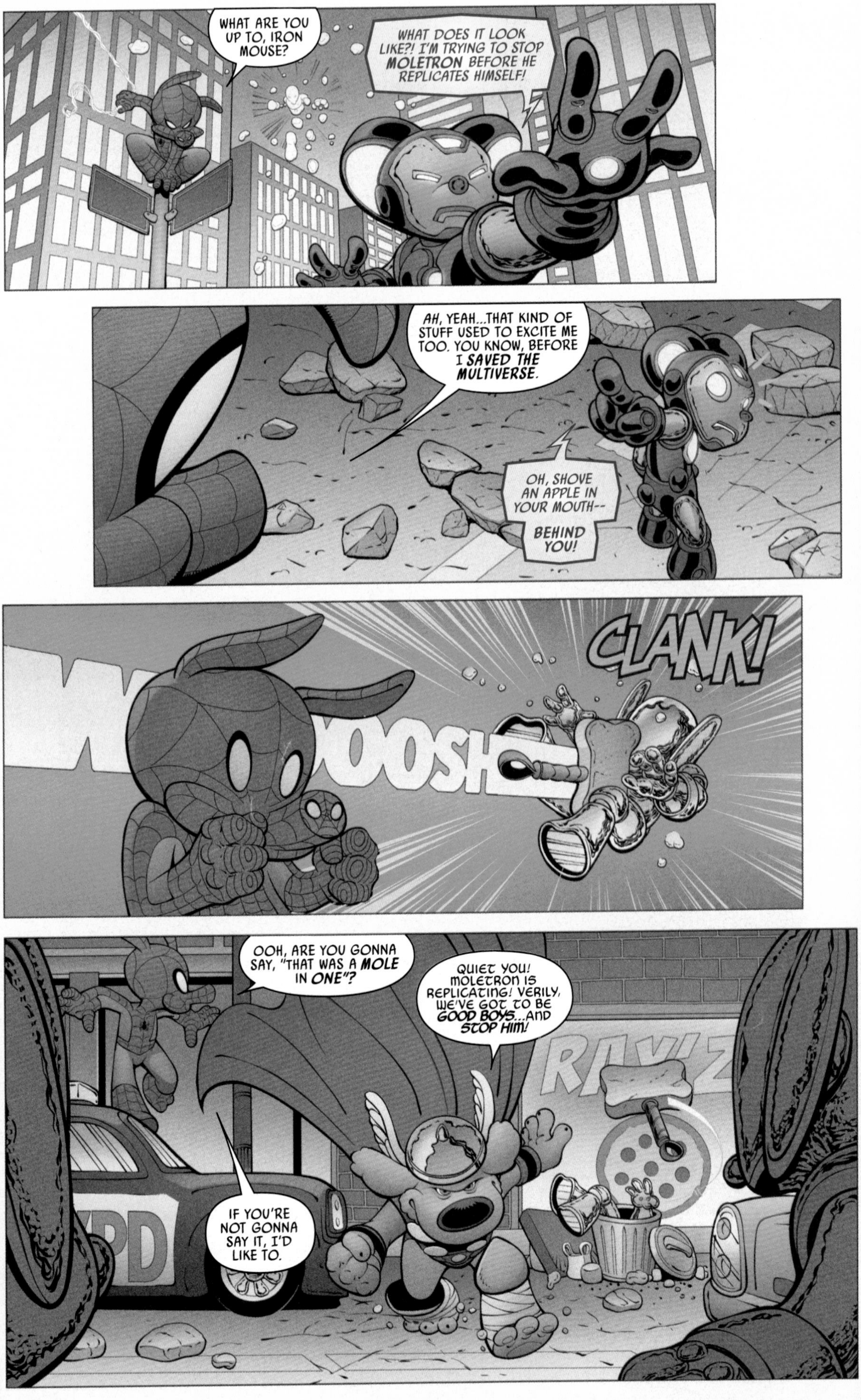
WHAT ARE YOU UP TO, IRON MOUSE?
WHAT DOES IT LOOK LIKE?! I'M TRYING TO STOP MOLETRON BEFORE HE REPLICATES HIMSELF!
AH, YEAH...THAT KIND OF STUFF USED TO EXCITE ME TOO. YOU KNOW, BEFORE I SAVED THE MULTIVERSE.
OH, SHOVE AN APPLE IN YOUR MOUTH--
BEHIND YOU!
WOOOSH
CLANK!
OOH, ARE YOU GONNA SAY, "THAT WAS A MOLE IN ONE"?
QUIET YOU! MOLETRON IS REPLICATING! VERILY, WE'VE GOT TO BE GOOD BOYS...AND STOP HIM!
IF YOU'RE NOT GONNA SAY IT, I'D LIKE TO.

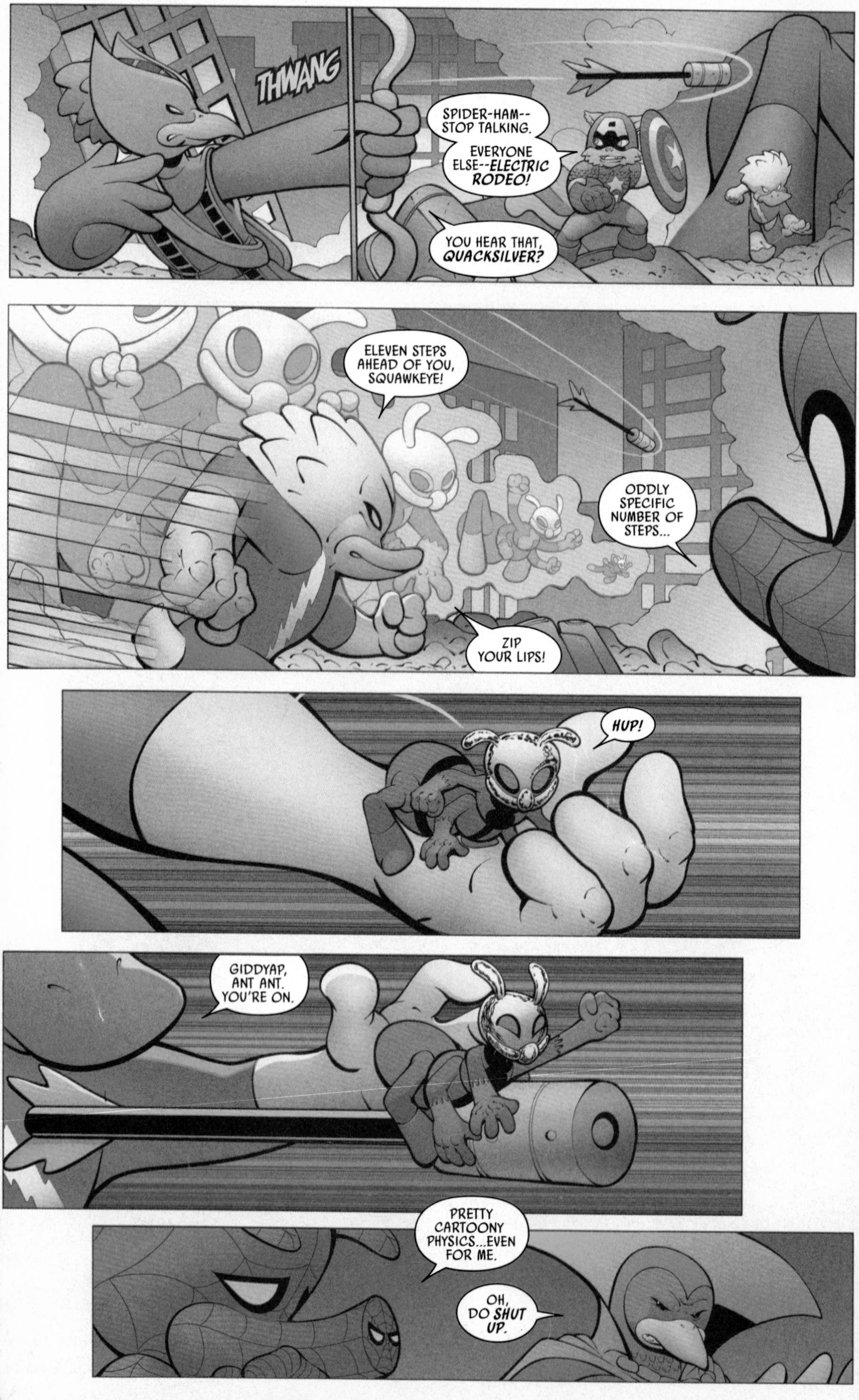
THWANG
SPIDER-HAM-- STOP TALKING.
EVERYONE ELSE--ELECTRIC RODEO!
YOU HEAR THAT, QUACKSILVER?
ELEVEN STEPS AHEAD OF YOU, SQUAWKEYE!
ODDLY SPECIFIC NUMBER OF STEPS...
ZIP YOUR LIPS!
HUP!
GIDDYAP, ANT ANT. YOU'RE ON.
PRETTY CARTOONY PHYSICS...EVEN FOR ME.
OH, DO SHUT UP.

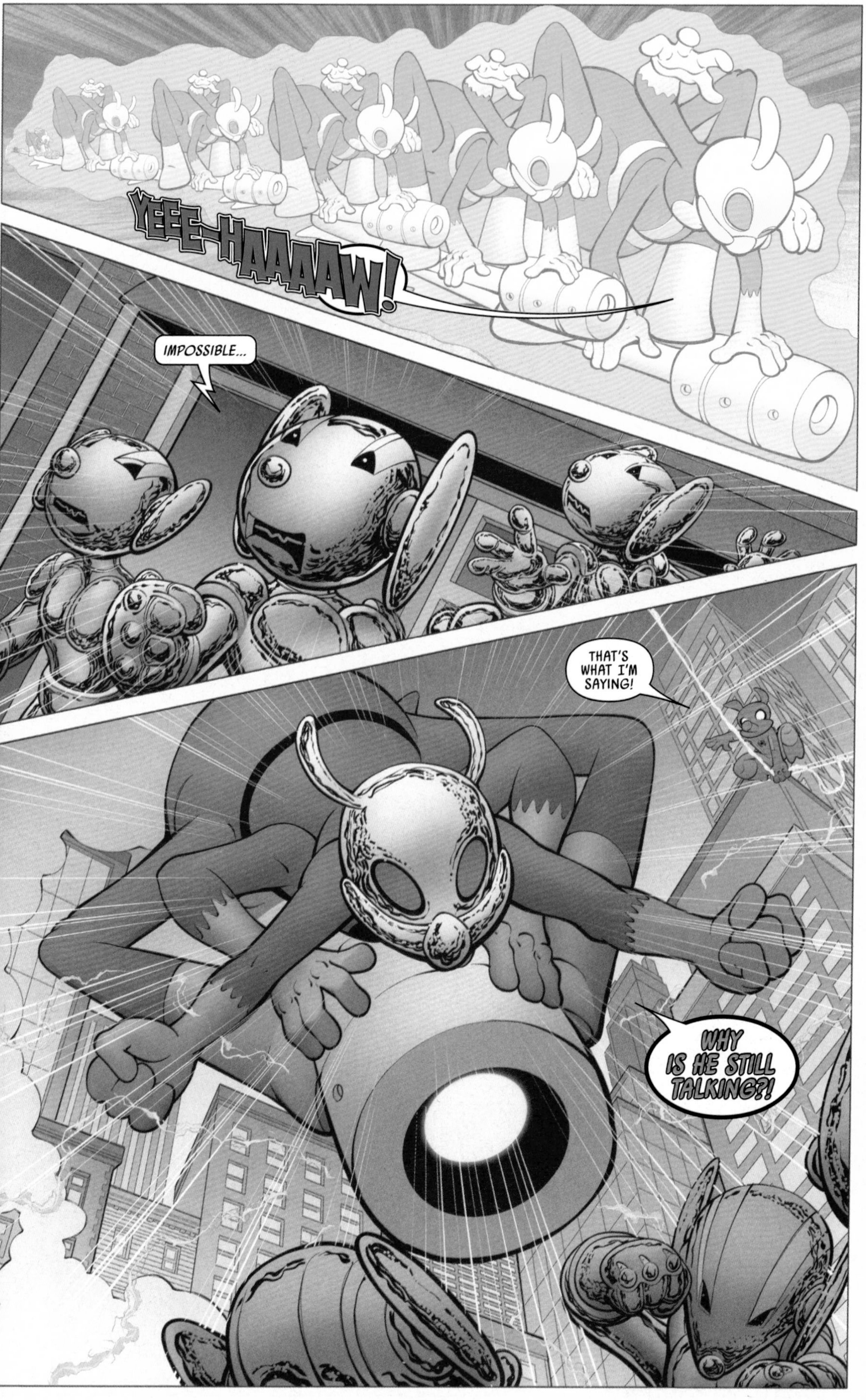
YEEE-HAAAAAW!
IMPOSSIBLE...
THAT'S WHAT I'M SAYING!
WHY IS HE STILL TALKING?!

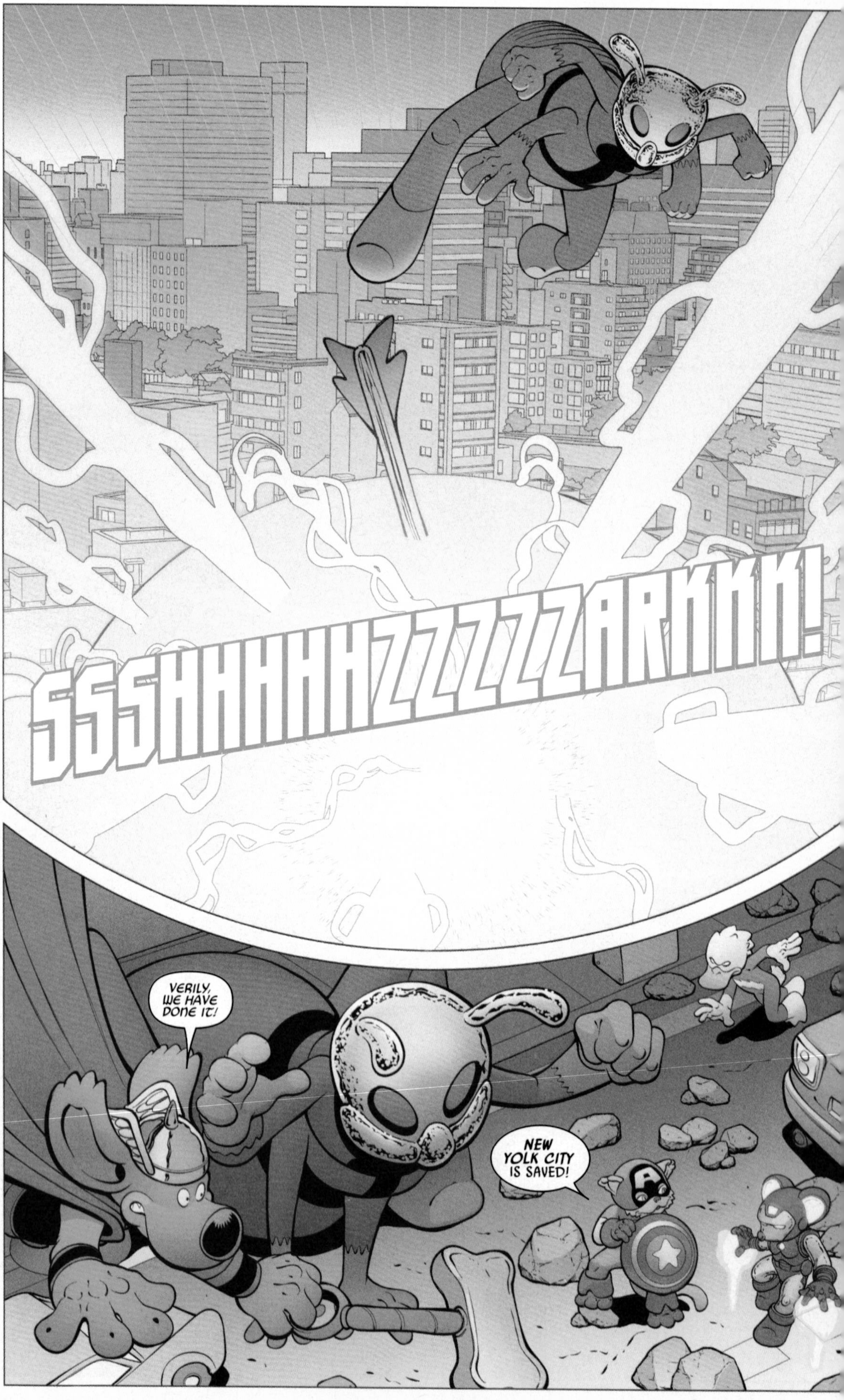
SSSHHHHHZZZZZZARKKKK!
VERILY, WE HAVE DONE IT!
NEW YOLK CITY IS SAVED!

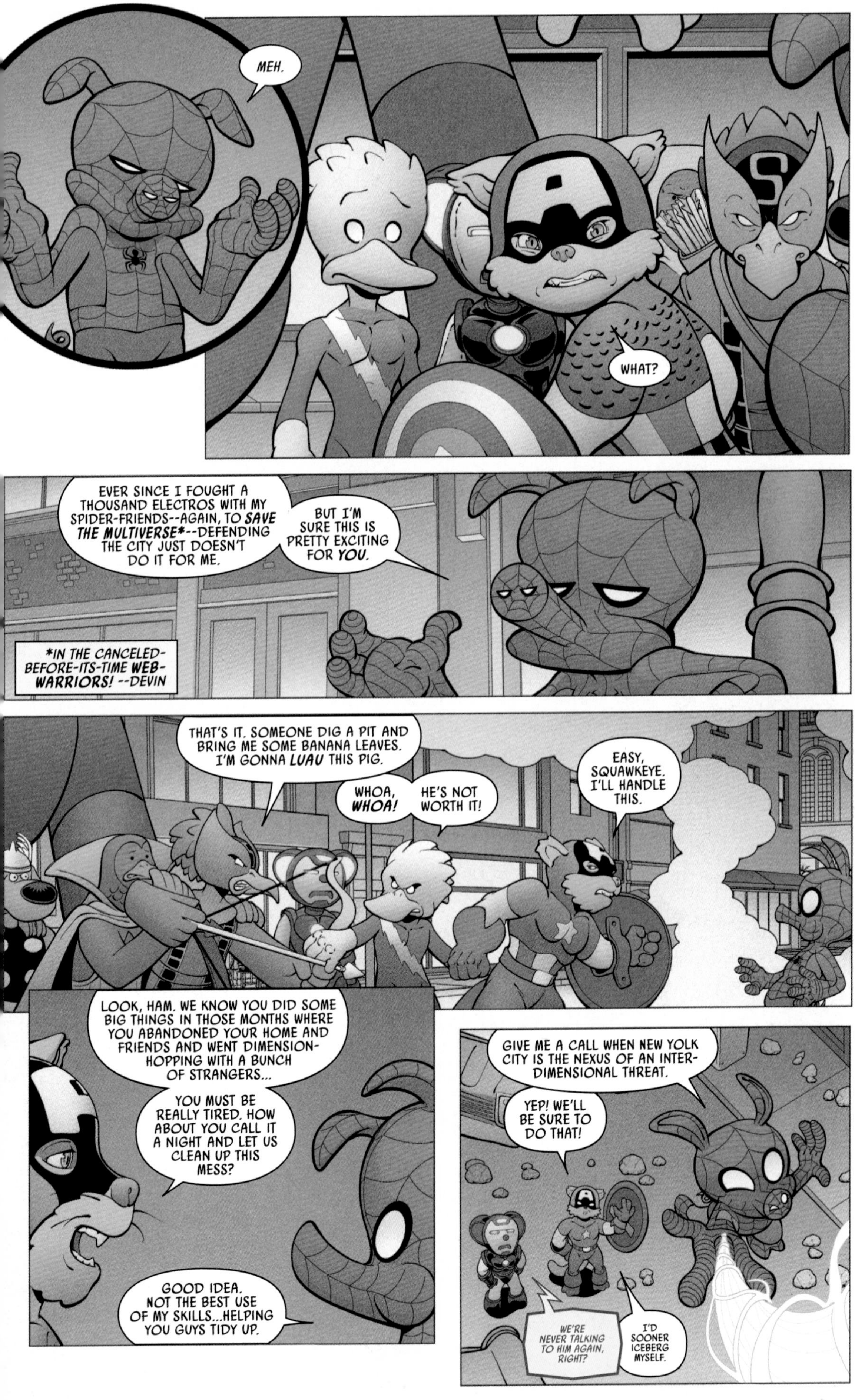
MEH.
WHAT?
EVER SINCE I FOUGHT A THOUSAND ELECTROS WITH MY SPIDER-FRIENDS--AGAIN, TO SAVE THE MULTIVERSE*--DEFENDING THE CITY JUST DOESN'T DO IT FOR ME.
BUT I'M SURE THIS IS PRETTY EXCITING FOR YOU.
*IN THE CANCELED-BEFORE-ITS-TIME WEB-WARRIORS! --DEVIN
THAT'S IT. SOMEONE DIG A PIT AND BRING ME SOME BANANA LEAVES. I'M GONNA LUAU THIS PIG.
WHOA, WHOA!
HE'S NOT WORTH IT!
EASY, SQUAWKEYE. I'LL HANDLE THIS.
LOOK, HAM. WE KNOW YOU DID SOME BIG THINGS IN THOSE MONTHS WHERE YOU ABANDONED YOUR HOME AND FRIENDS AND WENT DIMENSION-HOPPING WITH A BUNCH OF STRANGERS...
YOU MUST BE REALLY TIRED. HOW ABOUT YOU CALL IT A NIGHT AND LET US CLEAN UP THIS MESS?
GOOD IDEA. NOT THE BEST USE OF MY SKILLS...HELPING YOU GUYS TIDY UP.
GIVE ME A CALL WHEN NEW YOLK CITY IS THE NEXUS OF AN INTER-DIMENSIONAL THREAT.
YEP! WE'LL BE SURE TO DO THAT!
WE'RE NEVER TALKING TO HIM AGAIN, RIGHT?
I'D SOONER ICEBERG MYSELF.

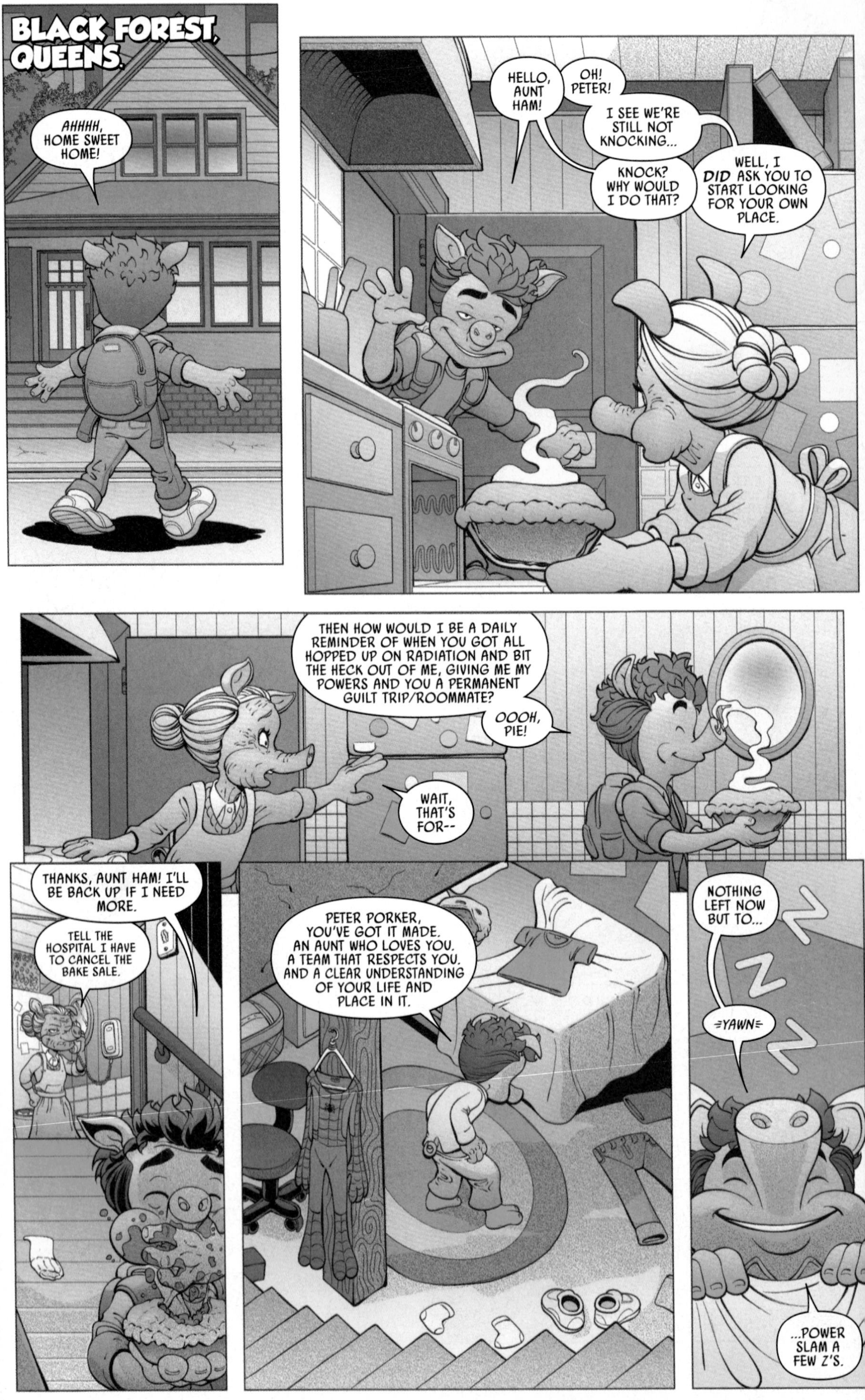
BLACK FOREST, QUEENS.
AHHHH, HOME SWEET HOME!
HELLO, AUNT HAM!
OH! PETER!
I SEE WE'RE STILL NOT KNOCKING...
KNOCK? WHY WOULD I DO THAT?
WELL, I DID ASK YOU TO START LOOKING FOR YOUR OWN PLACE.
THEN HOW WOULD I BE A DAILY REMINDER OF WHEN YOU GOT ALL HOPPED UP ON RADIATION AND BIT THE HECK OUT OF ME, GIVING ME MY POWERS AND YOU A PERMANENT GUILT TRIP/ROOMMATE?
OOOH, PIE!
WAIT, THAT'S FOR--
THANKS, AUNT HAM! I'LL BE BACK UP IF I NEED MORE.
TELL THE HOSPITAL I HAVE TO CANCEL THE BAKE SALE.
PETER PORKER, YOU'VE GOT IT MADE. AN AUNT WHO LOVES YOU. A TEAM THAT RESPECTS YOU. AND A CLEAR UNDERSTANDING OF YOUR LIFE AND PLACE IN IT.
NOTHING LEFT NOW BUT TO...
YAWN
...POWER SLAM A FEW Z'S.

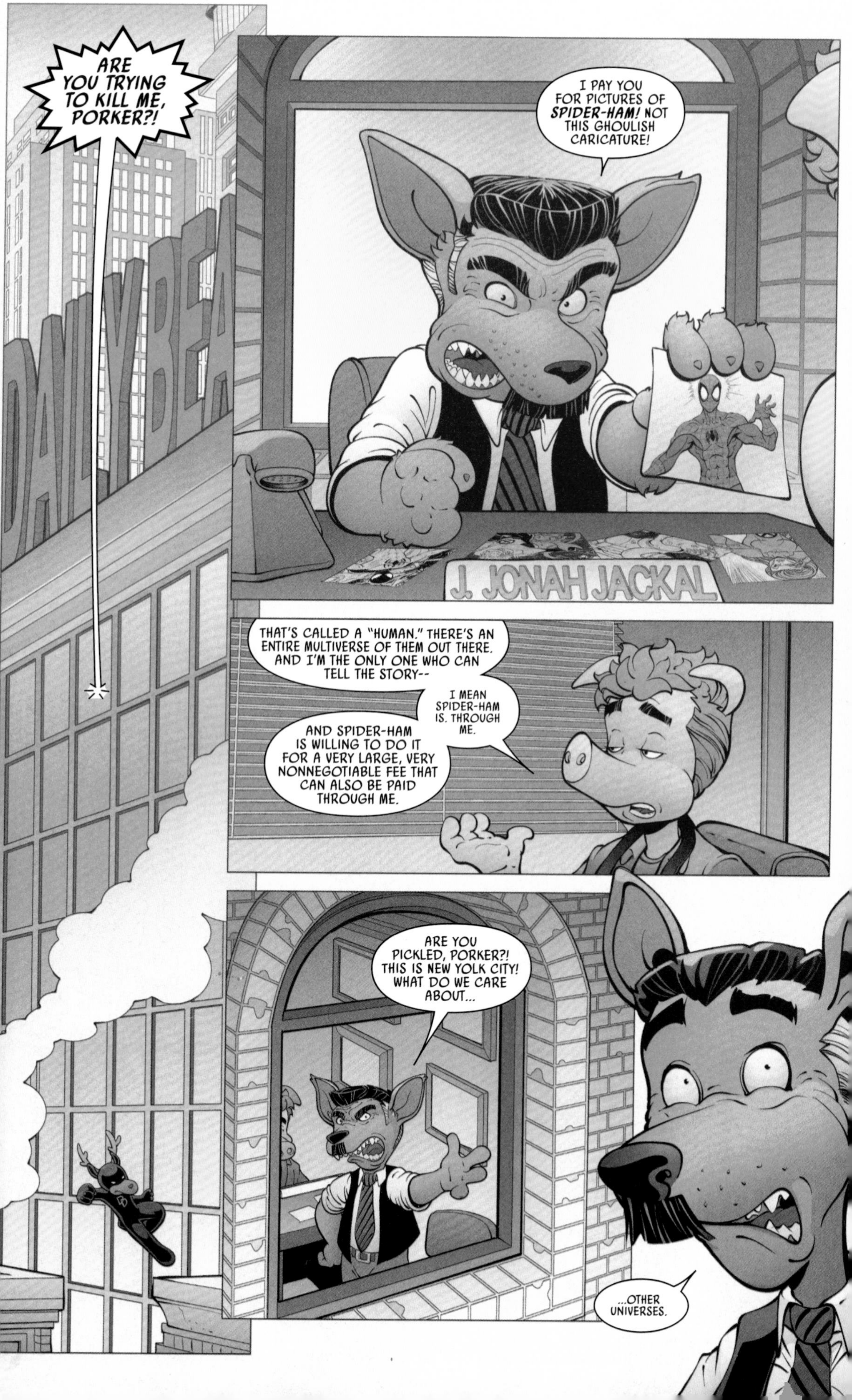
ARE YOU TRYING TO KILL ME, PORKER?!
I PAY YOU FOR PICTURES OF SPIDER-HAM! NOT THIS GHOULISH CARICATURE!
J. JONAH JACKAL
THAT'S CALLED A "HUMAN." THERE'S AN ENTIRE MULTIVERSE OF THEM OUT THERE. AND I'M THE ONLY ONE WHO CAN TELL THE STORY--
I MEAN SPIDER-HAM IS. THROUGH ME.
AND SPIDER-HAM IS WILLING TO DO IT FOR A VERY LARGE, VERY NONNEGOTIABLE FEE THAT CAN ALSO BE PAID THROUGH ME.
ARE YOU PICKLED, PORKER?! THIS IS NEW YOLK CITY! WHAT DO WE CARE ABOUT...
...OTHER UNIVERSES.

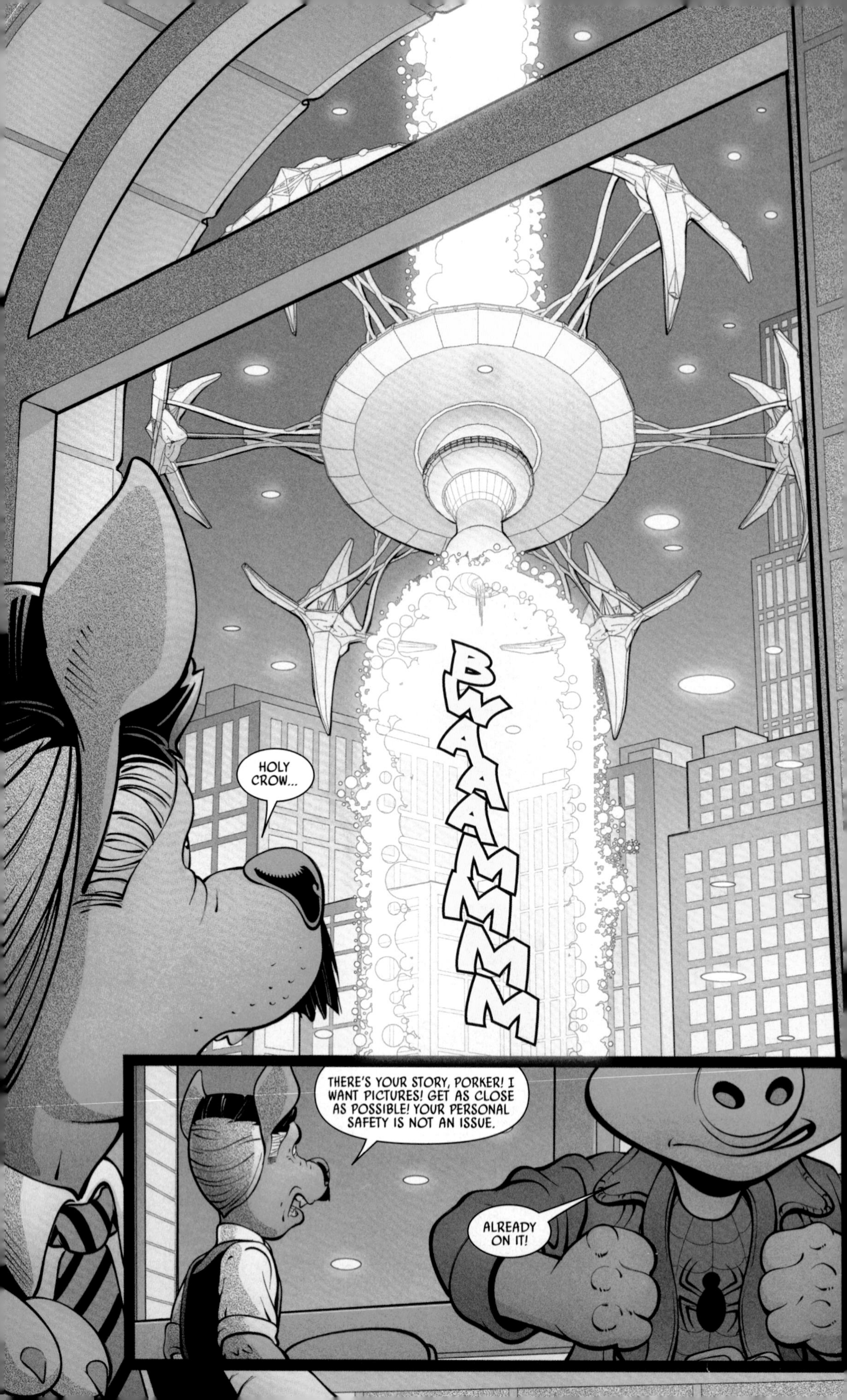
BWAAAMMMM
HOLY CROW...
THERE'S YOUR STORY, PORKER! I WANT PICTURES! GET AS CLOSE AS POSSIBLE! YOUR PERSONAL SAFETY IS NOT AN ISSUE.
ALREADY ON IT!

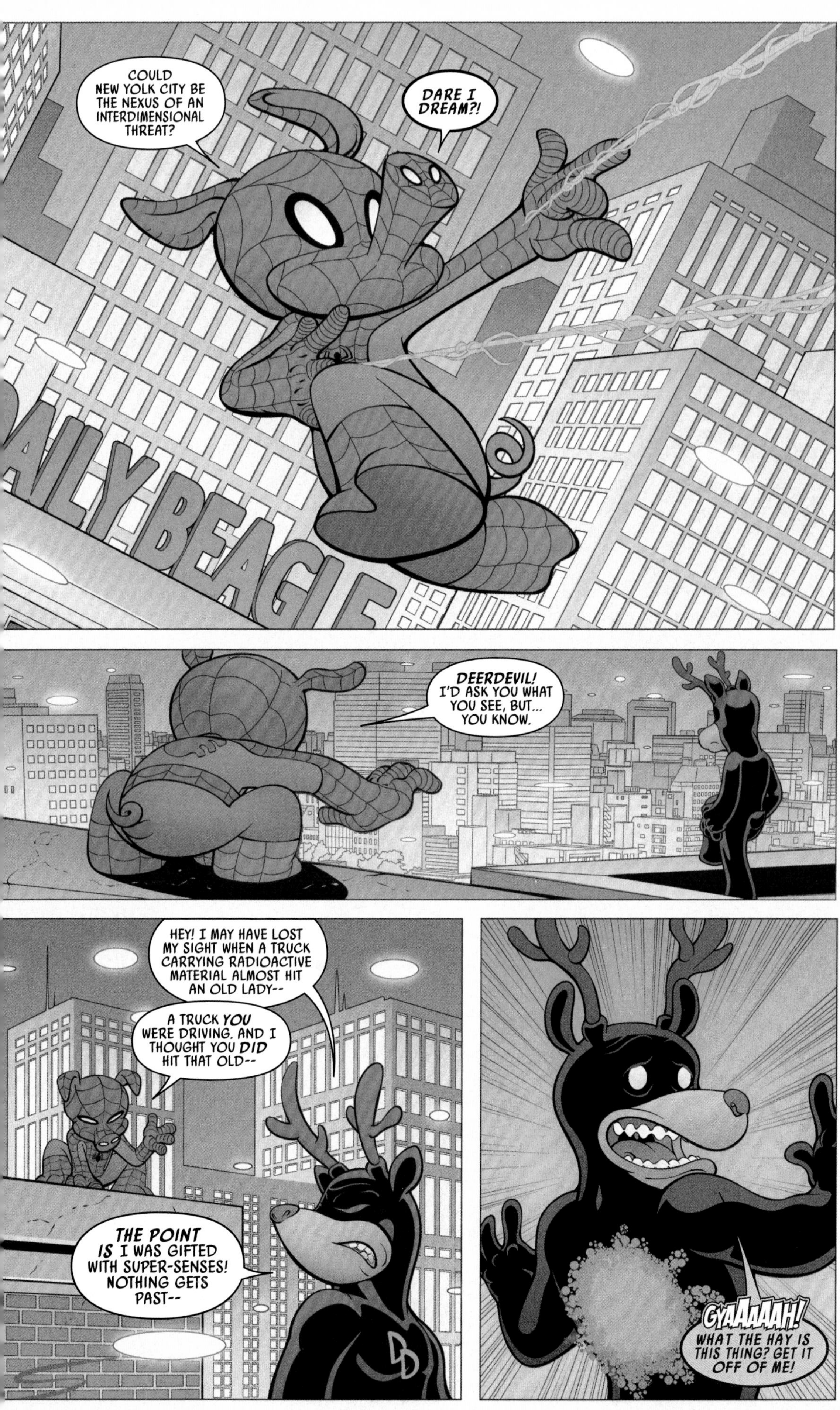

COULD NEW YOLK CITY BE THE NEXUS OF AN INTERDIMENSIONAL THREAT?
DARE I DREAM?!
DAILY BEAGLE
DEERDEVIL! I'D ASK YOU WHAT YOU SEE, BUT... YOU KNOW.
HEY! I MAY HAVE LOST MY SIGHT WHEN A TRUCK CARRYING RADIOACTIVE MATERIAL ALMOST HIT AN OLD LADY--
A TRUCK YOU WERE DRIVING, AND I THOUGHT YOU DID HIT THAT OLD--
THE POINT IS I WAS GIFTED WITH SUPER-SENSES! NOTHING GETS PAST--
GYAAAAAH!
WHAT THE HAY IS THIS THING? GET IT OFF OF ME!

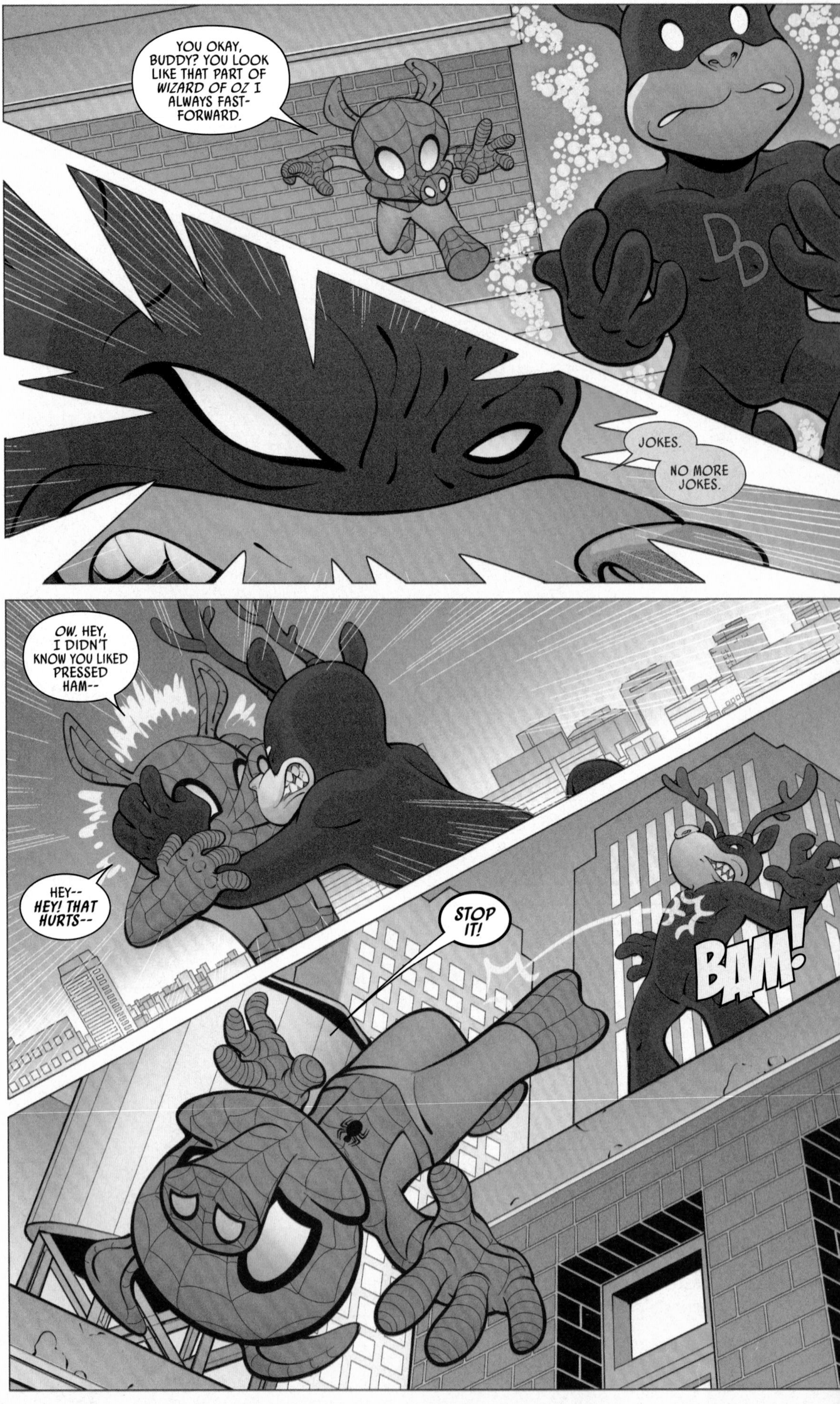

YOU OKAY, BUDDY? YOU LOOK LIKE THAT PART OF WIZARD OF OZ I ALWAYS FAST-FORWARD.
JOKES.
NO MORE JOKES.
OW. HEY, I DIDN'T KNOW YOU LIKED PRESSED HAM--
HEY-- HEY! THAT HURTS--
STOP IT!
BAM!

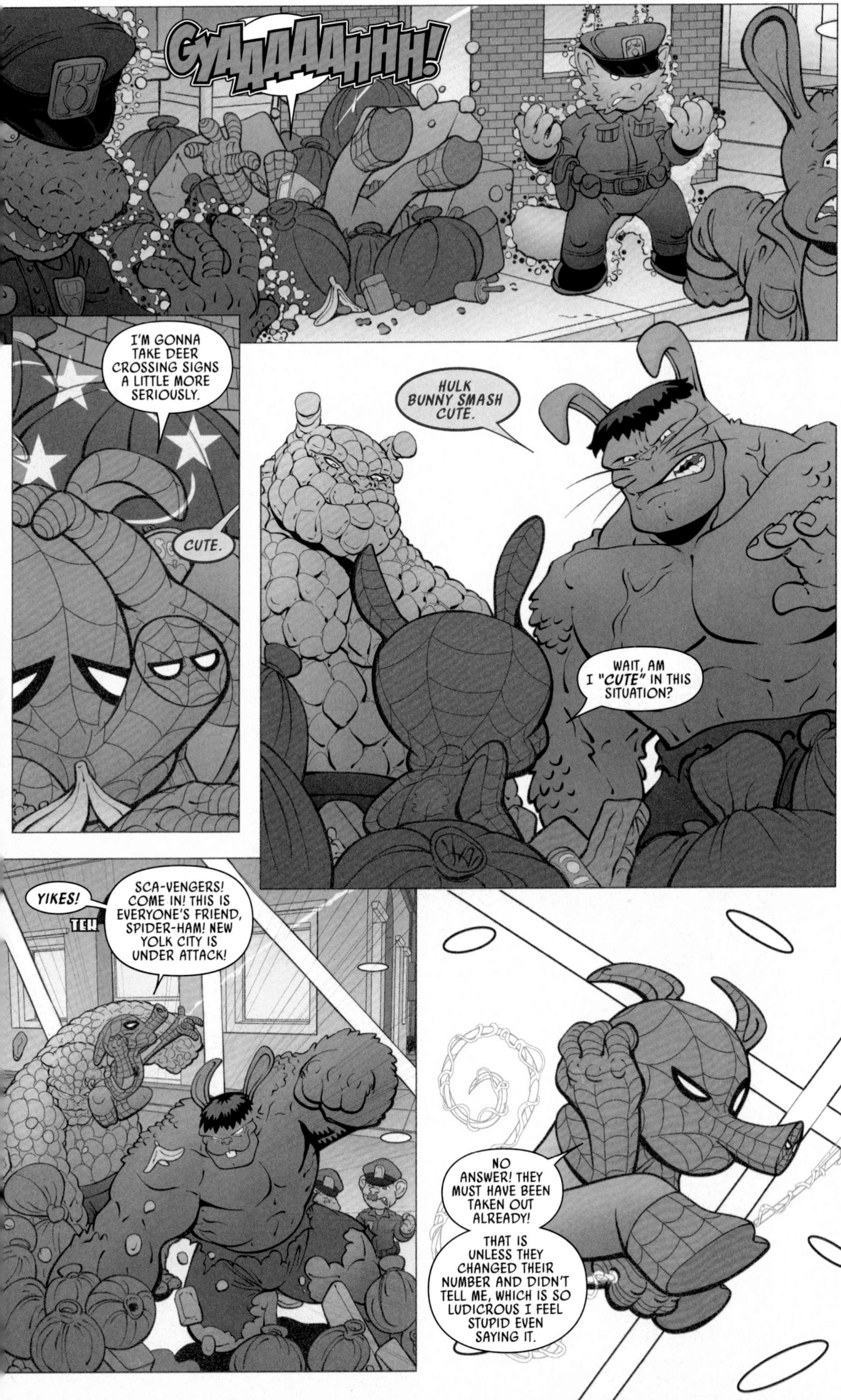
GYAAAAAHHH!
I'M GONNA TAKE DEER CROSSING SIGNS A LITTLE MORE SERIOUSLY.
CUTE.
HULK BUNNY SMASH CUTE.
WAIT, AM I "CUTE" IN THIS SITUATION?
YIKES!
SCA-VENGERS! COME IN! THIS IS EVERYONE'S FRIEND, SPIDER-HAM! NEW YOLK CITY IS UNDER ATTACK!
NO ANSWER! THEY MUST HAVE BEEN TAKEN OUT ALREADY!
THAT IS UNLESS THEY CHANGED THEIR NUMBER AND DIDN'T TELL ME, WHICH IS SO LUDICROUS I FEEL STUPID EVEN SAYING IT.

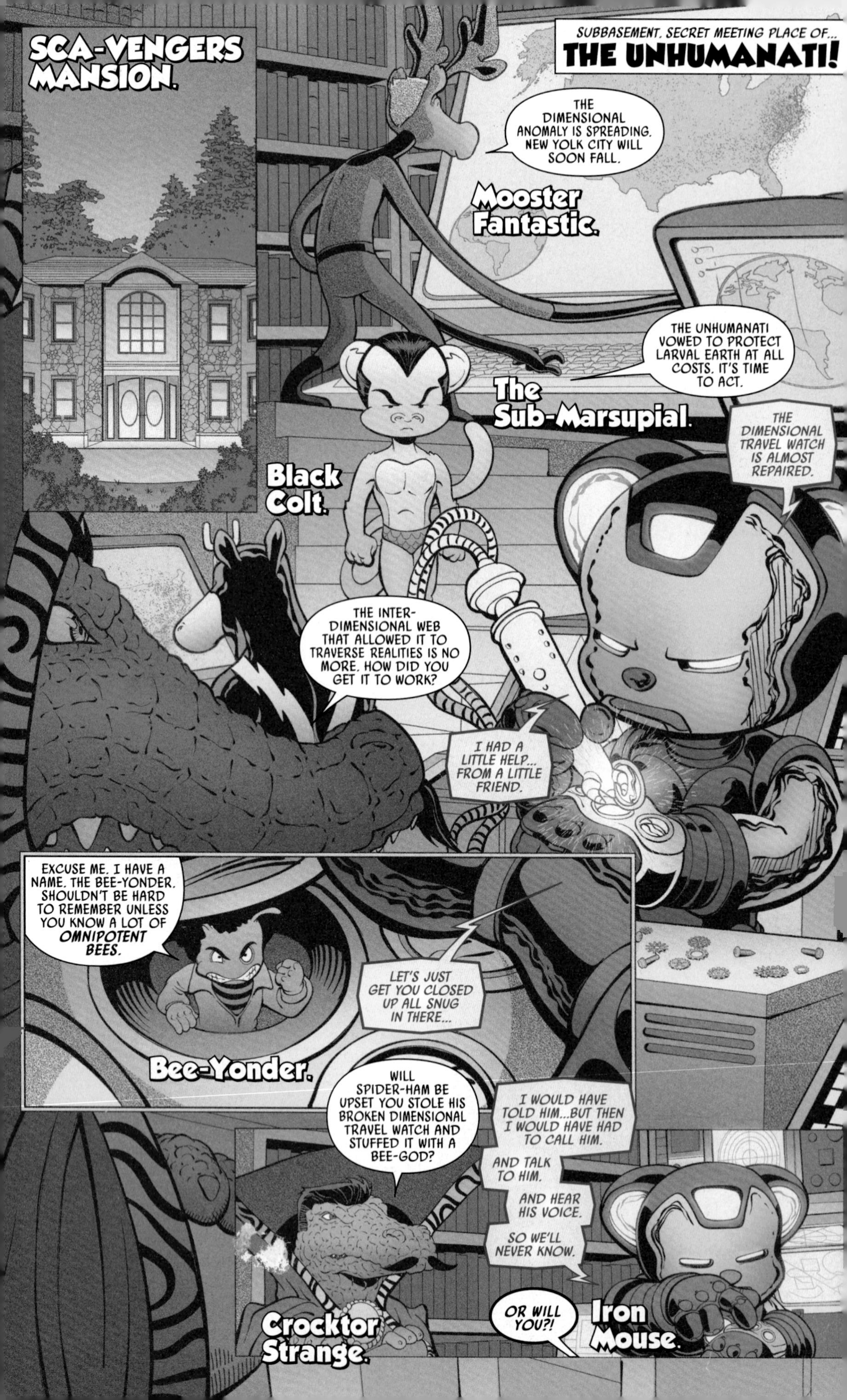
SCA-VENGERS MANSION.
SUBBASEMENT. SECRET MEETING PLACE OF... THE UNHUMANATI!
THE DIMENSIONAL ANOMALY IS SPREADING. NEW YOLK CITY WILL SOON FALL.
Mooster Fantastic.
THE UNHUMANATI VOWED TO PROTECT LARVAL EARTH AT ALL COSTS. IT'S TIME TO ACT.
The Sub-Marsupial.
Black Colt.
THE DIMENSIONAL TRAVEL WATCH IS ALMOST REPAIRED.
THE INTER-DIMENSIONAL WEB THAT ALLOWED IT TO TRAVERSE REALITIES IS NO MORE. HOW DID YOU GET IT TO WORK?
I HAD A LITTLE HELP... FROM A LITTLE FRIEND.
EXCUSE ME. I HAVE A NAME. THE BEE-YONDER. SHOULDN'T BE HARD TO REMEMBER UNLESS YOU KNOW A LOT OF OMNIPOTENT BEES.
LET'S JUST GET YOU CLOSED UP ALL SNUG IN THERE...
Bee-Yonder.
WILL SPIDER-HAM BE UPSET YOU STOLE HIS BROKEN DIMENSIONAL TRAVEL WATCH AND STUFFED IT WITH A BEE-GOD?
I WOULD HAVE TOLD HIM...BUT THEN I WOULD HAVE HAD TO CALL HIM.
AND TALK TO HIM.
AND HEAR HIS VOICE.
SO WE'LL NEVER KNOW.
OR WILL YOU?!
Crocktor Strange.
Iron Mouse.

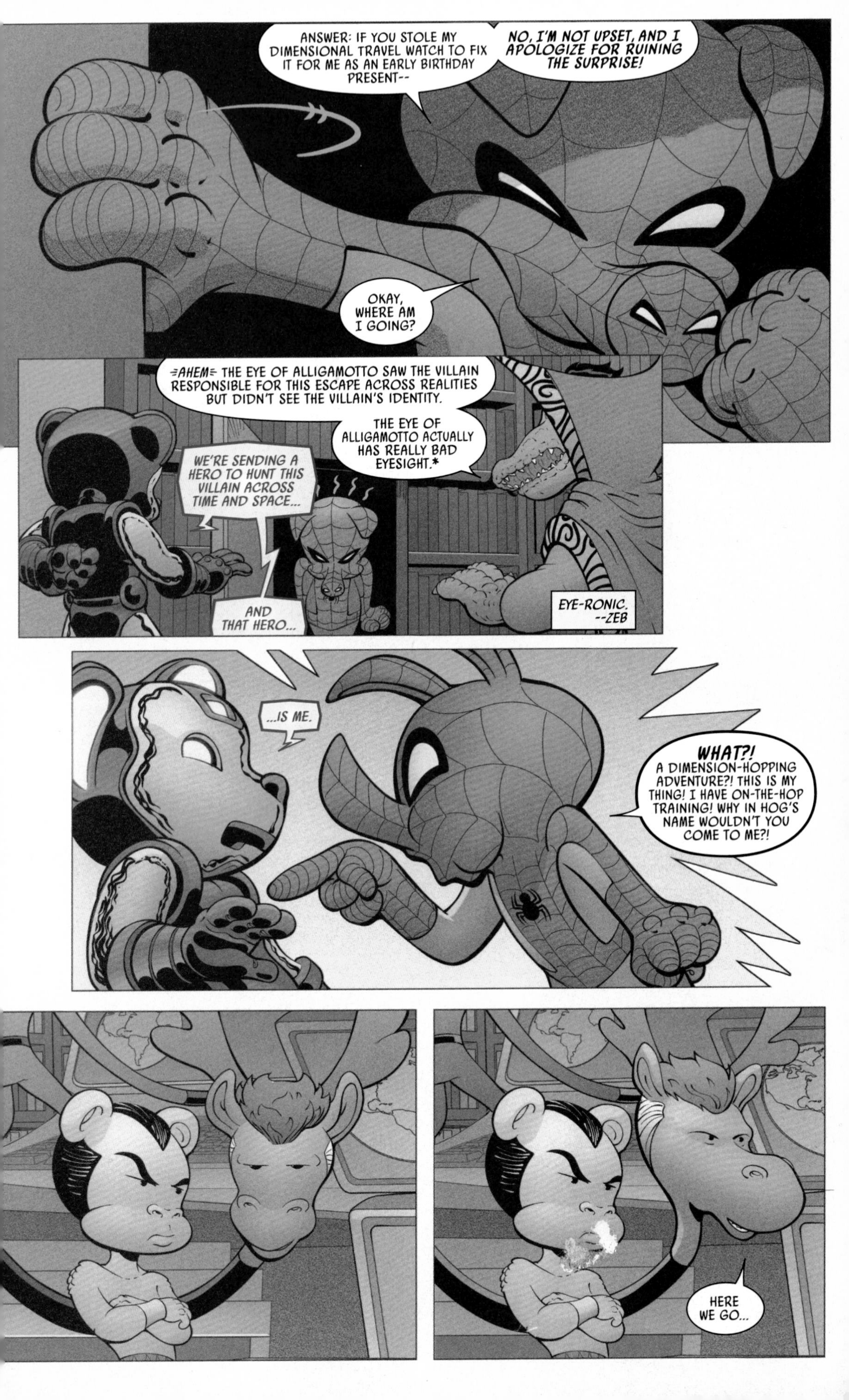
ANSWER: IF YOU STOLE MY DIMENSIONAL TRAVEL WATCH TO FIX IT FOR ME AS AN EARLY BIRTHDAY PRESENT--
NO, I'M NOT UPSET, AND I APOLOGIZE FOR RUINING THE SURPRISE!
OKAY, WHERE AM I GOING?
=AHEM= THE EYE OF ALLIGAMOTTO SAW THE VILLAIN RESPONSIBLE FOR THIS ESCAPE ACROSS REALITIES BUT DIDN'T SEE THE VILLAIN'S IDENTITY.
THE EYE OF ALLIGAMOTTO ACTUALLY HAS REALLY BAD EYESIGHT.*
WE'RE SENDING A HERO TO HUNT THIS VILLAIN ACROSS TIME AND SPACE...
AND THAT HERO...
EYE-RONIC. --ZEB
...IS ME.
WHAT?! A DIMENSION-HOPPING ADVENTURE?! THIS IS MY THING! I HAVE ON-THE-HOP TRAINING! WHY IN HOG'S NAME WOULDN'T YOU COME TO ME?!
HERE WE GO...

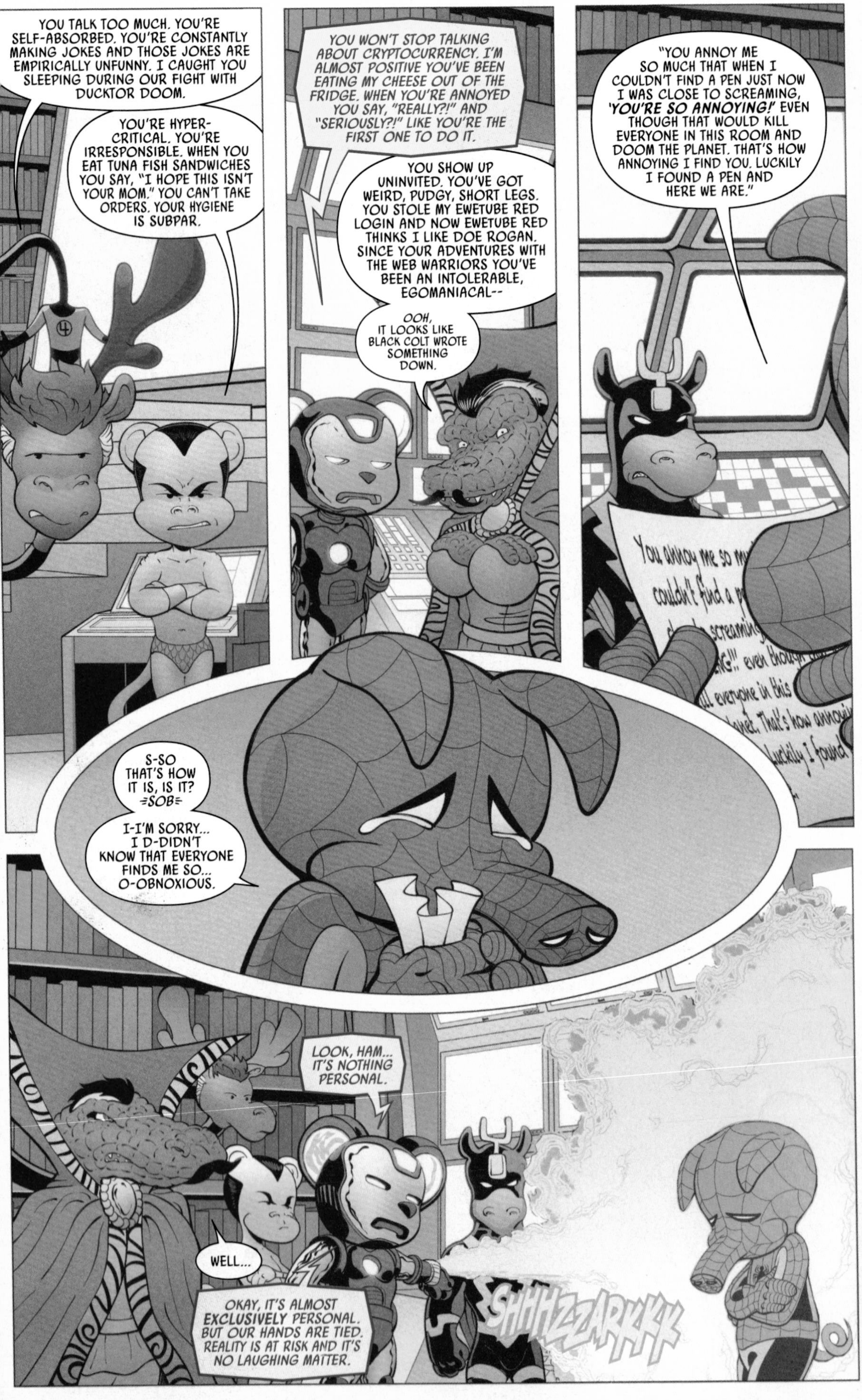

YOU TALK TOO MUCH. YOU'RE SELF-ABSORBED. YOU'RE CONSTANTLY MAKING JOKES AND THOSE JOKES ARE EMPIRICALLY UNFUNNY. I CAUGHT YOU SLEEPING DURING OUR FIGHT WITH DUCKTOR DOOM.
YOU'RE HYPER-CRITICAL. YOU'RE IRRESPONSIBLE. WHEN YOU EAT TUNA FISH SANDWICHES YOU SAY, "I HOPE THIS ISN'T YOUR MOM." YOU CAN'T TAKE ORDERS. YOUR HYGIENE IS SUBPAR.
YOU WON'T STOP TALKING ABOUT CRYPTOCURRENCY. I'M ALMOST POSITIVE YOU'VE BEEN EATING MY CHEESE OUT OF THE FRIDGE. WHEN YOU'RE ANNOYED YOU SAY, "REALLY?!" AND "SERIOUSLY?!" LIKE YOU'RE THE FIRST ONE TO DO IT.
YOU SHOW UP UNINVITED. YOU'VE GOT WEIRD, PUDGY, SHORT LEGS. YOU STOLE MY EWETUBE RED LOGIN AND NOW EWETUBE RED THINKS I LIKE DOE ROGAN. SINCE YOUR ADVENTURES WITH THE WEB WARRIORS YOU'VE BEEN AN INTOLERABLE, EGOMANIACAL--
OOH, IT LOOKS LIKE BLACK COLT WROTE SOMETHING DOWN.
"YOU ANNOY ME SO MUCH THAT WHEN I COULDN'T FIND A PEN JUST NOW I WAS CLOSE TO SCREAMING, **'YOU'RE SO ANNOYING!'** EVEN THOUGH THAT WOULD KILL EVERYONE IN THIS ROOM AND DOOM THE PLANET. THAT'S HOW ANNOYING I FIND YOU. LUCKILY I FOUND A PEN AND HERE WE ARE."
S-SO THAT'S HOW IT IS, IS IT? =SOB=
I-I'M SORRY... I D-DIDN'T KNOW THAT EVERYONE FINDS ME SO... O-OBNOXIOUS.
LOOK, HAM... IT'S NOTHING PERSONAL.
WELL...
OKAY, IT'S ALMOST **EXCLUSIVELY** PERSONAL. BUT OUR HANDS ARE TIED. REALITY IS AT RISK AND IT'S NO LAUGHING MATTER.
SHHHZZARKKK

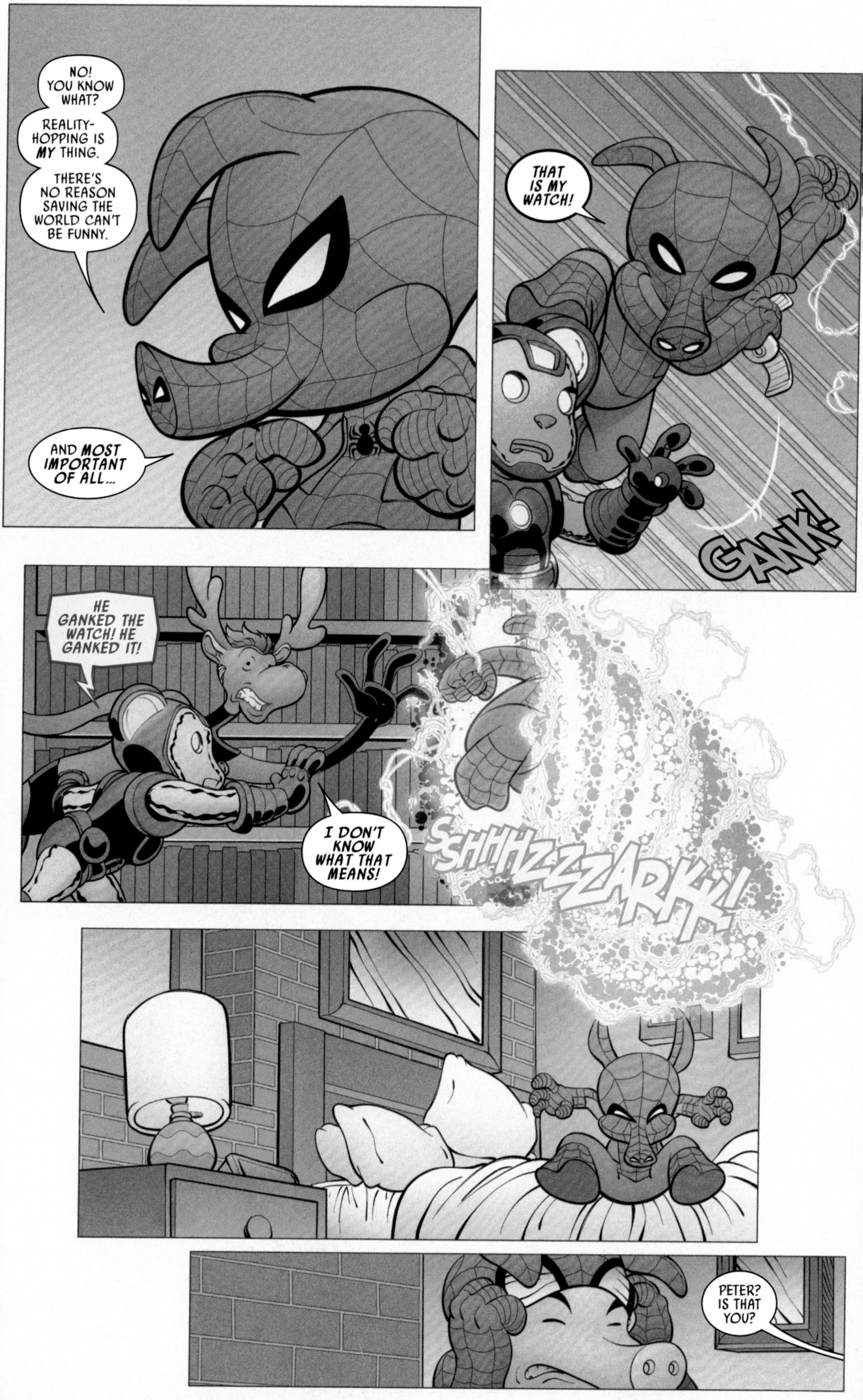
NO! YOU KNOW WHAT?
REALITY-HOPPING IS MY THING.
THERE'S NO REASON SAVING THE WORLD CAN'T BE FUNNY.
AND MOST IMPORTANT OF ALL...
THAT IS MY WATCH!
GANK!
HE GANKED THE WATCH! HE GANKED IT!
I DON'T KNOW WHAT THAT MEANS!
SHHHZZZARK!
PETER? IS THAT YOU?

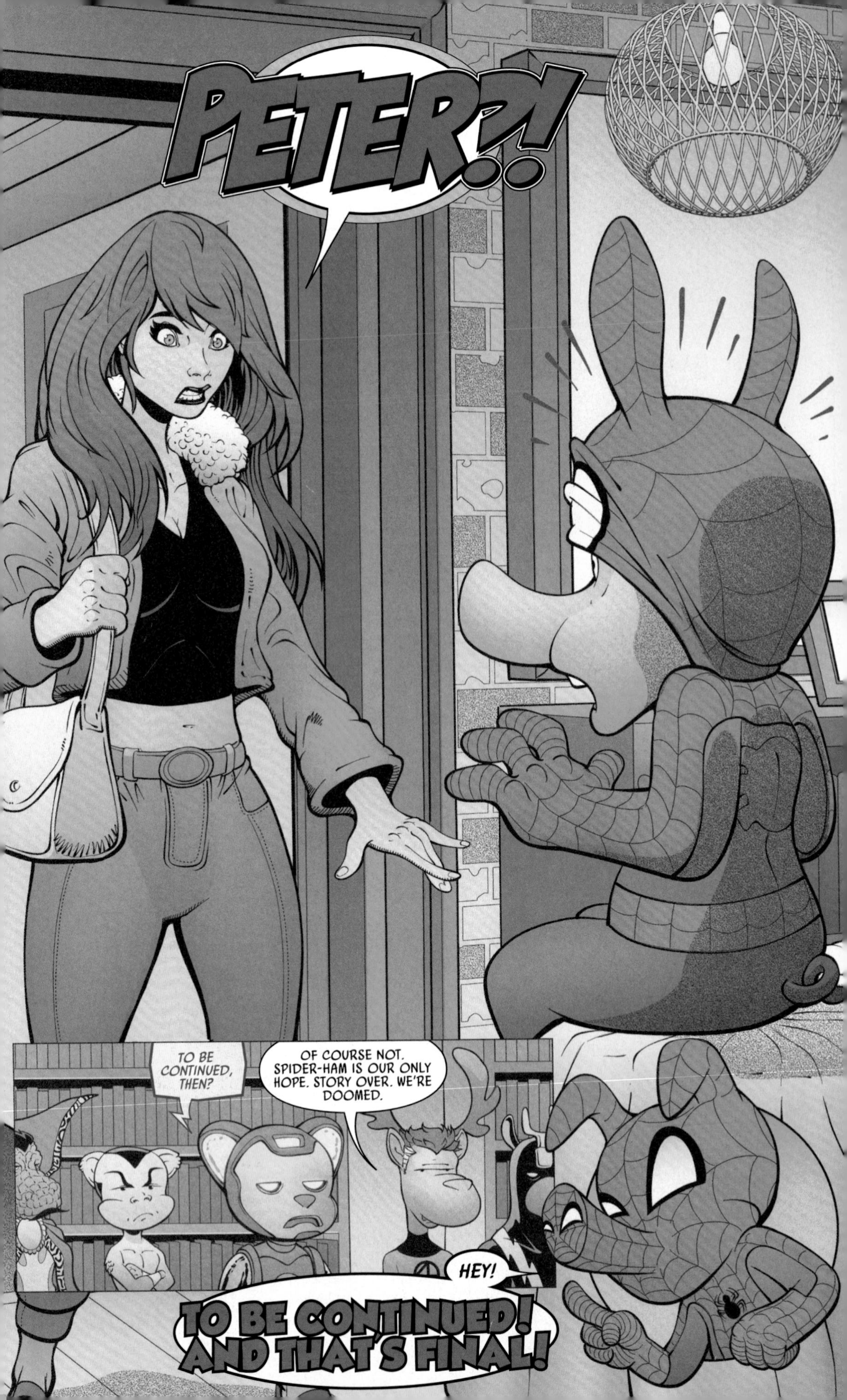
PETER?!
TO BE CONTINUED, THEN?
OF COURSE NOT. SPIDER-HAM IS OUR ONLY HOPE. STORY OVER. WE'RE DOOMED.
HEY!
TO BE CONTINUED! AND THAT'S FINAL!

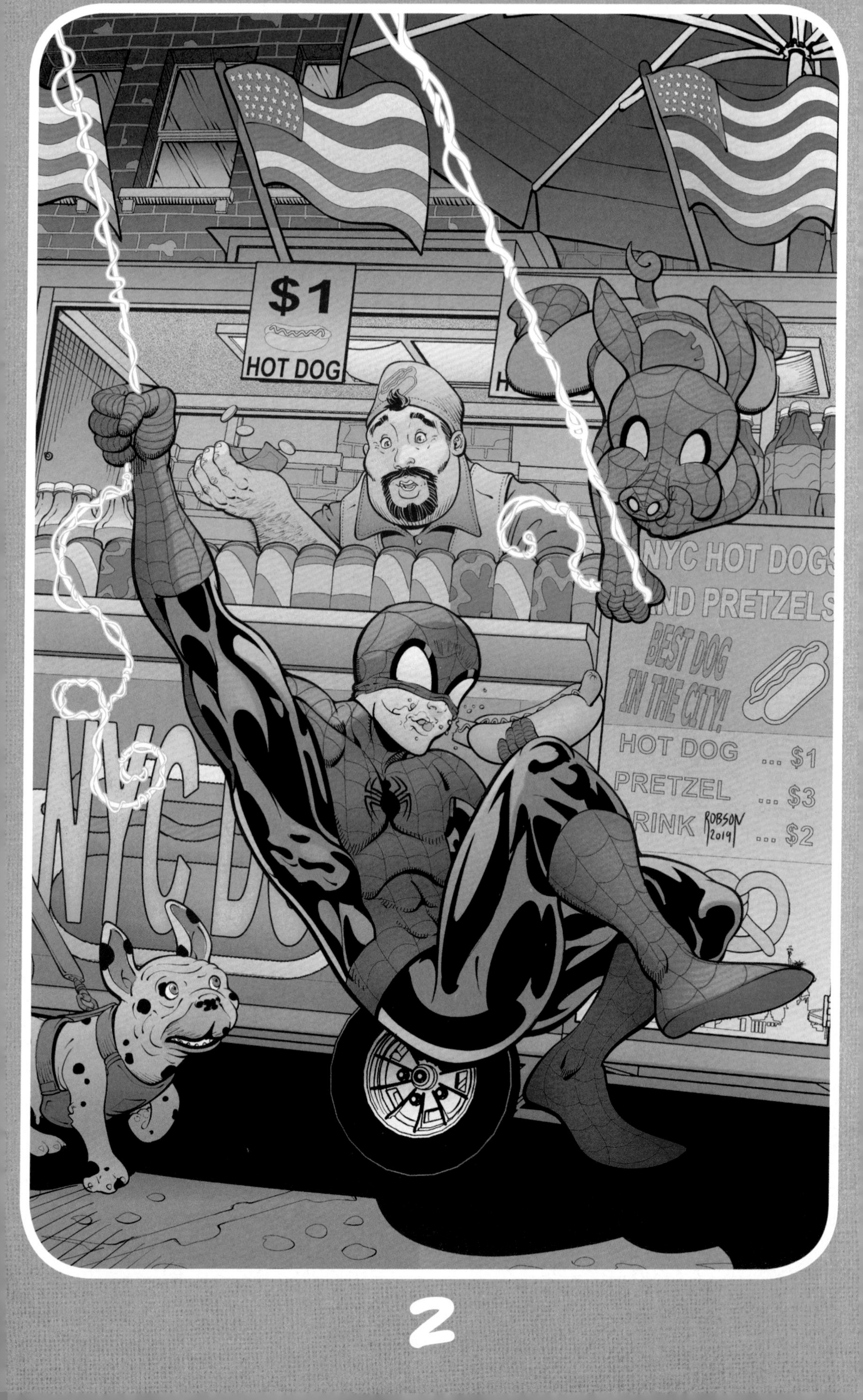
$1
HOT DOG
NYC HOT DOGS
ND PRETZELS
BEST DOG IN THE CITY!
HOT DOG ... $1
PRETZEL ... $3
RINK ... $2
ROBSON 2019

2

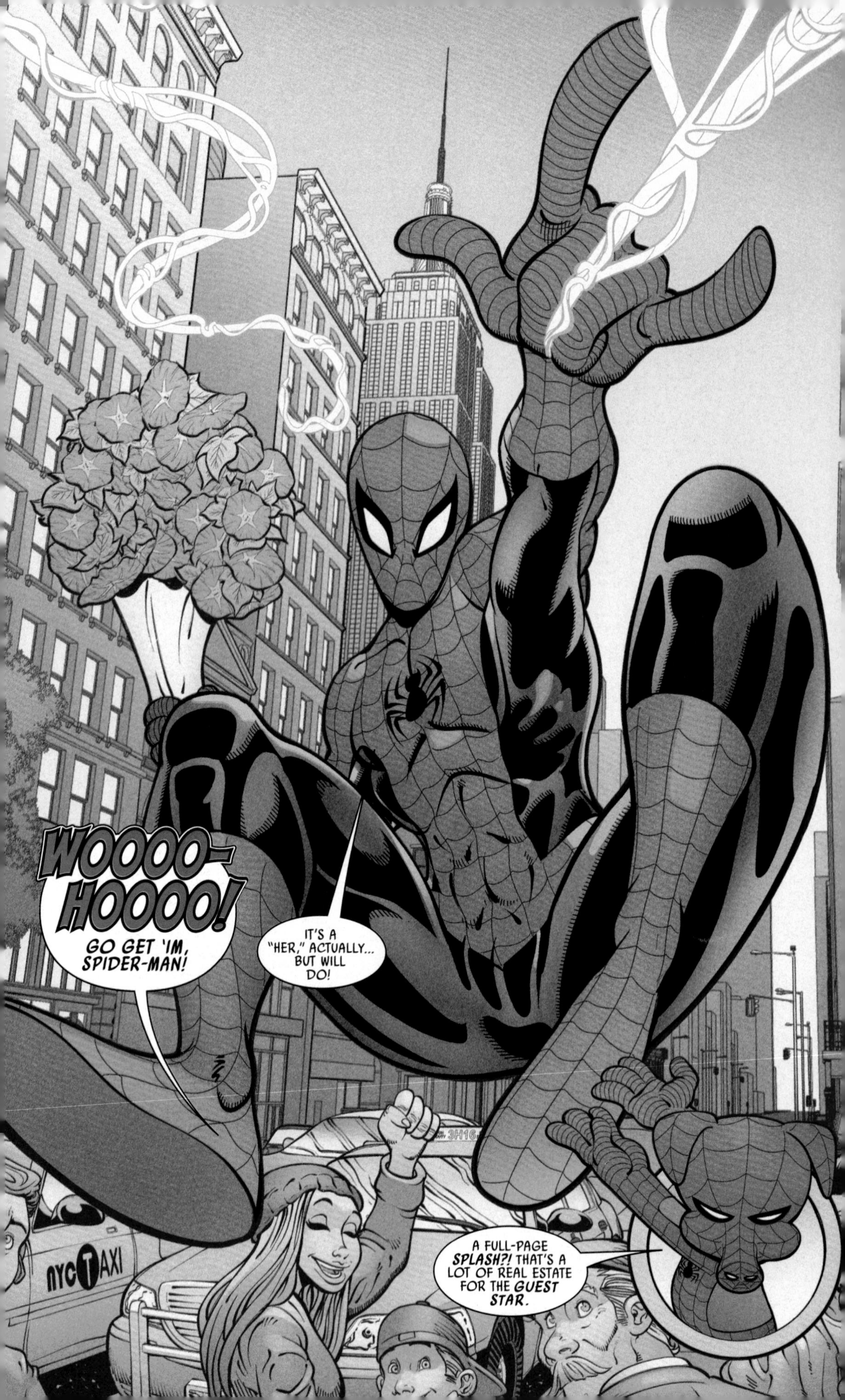
WOOOO-HOOOOO!
GO GET 'IM, SPIDER-MAN!
IT'S A "HER," ACTUALLY... BUT WILL DO!
A FULL-PAGE SPLASH?! THAT'S A LOT OF REAL ESTATE FOR THE GUEST STAR.
NYC TAXI

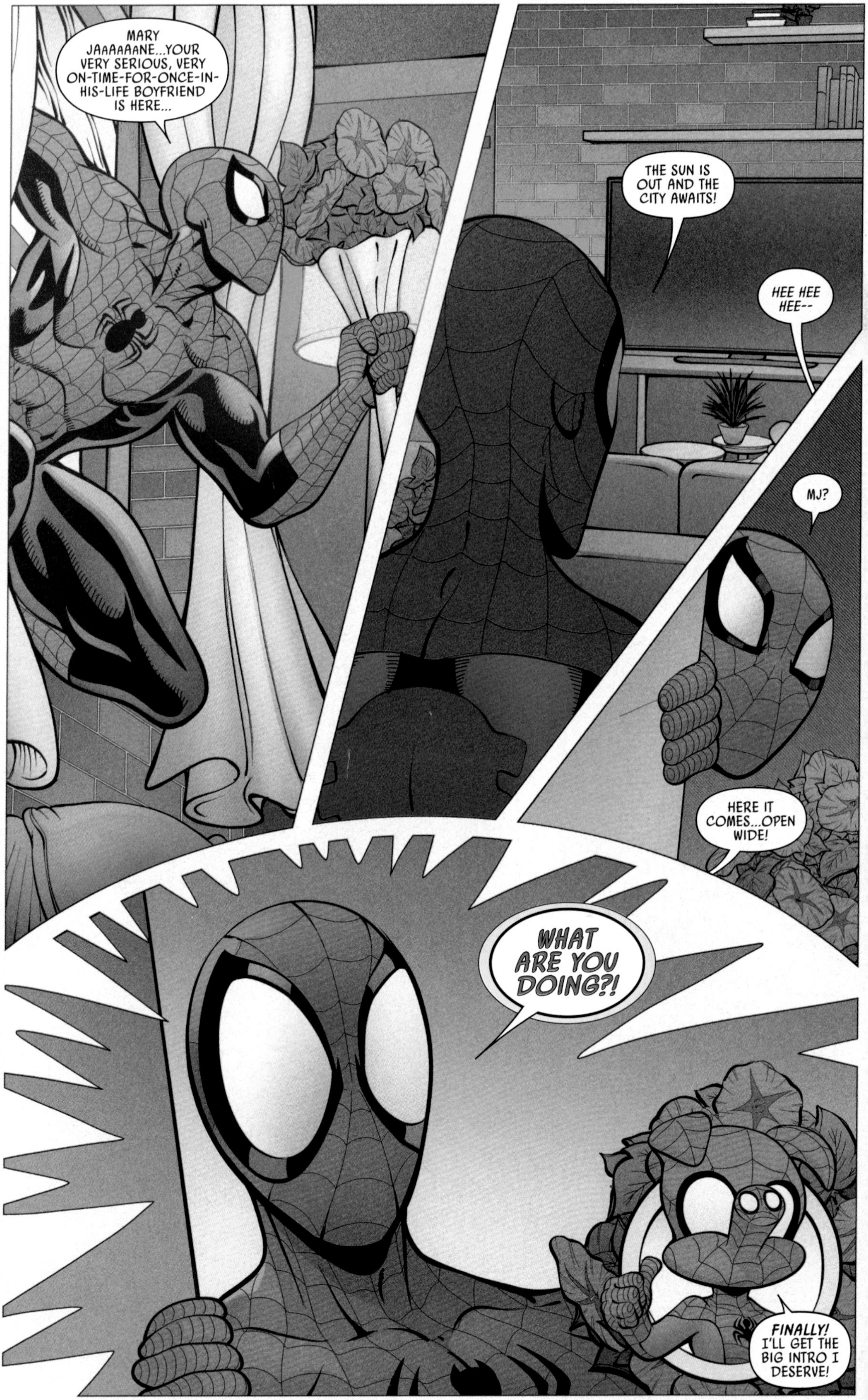
MARY JAAAAAANE...YOUR VERY SERIOUS, VERY ON-TIME-FOR-ONCE-IN-HIS-LIFE BOYFRIEND IS HERE...
THE SUN IS OUT AND THE CITY AWAITS!
HEE HEE HEE--
MJ?
HERE IT COMES...OPEN WIDE!
WHAT ARE YOU DOING?!
FINALLY! I'LL GET THE BIG INTRO I DESERVE!

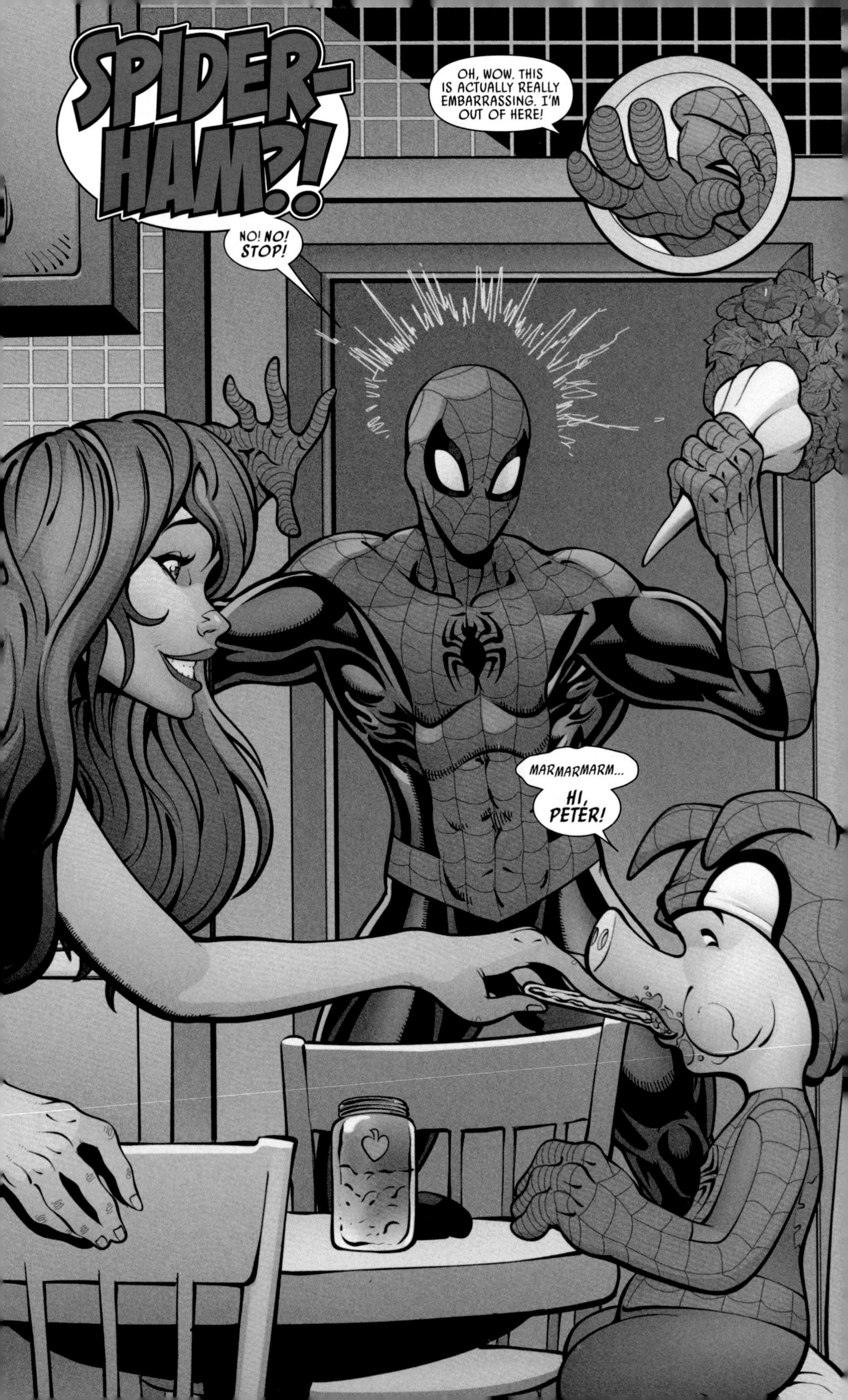
SPIDER-HAM?!
OH, WOW. THIS IS ACTUALLY REALLY EMBARRASSING. I'M OUT OF HERE!
NO! NO! STOP!
MARMARMARM... HI, PETER!

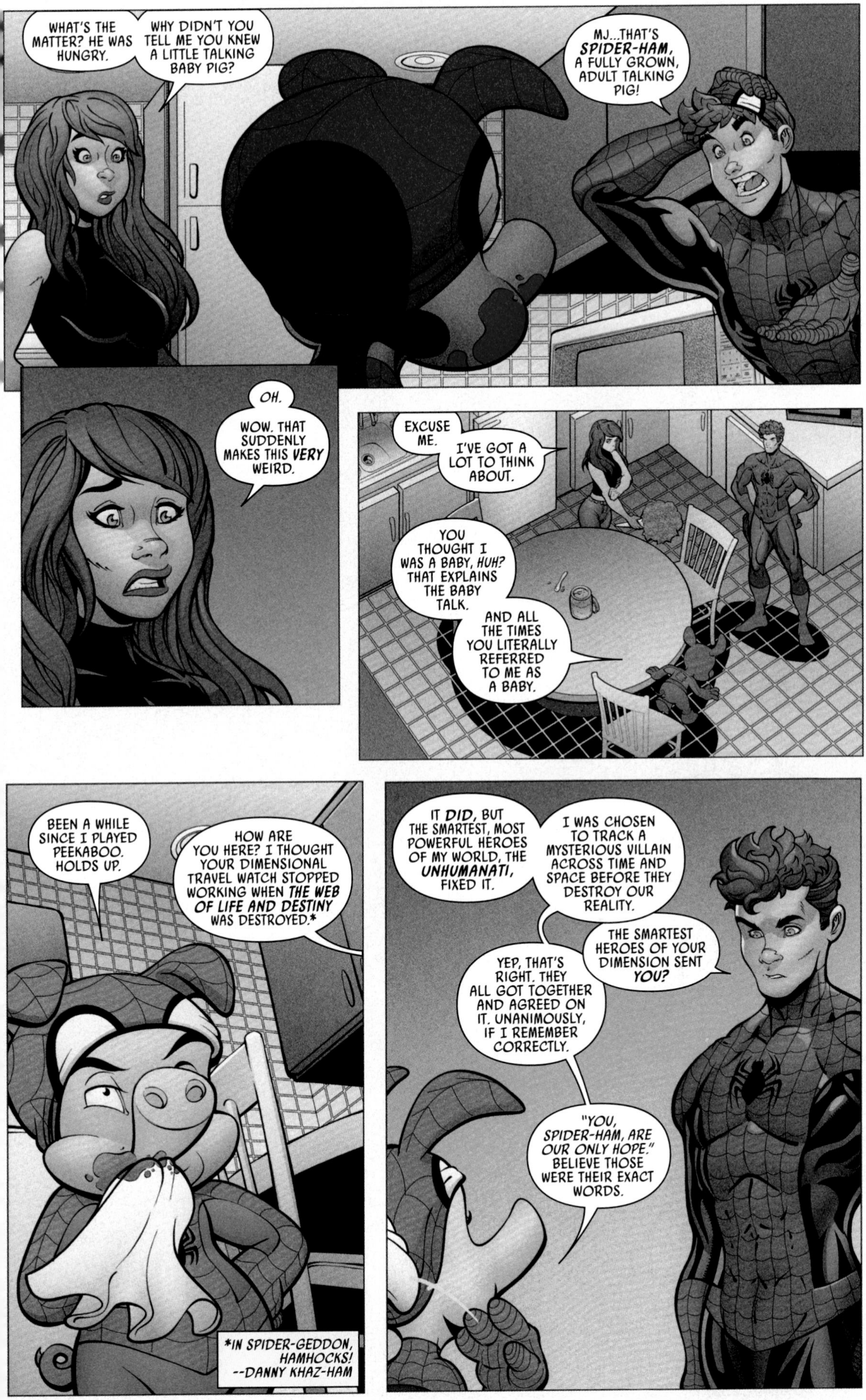
WHAT'S THE MATTER? HE WAS HUNGRY.
WHY DIDN'T YOU TELL ME YOU KNEW A LITTLE TALKING BABY PIG?
MJ...THAT'S SPIDER-HAM, A FULLY GROWN, ADULT TALKING PIG!
OH.
WOW. THAT SUDDENLY MAKES THIS VERY WEIRD.
EXCUSE ME.
I'VE GOT A LOT TO THINK ABOUT.
YOU THOUGHT I WAS A BABY, HUH? THAT EXPLAINS THE BABY TALK.
AND ALL THE TIMES YOU LITERALLY REFERRED TO ME AS A BABY.
BEEN A WHILE SINCE I PLAYED PEEKABOO. HOLDS UP.
HOW ARE YOU HERE? I THOUGHT YOUR DIMENSIONAL TRAVEL WATCH STOPPED WORKING WHEN THE WEB OF LIFE AND DESTINY WAS DESTROYED.*
*IN SPIDER-GEDDON, HAMHOCKS! --DANNY KHAZ-HAM
IT DID, BUT THE SMARTEST, MOST POWERFUL HEROES OF MY WORLD, THE UNHUMANATI, FIXED IT.
I WAS CHOSEN TO TRACK A MYSTERIOUS VILLAIN ACROSS TIME AND SPACE BEFORE THEY DESTROY OUR REALITY.
THE SMARTEST HEROES OF YOUR DIMENSION SENT YOU?
YEP, THAT'S RIGHT. THEY ALL GOT TOGETHER AND AGREED ON IT. UNANIMOUSLY, IF I REMEMBER CORRECTLY.
"YOU, SPIDER-HAM, ARE OUR ONLY HOPE." BELIEVE THOSE WERE THEIR EXACT WORDS.

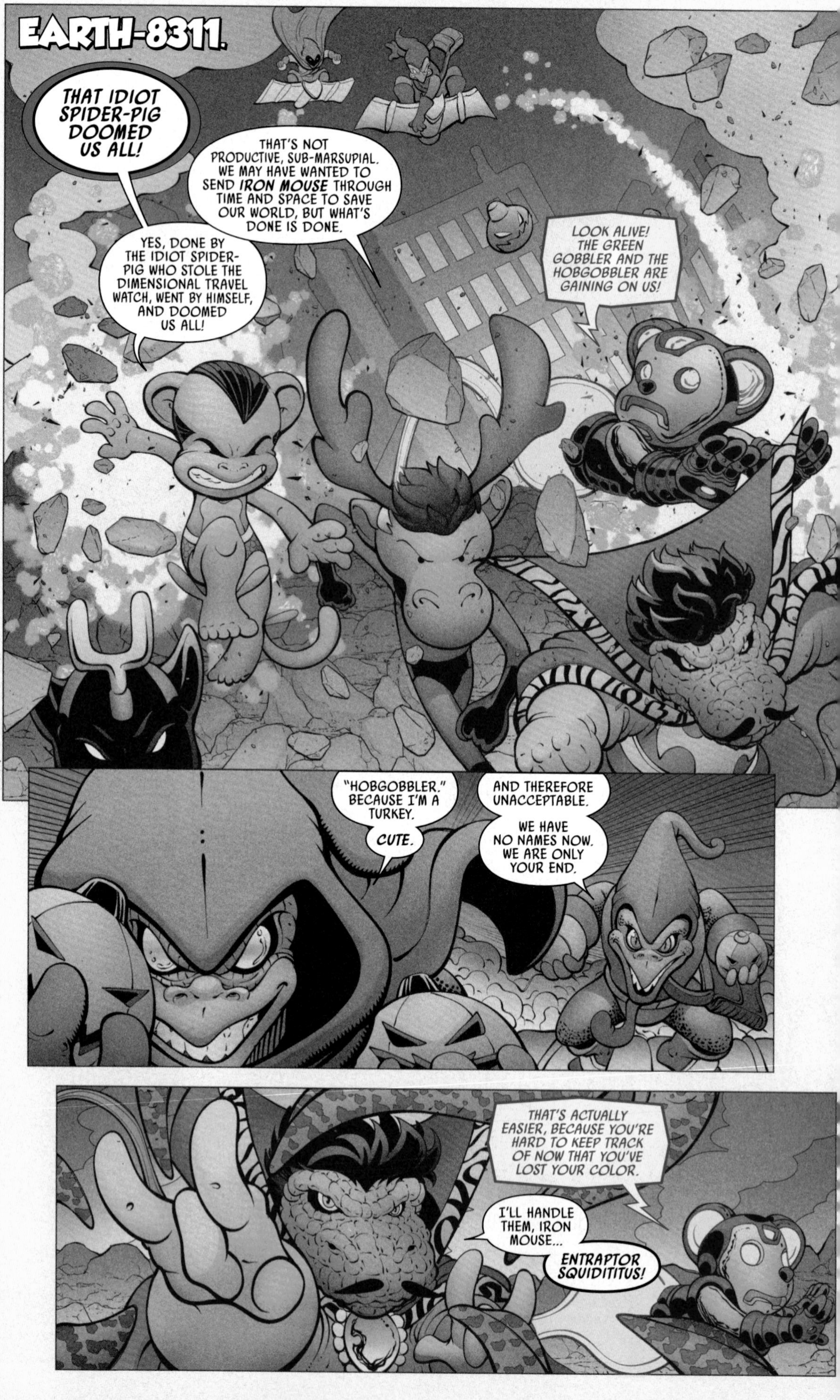
EARTH-8311.
THAT IDIOT SPIDER-PIG DOOMED US ALL!
THAT'S NOT PRODUCTIVE, SUB-MARSUPIAL. WE MAY HAVE WANTED TO SEND IRON MOUSE THROUGH TIME AND SPACE TO SAVE OUR WORLD, BUT WHAT'S DONE IS DONE.
YES, DONE BY THE IDIOT SPIDER-PIG WHO STOLE THE DIMENSIONAL TRAVEL WATCH, WENT BY HIMSELF, AND DOOMED US ALL!
LOOK ALIVE! THE GREEN GOBBLER AND THE HOBGOBBLER ARE GAINING ON US!
"HOBGOBBLER." BECAUSE I'M A TURKEY.
CUTE.
AND THEREFORE UNACCEPTABLE.
WE HAVE NO NAMES NOW. WE ARE ONLY YOUR END.
THAT'S ACTUALLY EASIER, BECAUSE YOU'RE HARD TO KEEP TRACK OF NOW THAT YOU'VE LOST YOUR COLOR.
I'LL HANDLE THEM, IRON MOUSE...
ENTRAPTOR SQUIDITITUS!

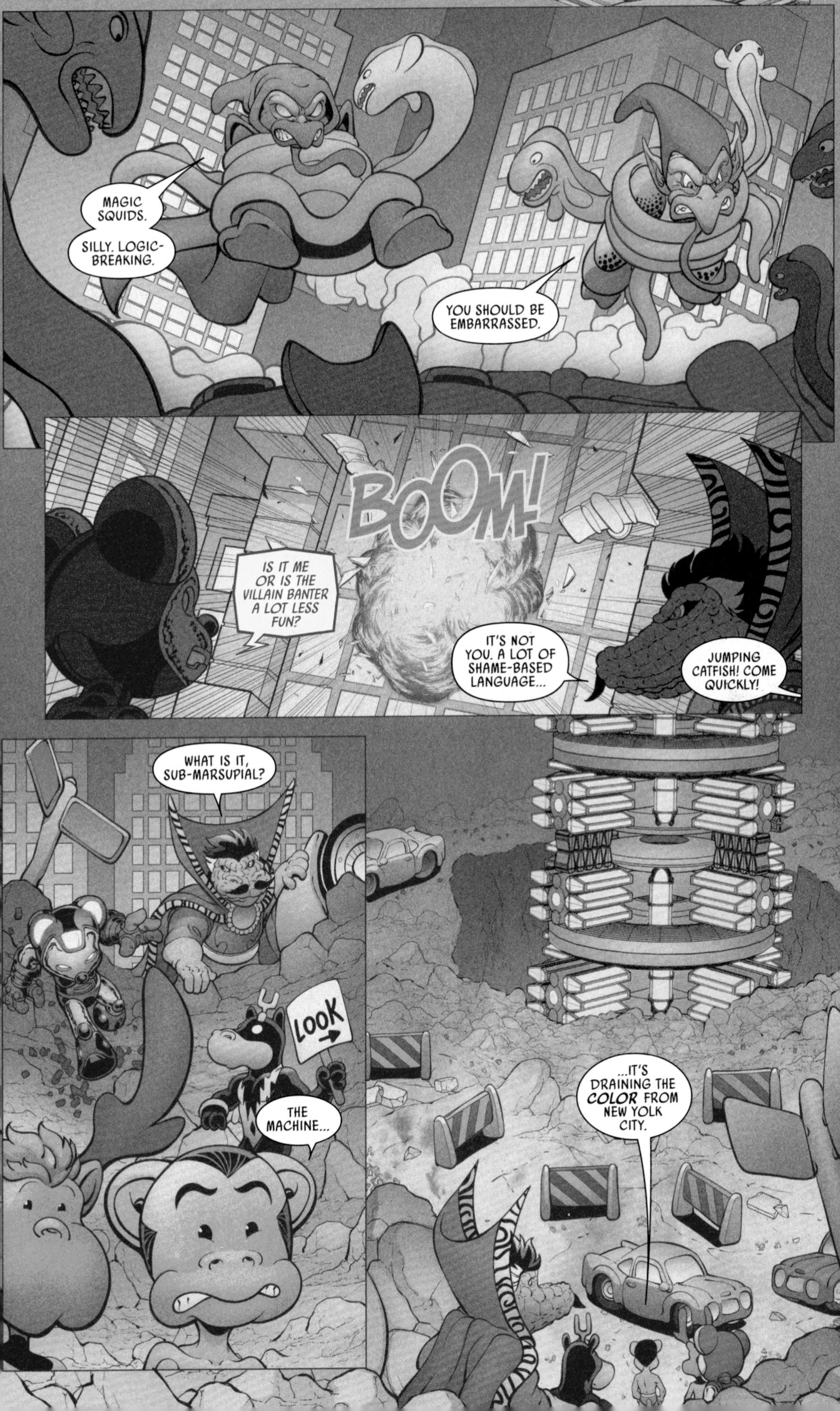

MAGIC SQUIDS.
SILLY. LOGIC-BREAKING.
YOU SHOULD BE EMBARRASSED.
BOOM!
IS IT ME OR IS THE VILLAIN BANTER A LOT LESS FUN?
IT'S NOT YOU. A LOT OF SHAME-BASED LANGUAGE...
JUMPING CATFISH! COME QUICKLY!
WHAT IS IT, SUB-MARSUPIAL?
LOOK
THE MACHINE...
...IT'S DRAINING THE COLOR FROM NEW YOLK CITY.

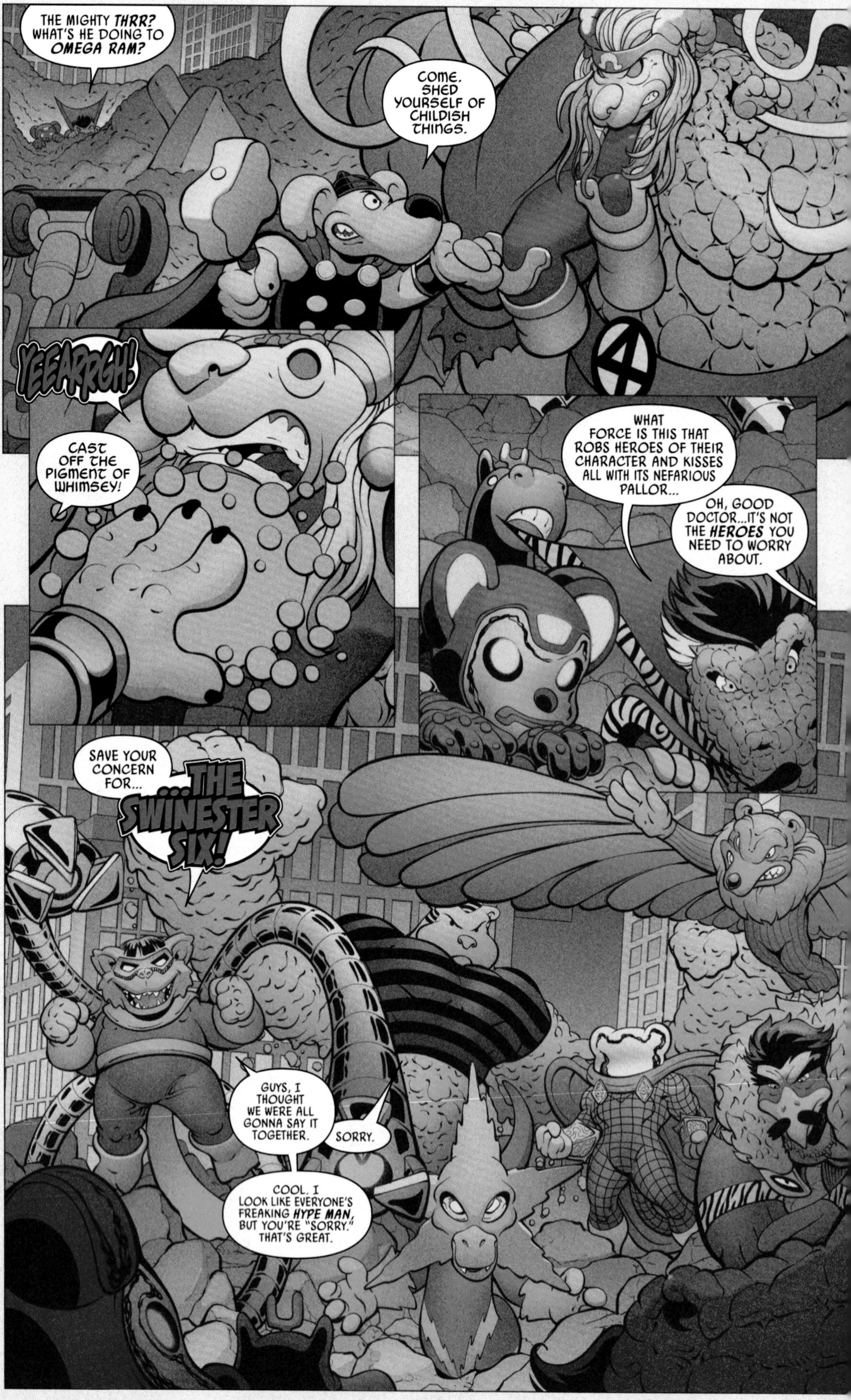

THE MIGHTY THRR? WHAT'S HE DOING TO OMEGA RAM?
COME. SHED YOURSELF OF CHILDISH THINGS.
YEEARRGH!
CAST OFF THE PIGMENT OF WHIMSEY!
WHAT FORCE IS THIS THAT ROBS HEROES OF THEIR CHARACTER AND KISSES ALL WITH ITS NEFARIOUS PALLOR...
OH, GOOD DOCTOR...IT'S NOT THE HEROES YOU NEED TO WORRY ABOUT.
SAVE YOUR CONCERN FOR...
...THE SWINESTER SIX!
GUYS, I THOUGHT WE WERE ALL GONNA SAY IT TOGETHER.
SORRY.
COOL. I LOOK LIKE EVERYONE'S FREAKING HYPE MAN, BUT YOU'RE "SORRY." THAT'S GREAT.

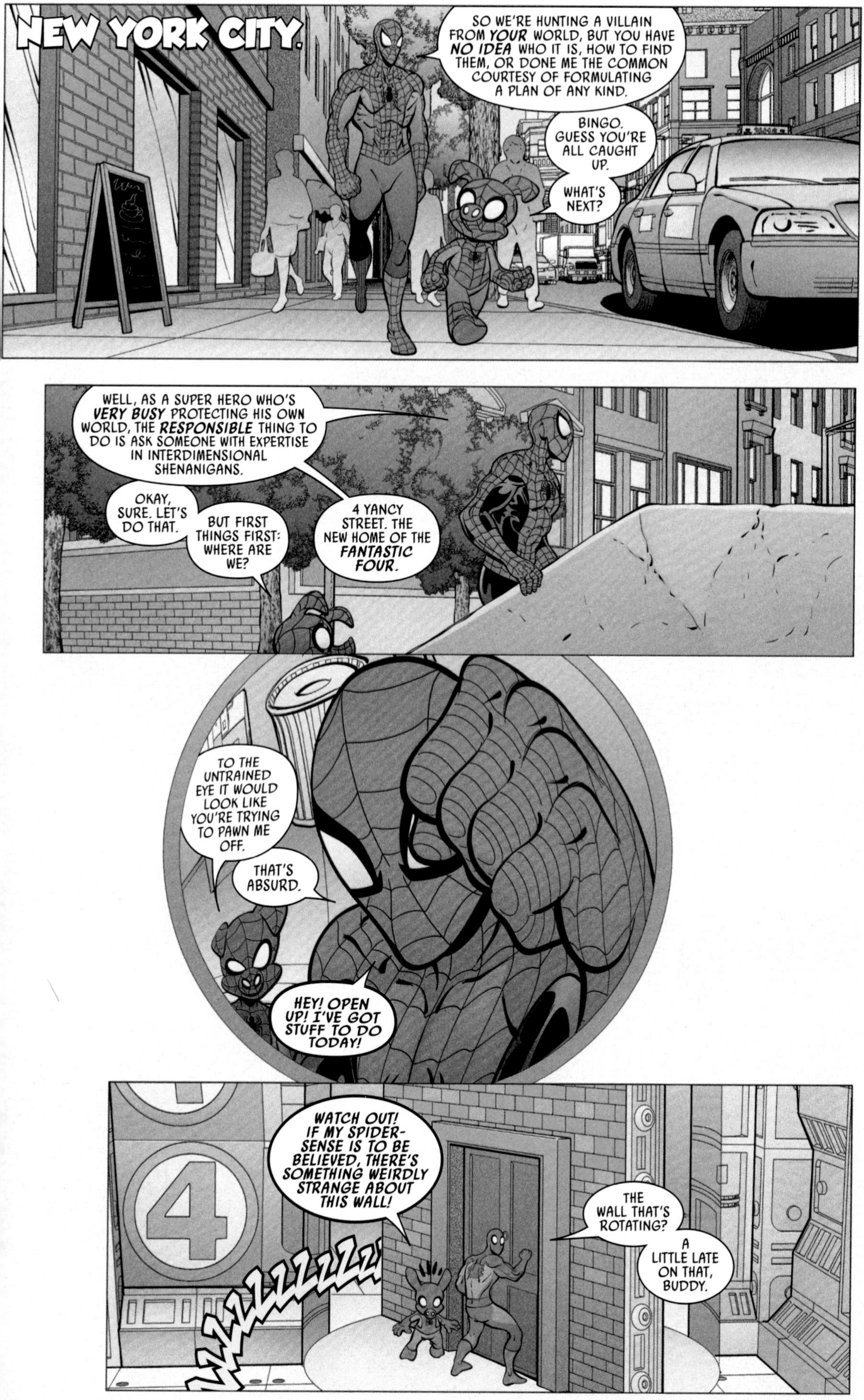
NEW YORK CITY.
SO WE'RE HUNTING A VILLAIN FROM YOUR WORLD, BUT YOU HAVE NO IDEA WHO IT IS, HOW TO FIND THEM, OR DONE ME THE COMMON COURTESY OF FORMULATING A PLAN OF ANY KIND.
BINGO. GUESS YOU'RE ALL CAUGHT UP.
WHAT'S NEXT?
WELL, AS A SUPER HERO WHO'S VERY BUSY PROTECTING HIS OWN WORLD, THE RESPONSIBLE THING TO DO IS ASK SOMEONE WITH EXPERTISE IN INTERDIMENSIONAL SHENANIGANS.
OKAY, SURE. LET'S DO THAT.
BUT FIRST THINGS FIRST: WHERE ARE WE?
4 YANCY STREET. THE NEW HOME OF THE FANTASTIC FOUR.
TO THE UNTRAINED EYE IT WOULD LOOK LIKE YOU'RE TRYING TO PAWN ME OFF.
THAT'S ABSURD.
HEY! OPEN UP! I'VE GOT STUFF TO DO TODAY!
WATCH OUT! IF MY SPIDER-SENSE IS TO BE BELIEVED, THERE'S SOMETHING WEIRDLY STRANGE ABOUT THIS WALL!
THE WALL THAT'S ROTATING?
A LITTLE LATE ON THAT, BUDDY.
4
WZZZZZZZZ

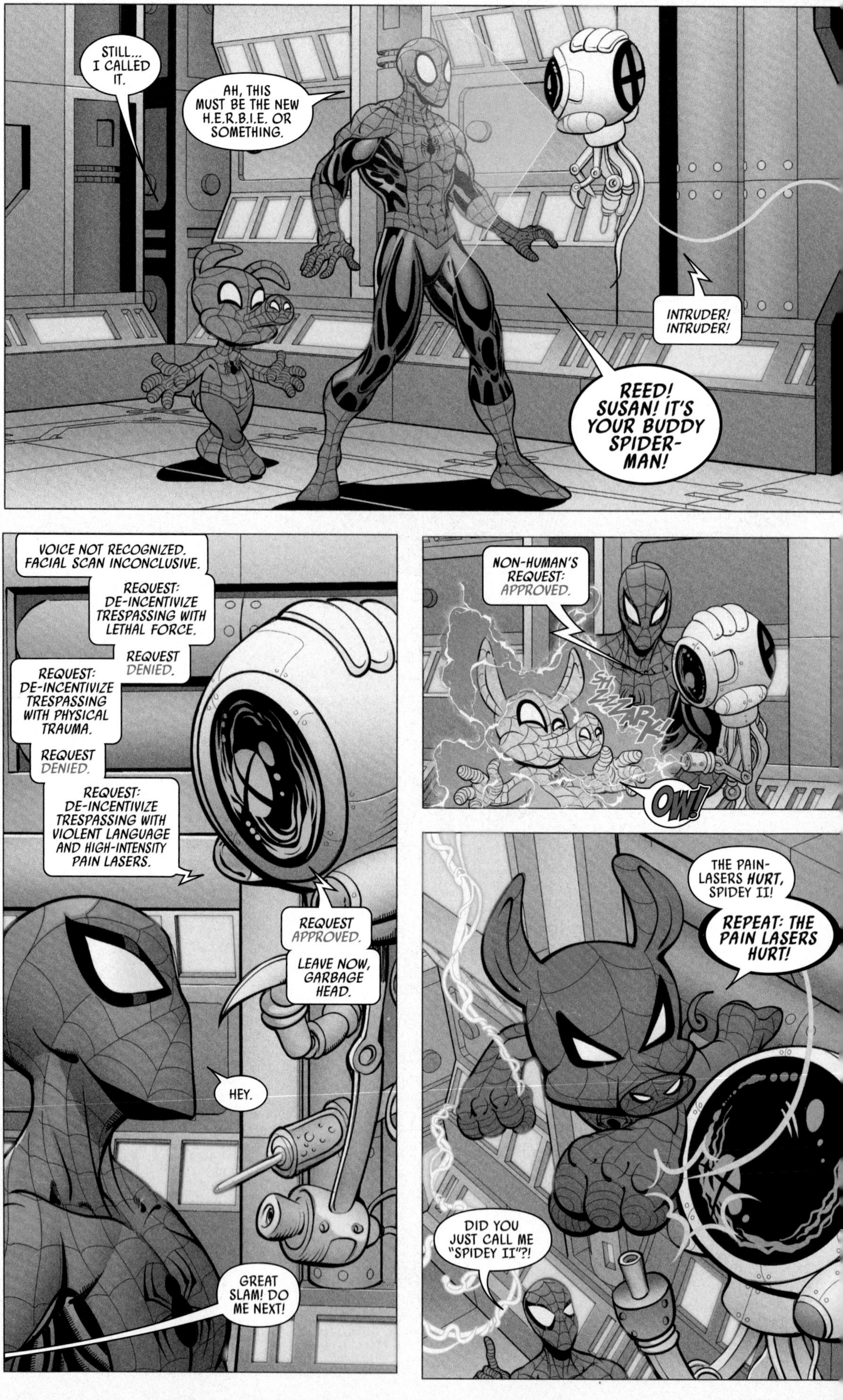
STILL... I CALLED IT.
AH, THIS MUST BE THE NEW H.E.R.B.I.E. OR SOMETHING.
INTRUDER! INTRUDER!
REED! SUSAN! IT'S YOUR BUDDY SPIDER-MAN!
VOICE NOT RECOGNIZED. FACIAL SCAN INCONCLUSIVE.
REQUEST: DE-INCENTIVIZE TRESPASSING WITH LETHAL FORCE.
REQUEST DENIED.
REQUEST: DE-INCENTIVIZE TRESPASSING WITH PHYSICAL TRAUMA.
REQUEST DENIED.
REQUEST: DE-INCENTIVIZE TRESPASSING WITH VIOLENT LANGUAGE AND HIGH-INTENSITY PAIN LASERS.
REQUEST APPROVED.
LEAVE NOW, GARBAGE HEAD.
HEY.
GREAT SLAM! DO ME NEXT!
NON-HUMAN'S REQUEST: APPROVED.
SHZZZARK!
OW!
THE PAIN-LASERS HURT, SPIDEY II!
REPEAT: THE PAIN LASERS HURT!
DID YOU JUST CALL ME "SPIDEY II"?!

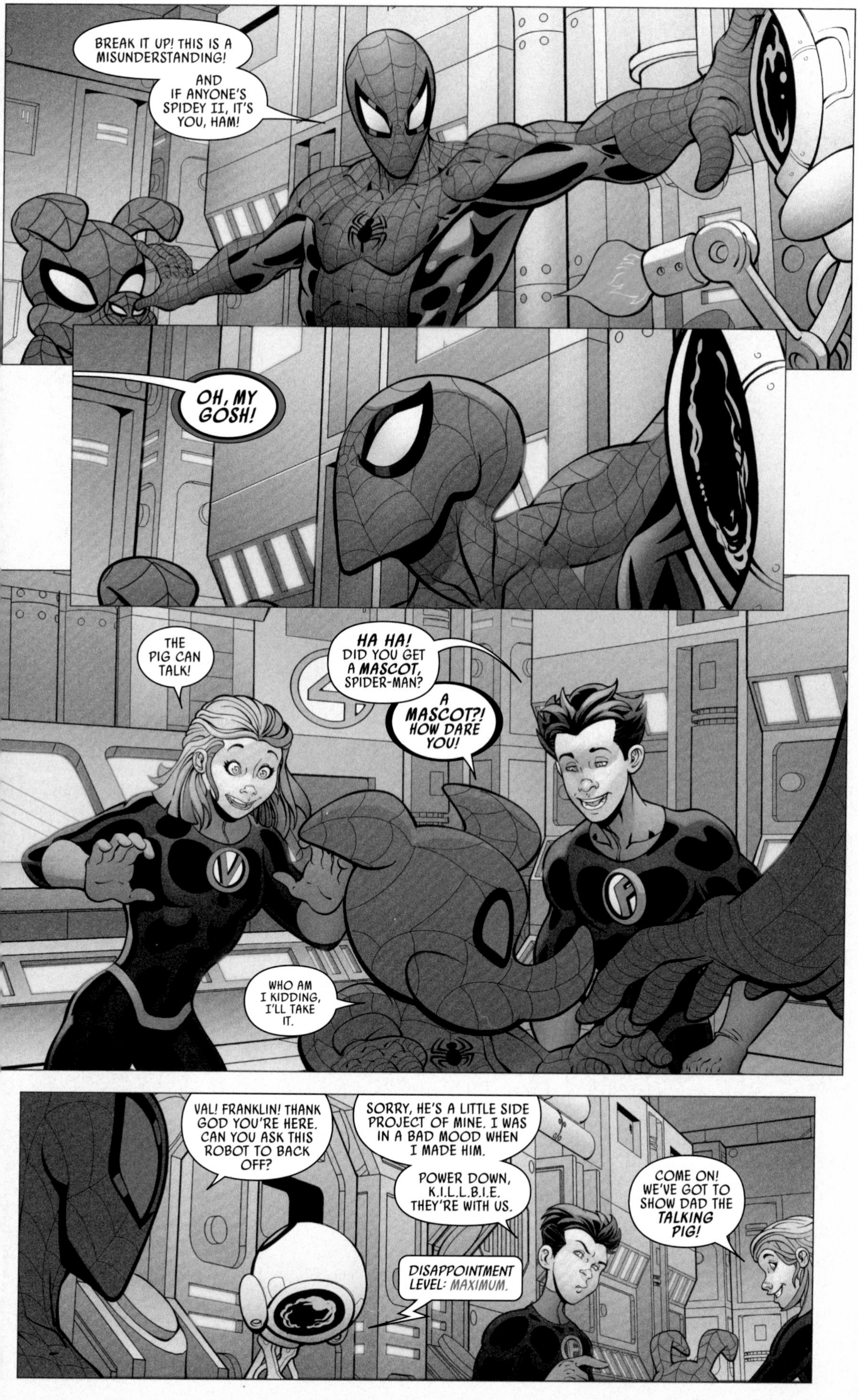
BREAK IT UP! THIS IS A MISUNDERSTANDING!
AND IF ANYONE'S SPIDEY II, IT'S YOU, HAM!
OH, MY GOSH!
THE PIG CAN TALK!
HA HA! DID YOU GET A MASCOT, SPIDER-MAN?
A MASCOT?! HOW DARE YOU!
WHO AM I KIDDING, I'LL TAKE IT.
VAL! FRANKLIN! THANK GOD YOU'RE HERE. CAN YOU ASK THIS ROBOT TO BACK OFF?
SORRY, HE'S A LITTLE SIDE PROJECT OF MINE. I WAS IN A BAD MOOD WHEN I MADE HIM.
POWER DOWN, K.I.L.L.B.I.E. THEY'RE WITH US.
COME ON! WE'VE GOT TO SHOW DAD THE TALKING PIG!
DISAPPOINTMENT LEVEL: MAXIMUM.

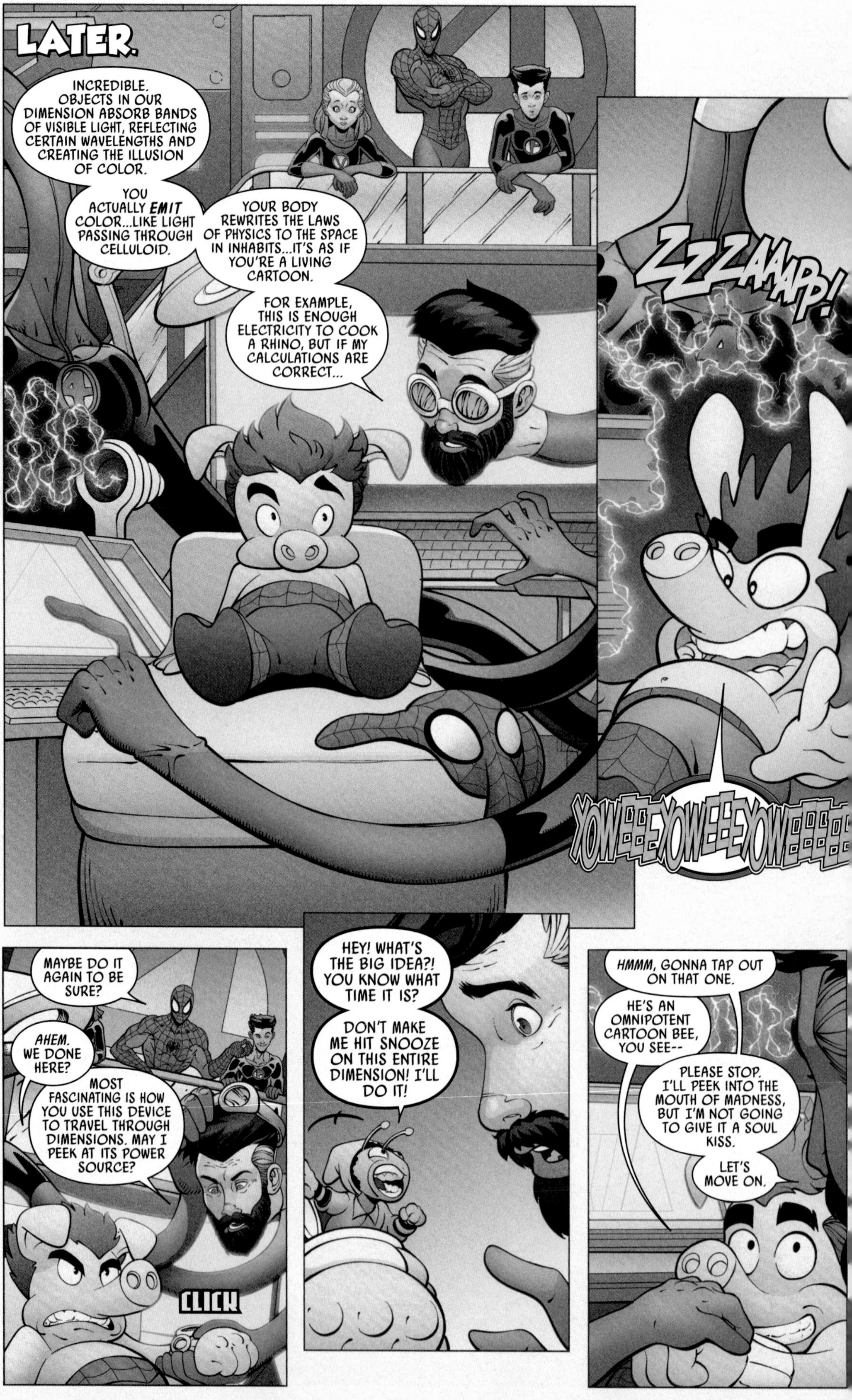
LATER.
INCREDIBLE. OBJECTS IN OUR DIMENSION ABSORB BANDS OF VISIBLE LIGHT, REFLECTING CERTAIN WAVELENGTHS AND CREATING THE ILLUSION OF COLOR.
YOU ACTUALLY EMIT COLOR...LIKE LIGHT PASSING THROUGH CELLULOID.
YOUR BODY REWRITES THE LAWS OF PHYSICS TO THE SPACE IN INHABITS...IT'S AS IF YOU'RE A LIVING CARTOON.
FOR EXAMPLE, THIS IS ENOUGH ELECTRICITY TO COOK A RHINO, BUT IF MY CALCULATIONS ARE CORRECT...
ZZZAAAPP!
YOWEEEYOWEEEYOWEEEE
MAYBE DO IT AGAIN TO BE SURE?
AHEM. WE DONE HERE?
MOST FASCINATING IS HOW YOU USE THIS DEVICE TO TRAVEL THROUGH DIMENSIONS. MAY I PEEK AT ITS POWER SOURCE?
CLICK
HEY! WHAT'S THE BIG IDEA?! YOU KNOW WHAT TIME IT IS?
DON'T MAKE ME HIT SNOOZE ON THIS ENTIRE DIMENSION! I'LL DO IT!
HMMM, GONNA TAP OUT ON THAT ONE.
HE'S AN OMNIPOTENT CARTOON BEE, YOU SEE--
PLEASE STOP. I'LL PEEK INTO THE MOUTH OF MADNESS, BUT I'M NOT GOING TO GIVE IT A SOUL KISS.
LET'S MOVE ON.

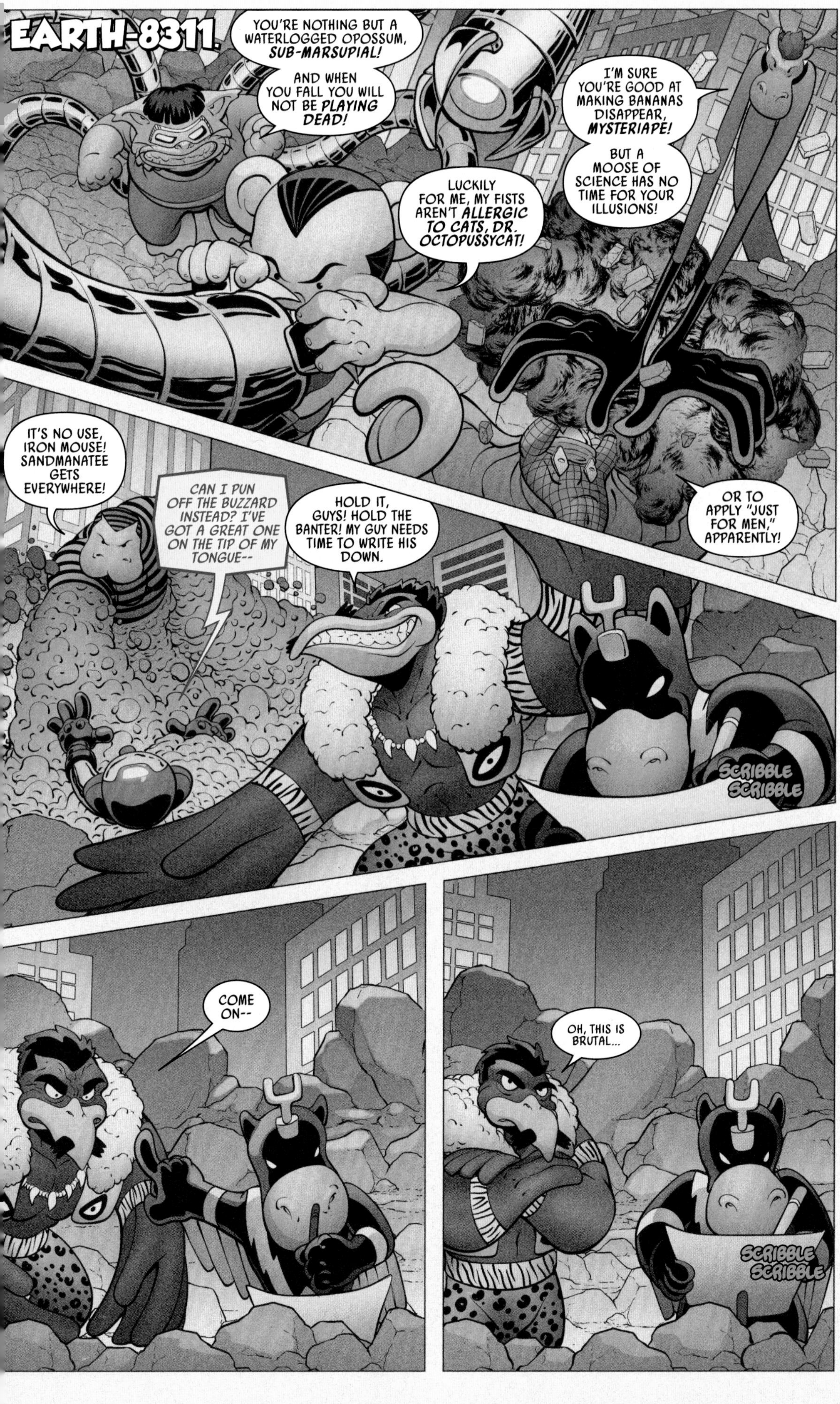
EARTH-8311.
YOU'RE NOTHING BUT A WATERLOGGED OPOSSUM, SUB-MARSUPIAL!
AND WHEN YOU FALL YOU WILL NOT BE PLAYING DEAD!
LUCKILY FOR ME, MY FISTS AREN'T ALLERGIC TO CATS, DR. OCTOPUSSYCAT!
I'M SURE YOU'RE GOOD AT MAKING BANANAS DISAPPEAR, MYSTERIAPE!
BUT A MOOSE OF SCIENCE HAS NO TIME FOR YOUR ILLUSIONS!
OR TO APPLY "JUST FOR MEN," APPARENTLY!
IT'S NO USE, IRON MOUSE! SANDMANATEE GETS EVERYWHERE!
CAN I PUN OFF THE BUZZARD INSTEAD? I'VE GOT A GREAT ONE ON THE TIP OF MY TONGUE--
HOLD IT, GUYS! HOLD THE BANTER! MY GUY NEEDS TIME TO WRITE HIS DOWN.
SCRIBBLE SCRIBBLE
COME ON--
OH, THIS IS BRUTAL...
SCRIBBLE SCRIBBLE

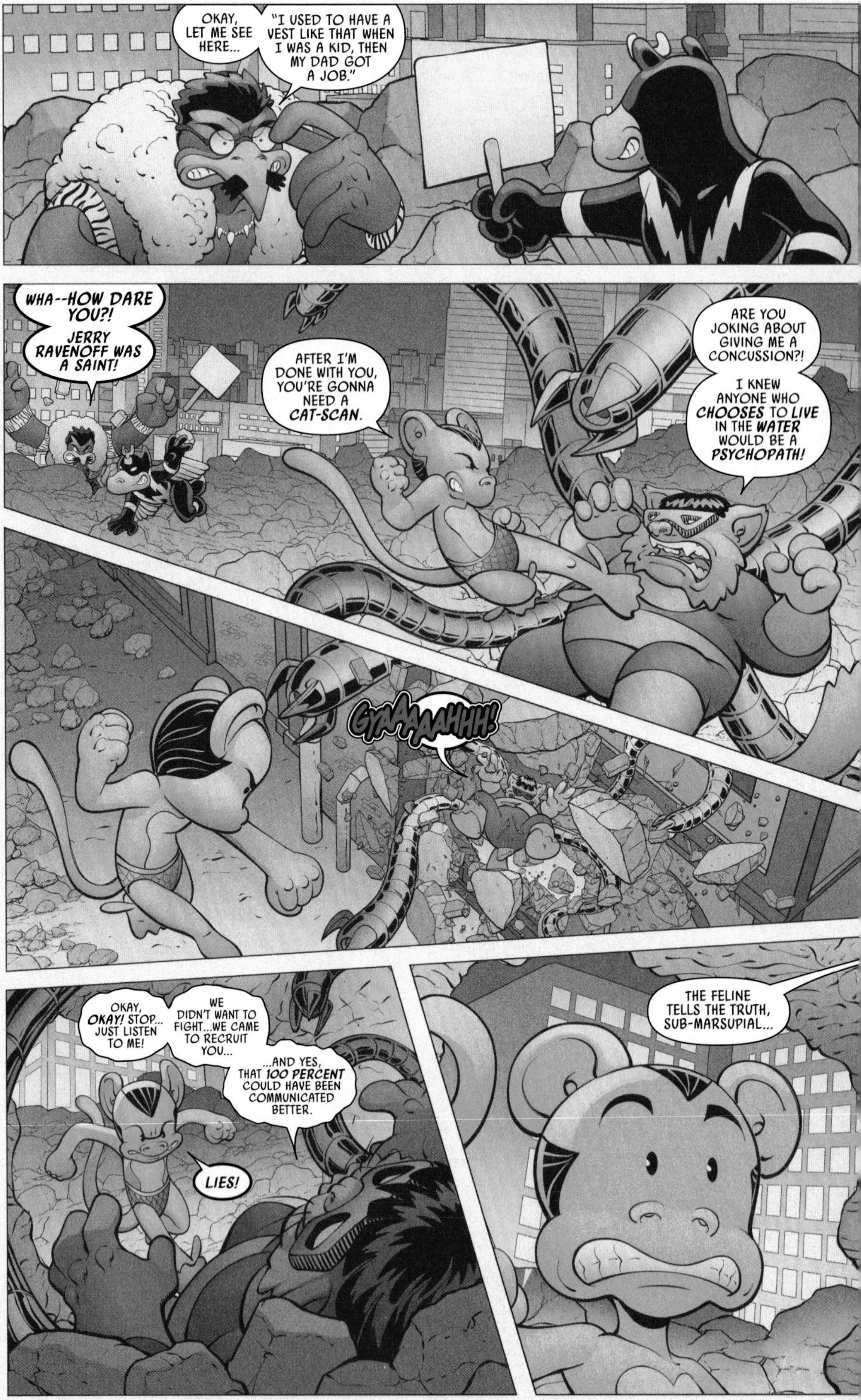
OKAY, LET ME SEE HERE...
"I USED TO HAVE A VEST LIKE THAT WHEN I WAS A KID, THEN MY DAD GOT A JOB."
WHA--HOW DARE YOU?! JERRY RAVENOFF WAS A SAINT!
AFTER I'M DONE WITH YOU, YOU'RE GONNA NEED A CAT-SCAN.
ARE YOU JOKING ABOUT GIVING ME A CONCUSSION?!
I KNEW ANYONE WHO CHOOSES TO LIVE IN THE WATER WOULD BE A PSYCHOPATH!
GYAAAAAHHH!
OKAY, OKAY! STOP... JUST LISTEN TO ME!
WE DIDN'T WANT TO FIGHT...WE CAME TO RECRUIT YOU...
...AND YES, THAT 100 PERCENT COULD HAVE BEEN COMMUNICATED BETTER.
LIES!
THE FELINE TELLS THE TRUTH, SUB-MARSUPIAL...

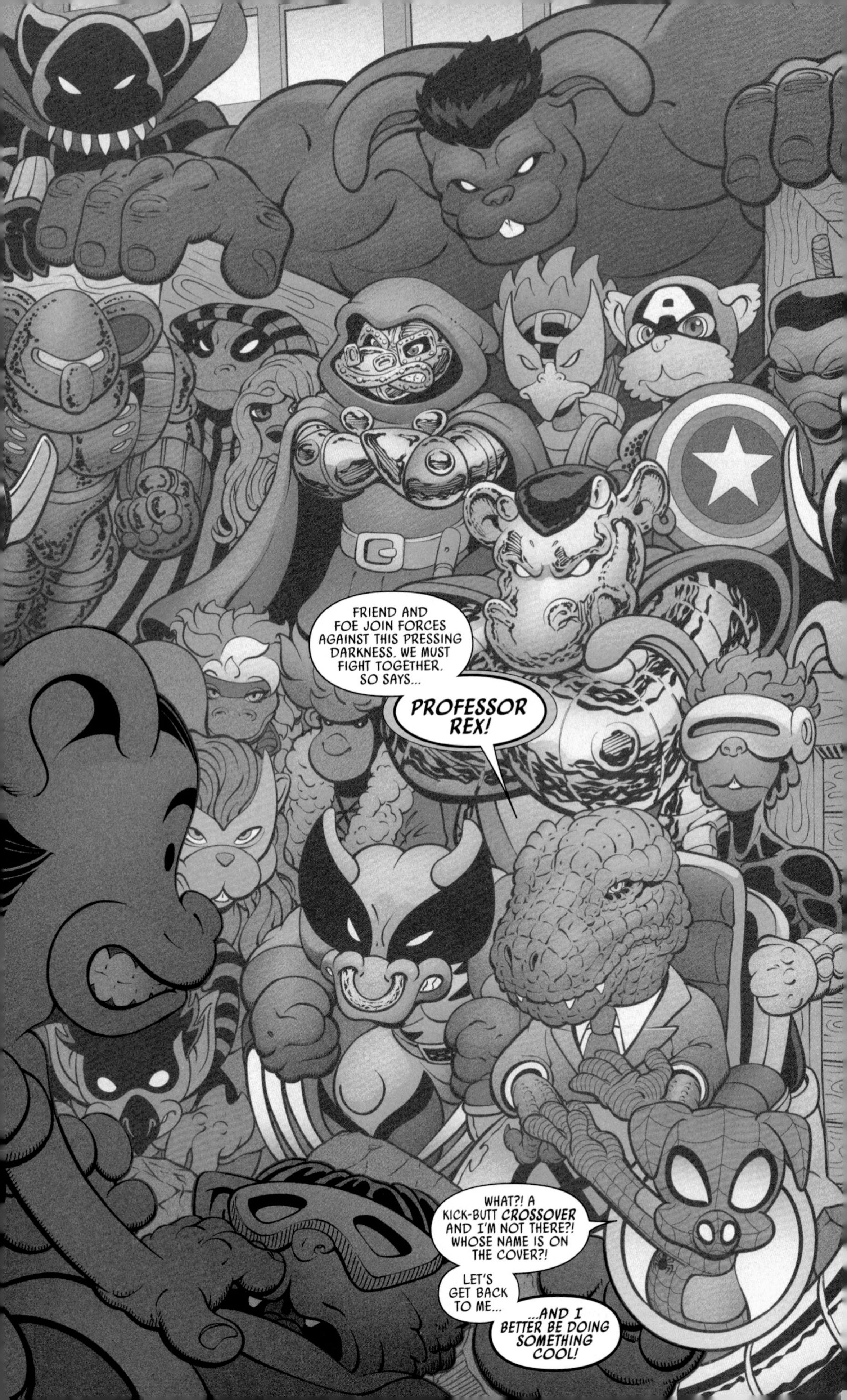
FRIEND AND FOE JOIN FORCES AGAINST THIS PRESSING DARKNESS. WE MUST FIGHT TOGETHER. SO SAYS...
PROFESSOR REX!
WHAT?! A KICK-BUTT CROSSOVER AND I'M NOT THERE?! WHOSE NAME IS ON THE COVER?!
LET'S GET BACK TO ME...
...AND I BETTER BE DOING SOMETHING COOL!

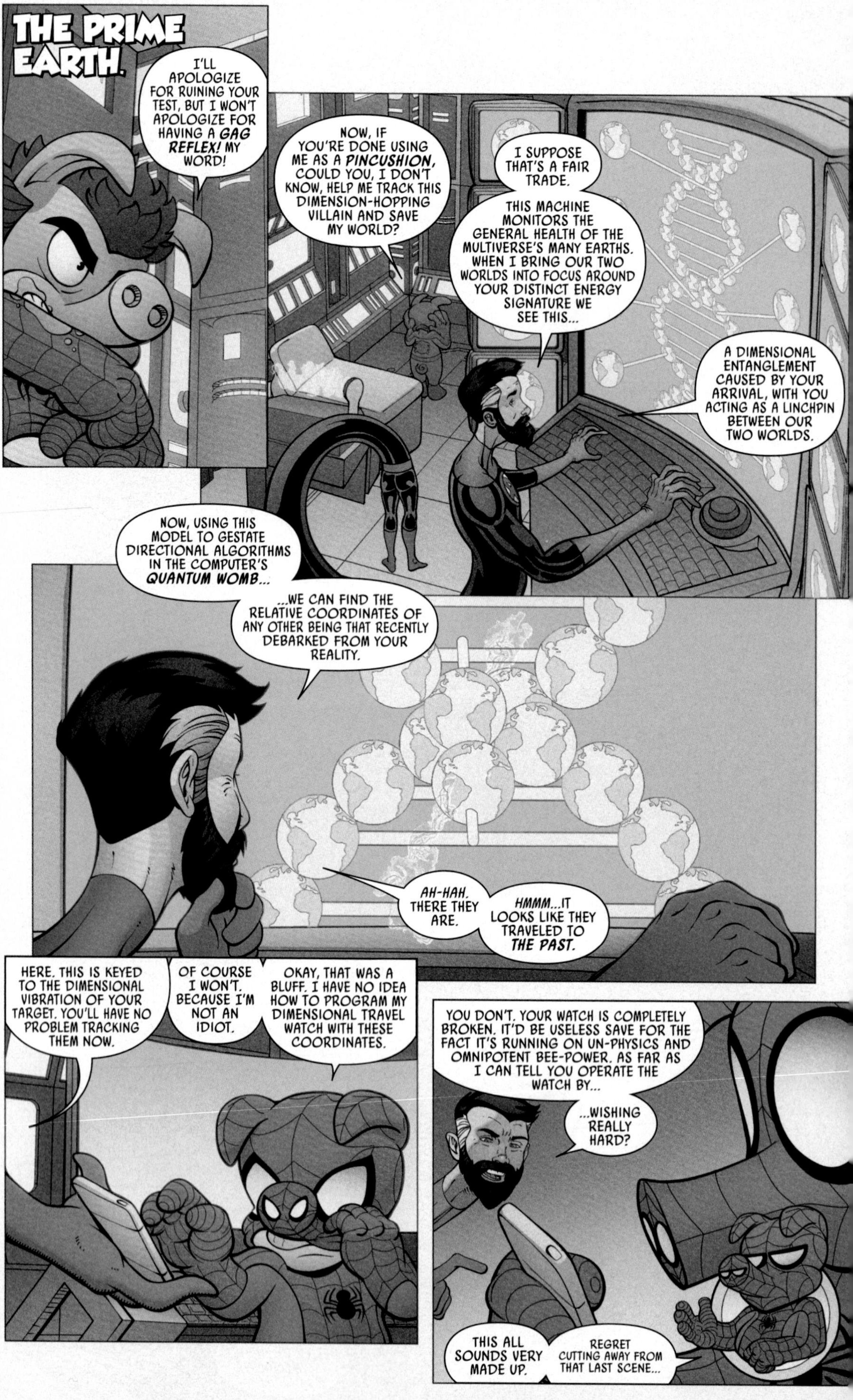
THE PRIME EARTH.
I'LL APOLOGIZE FOR RUINING YOUR TEST, BUT I WON'T APOLOGIZE FOR HAVING A GAG REFLEX! MY WORD!
NOW, IF YOU'RE DONE USING ME AS A PINCUSHION, COULD YOU, I DON'T KNOW, HELP ME TRACK THIS DIMENSION-HOPPING VILLAIN AND SAVE MY WORLD?
I SUPPOSE THAT'S A FAIR TRADE.
THIS MACHINE MONITORS THE GENERAL HEALTH OF THE MULTIVERSE'S MANY EARTHS. WHEN I BRING OUR TWO WORLDS INTO FOCUS AROUND YOUR DISTINCT ENERGY SIGNATURE WE SEE THIS...
A DIMENSIONAL ENTANGLEMENT CAUSED BY YOUR ARRIVAL, WITH YOU ACTING AS A LINCHPIN BETWEEN OUR TWO WORLDS.
NOW, USING THIS MODEL TO GESTATE DIRECTIONAL ALGORITHMS IN THE COMPUTER'S QUANTUM WOMB...
...WE CAN FIND THE RELATIVE COORDINATES OF ANY OTHER BEING THAT RECENTLY DEBARKED FROM YOUR REALITY.
AH-HAH. THERE THEY ARE.
HMMM...IT LOOKS LIKE THEY TRAVELED TO THE PAST.
HERE. THIS IS KEYED TO THE DIMENSIONAL VIBRATION OF YOUR TARGET. YOU'LL HAVE NO PROBLEM TRACKING THEM NOW.
OF COURSE I WON'T. BECAUSE I'M NOT AN IDIOT.
OKAY, THAT WAS A BLUFF. I HAVE NO IDEA HOW TO PROGRAM MY DIMENSIONAL TRAVEL WATCH WITH THESE COORDINATES.
YOU DON'T. YOUR WATCH IS COMPLETELY BROKEN. IT'D BE USELESS SAVE FOR THE FACT IT'S RUNNING ON UN-PHYSICS AND OMNIPOTENT BEE-POWER. AS FAR AS I CAN TELL YOU OPERATE THE WATCH BY...
...WISHING REALLY HARD?
THIS ALL SOUNDS VERY MADE UP.
REGRET CUTTING AWAY FROM THAT LAST SCENE...

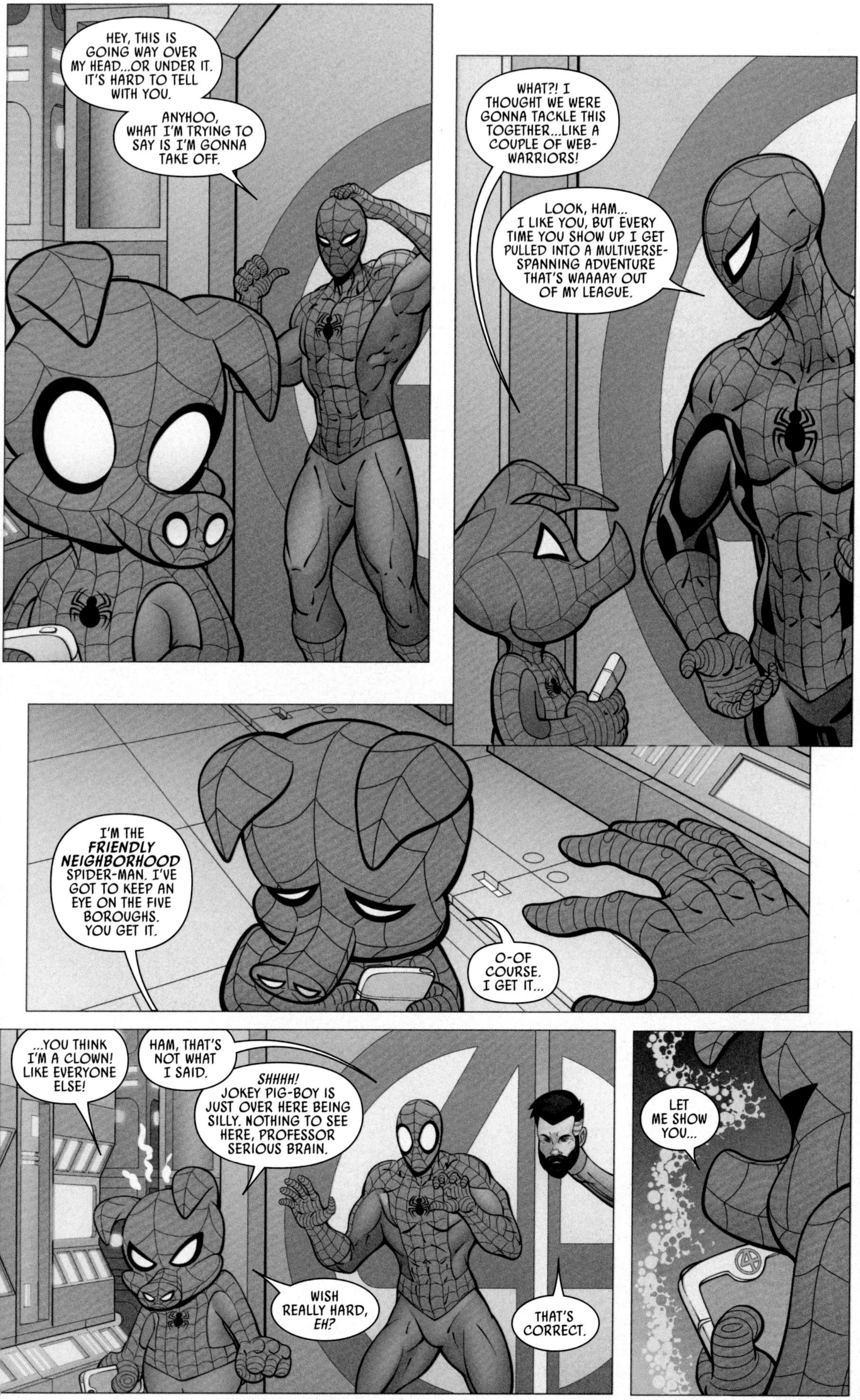
HEY, THIS IS GOING WAY OVER MY HEAD...OR UNDER IT. IT'S HARD TO TELL WITH YOU.
ANYHOO, WHAT I'M TRYING TO SAY IS I'M GONNA TAKE OFF.
WHAT?! I THOUGHT WE WERE GONNA TACKLE THIS TOGETHER...LIKE A COUPLE OF WEB-WARRIORS!
LOOK, HAM... I LIKE YOU, BUT EVERY TIME YOU SHOW UP I GET PULLED INTO A MULTIVERSE-SPANNING ADVENTURE THAT'S WAAAAY OUT OF MY LEAGUE.
I'M THE FRIENDLY NEIGHBORHOOD SPIDER-MAN. I'VE GOT TO KEEP AN EYE ON THE FIVE BOROUGHS. YOU GET IT.
O-OF COURSE. I GET IT...
...YOU THINK I'M A CLOWN! LIKE EVERYONE ELSE!
HAM, THAT'S NOT WHAT I SAID.
SHHHH! JOKEY PIG-BOY IS JUST OVER HERE BEING SILLY. NOTHING TO SEE HERE, PROFESSOR SERIOUS BRAIN.
WISH REALLY HARD, EH?
THAT'S CORRECT.
LET ME SHOW YOU...

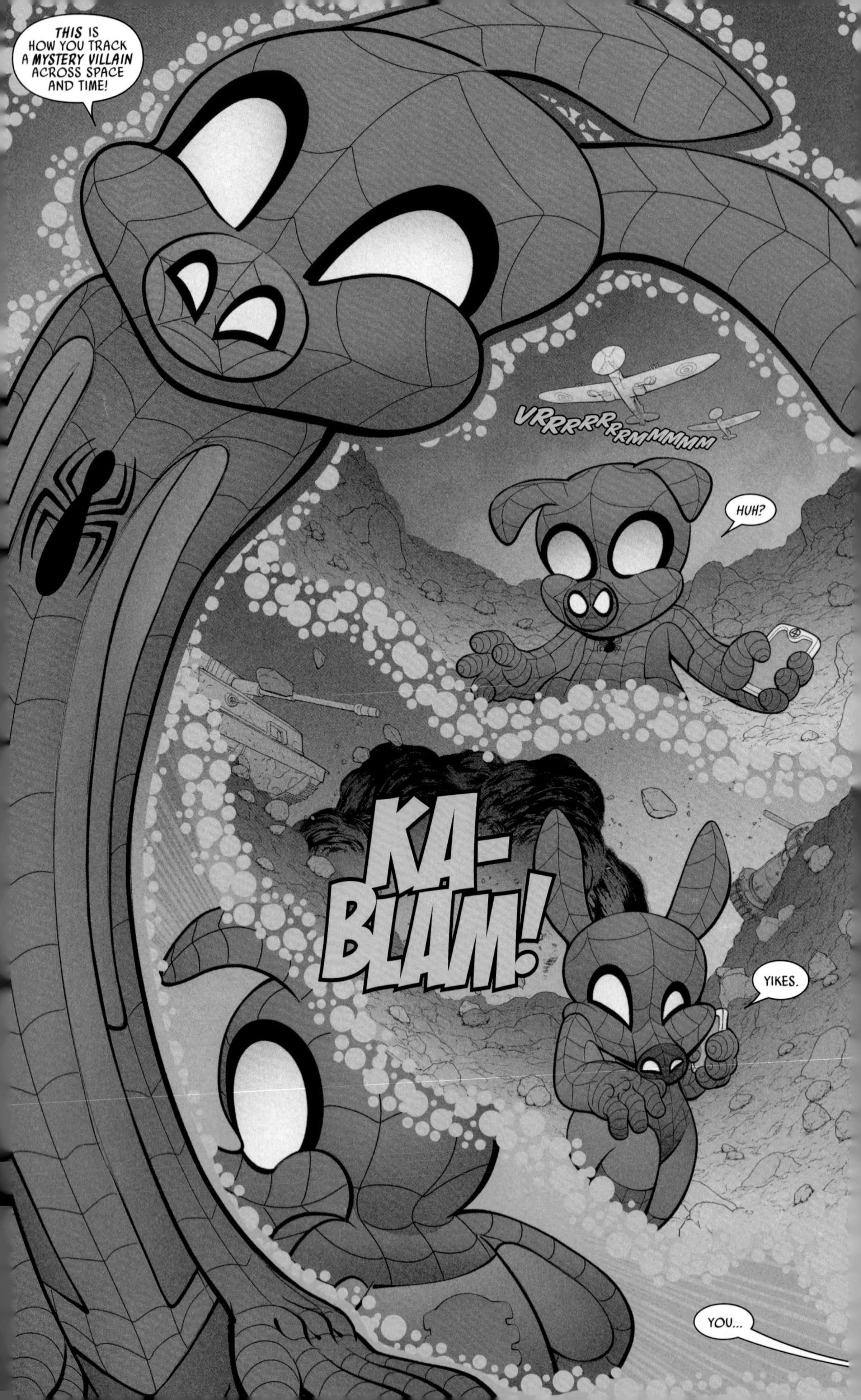
THIS IS HOW YOU TRACK A MYSTERY VILLAIN ACROSS SPACE AND TIME!
VRRRRRRRMMMMM
HUH?
KA-BLAM!
YIKES.
YOU...

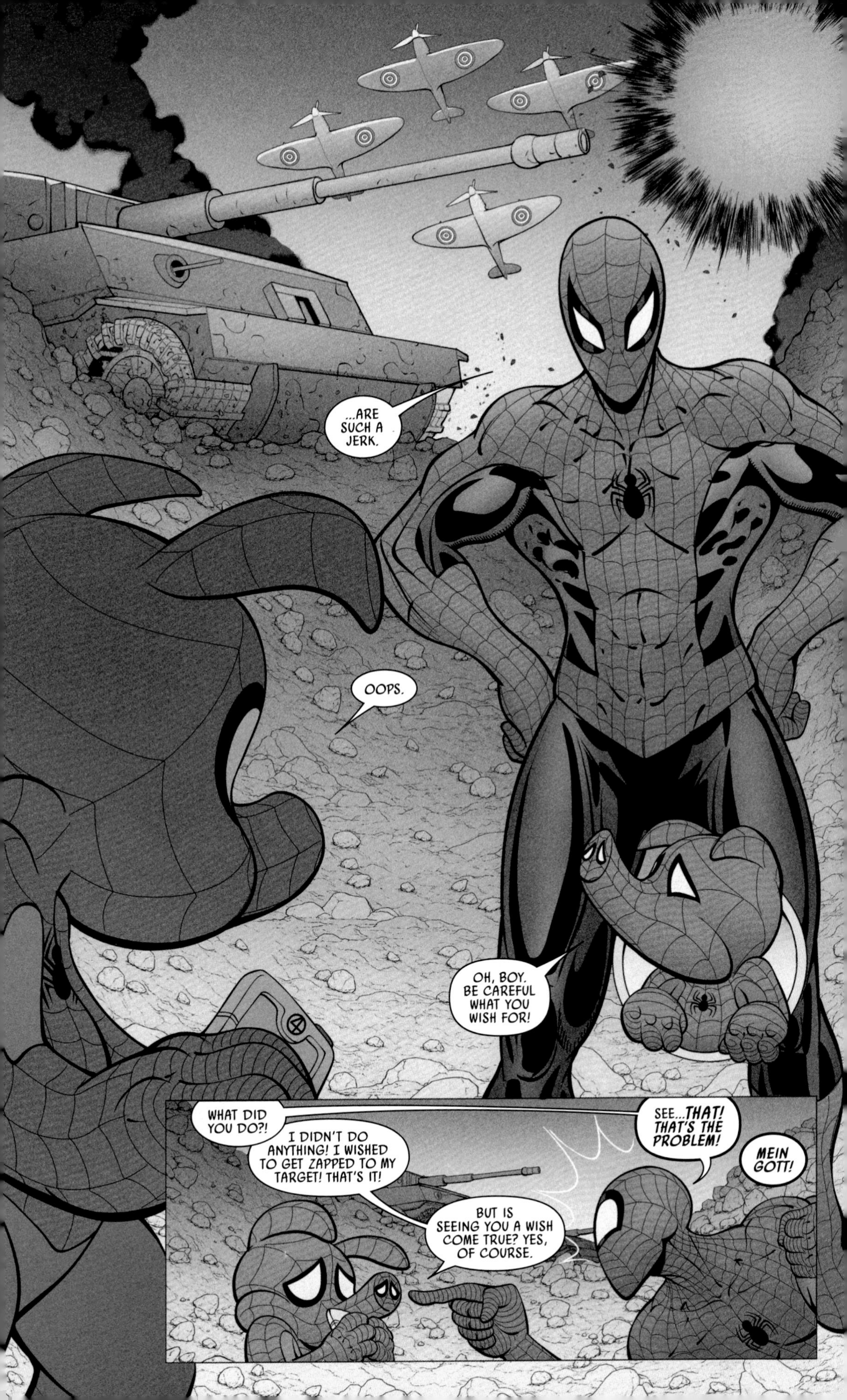
...ARE SUCH A JERK.
OOPS.
OH, BOY. BE CAREFUL WHAT YOU WISH FOR!
WHAT DID YOU DO?!
I DIDN'T DO ANYTHING! I WISHED TO GET ZAPPED TO MY TARGET! THAT'S IT!
SEE...THAT! THAT'S THE PROBLEM!
BUT IS SEEING YOU A WISH COME TRUE? YES, OF COURSE.
MEIN GOTT!

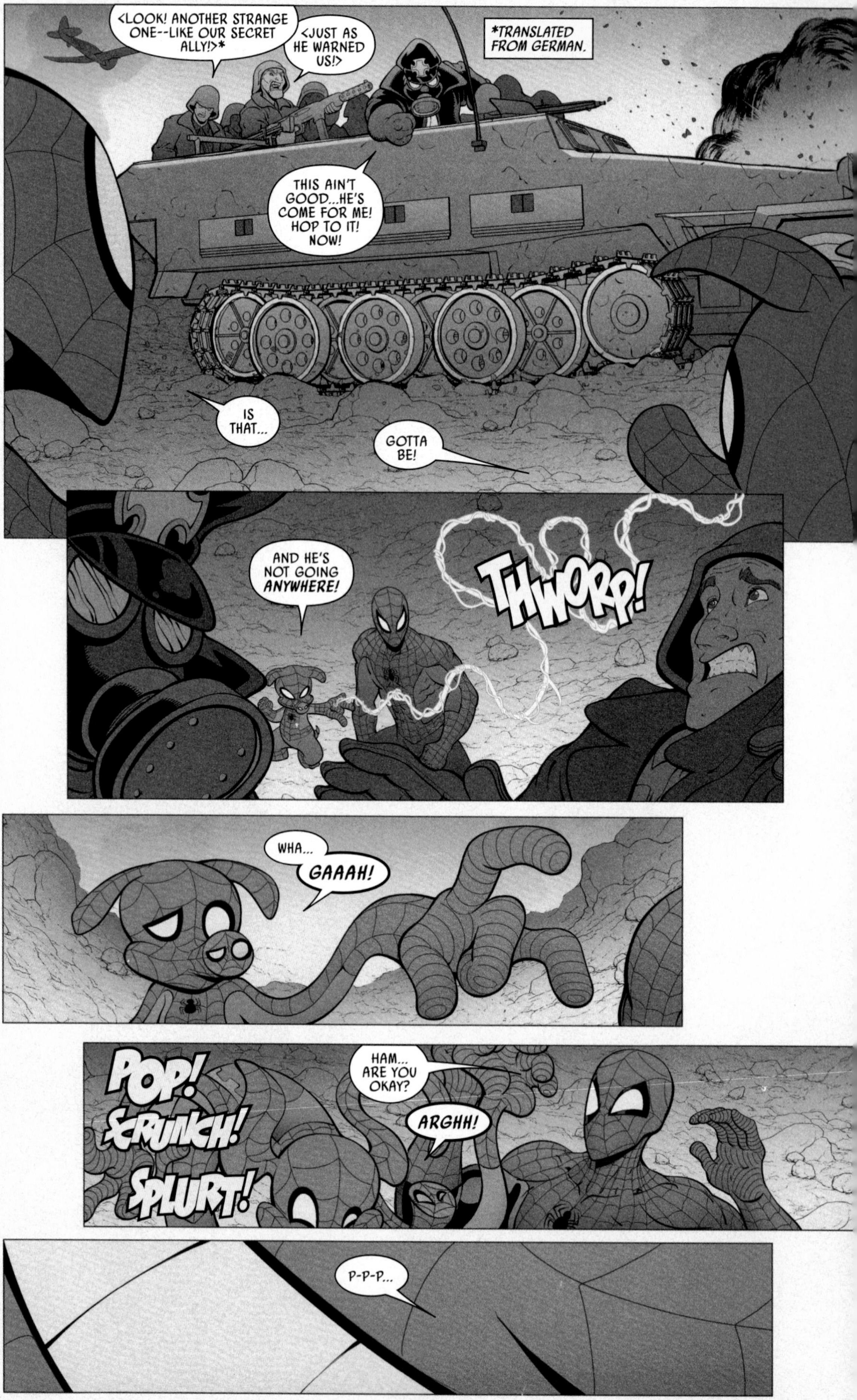

<LOOK! ANOTHER STRANGE ONE--LIKE OUR SECRET ALLY!>*
<JUST AS HE WARNED US!>
*TRANSLATED FROM GERMAN.
THIS AIN'T GOOD...HE'S COME FOR ME! HOP TO IT! NOW!
IS THAT...
GOTTA BE!
AND HE'S NOT GOING ANYWHERE!
THWORP!
WHA... GAAAH!
POP!
SCRUNCH!
SPLURT!
HAM... ARE YOU OKAY?
ARGHH!
P-P-P...

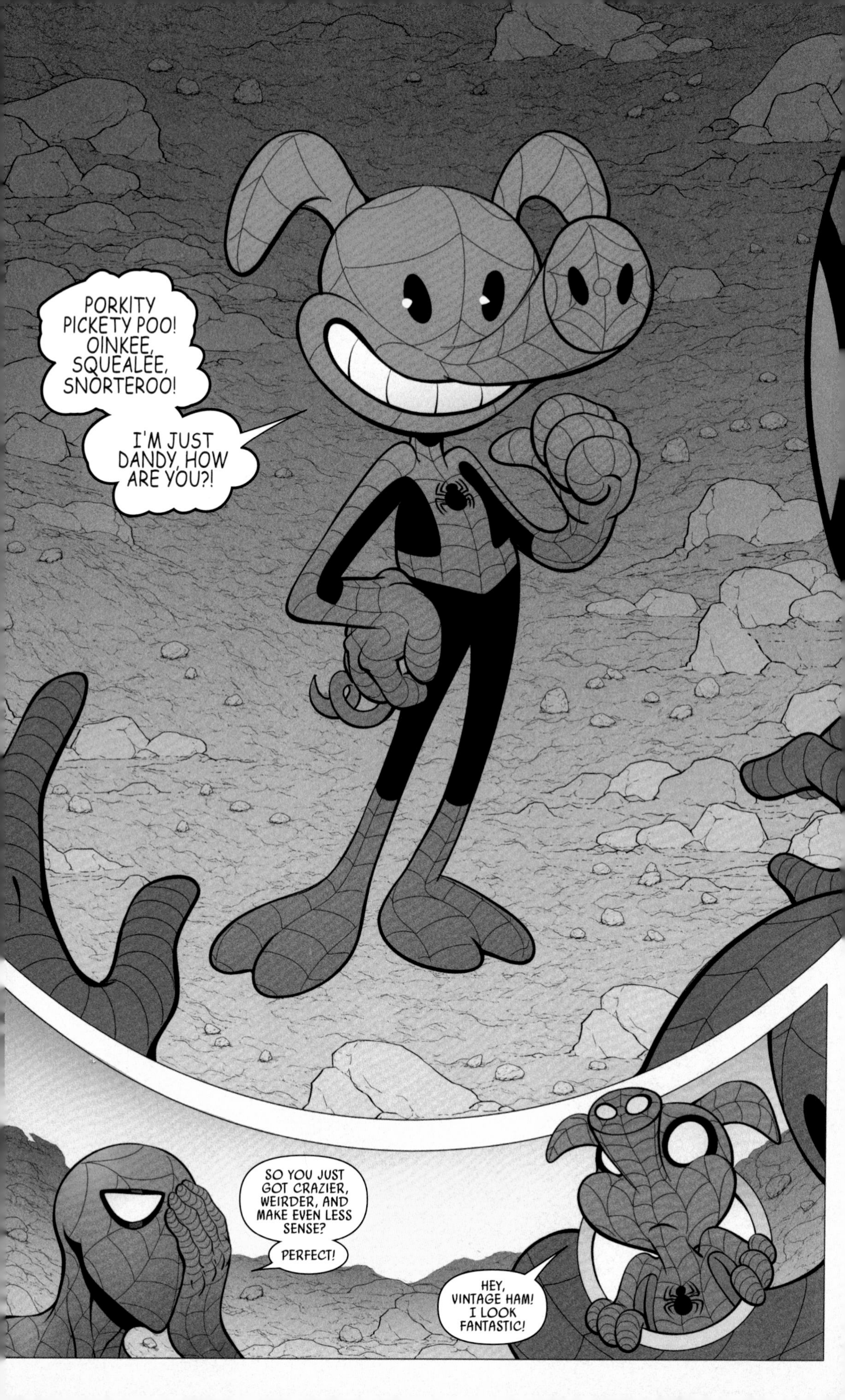
PORKITY PICKETY POO! OINKEE, SQUEALEE, SNORTEROO!
I'M JUST DANDY, HOW ARE YOU?!
SO YOU JUST GOT CRAZIER, WEIRDER, AND MAKE EVEN LESS SENSE?
PERFECT!
HEY, VINTAGE HAM! I LOOK FANTASTIC!

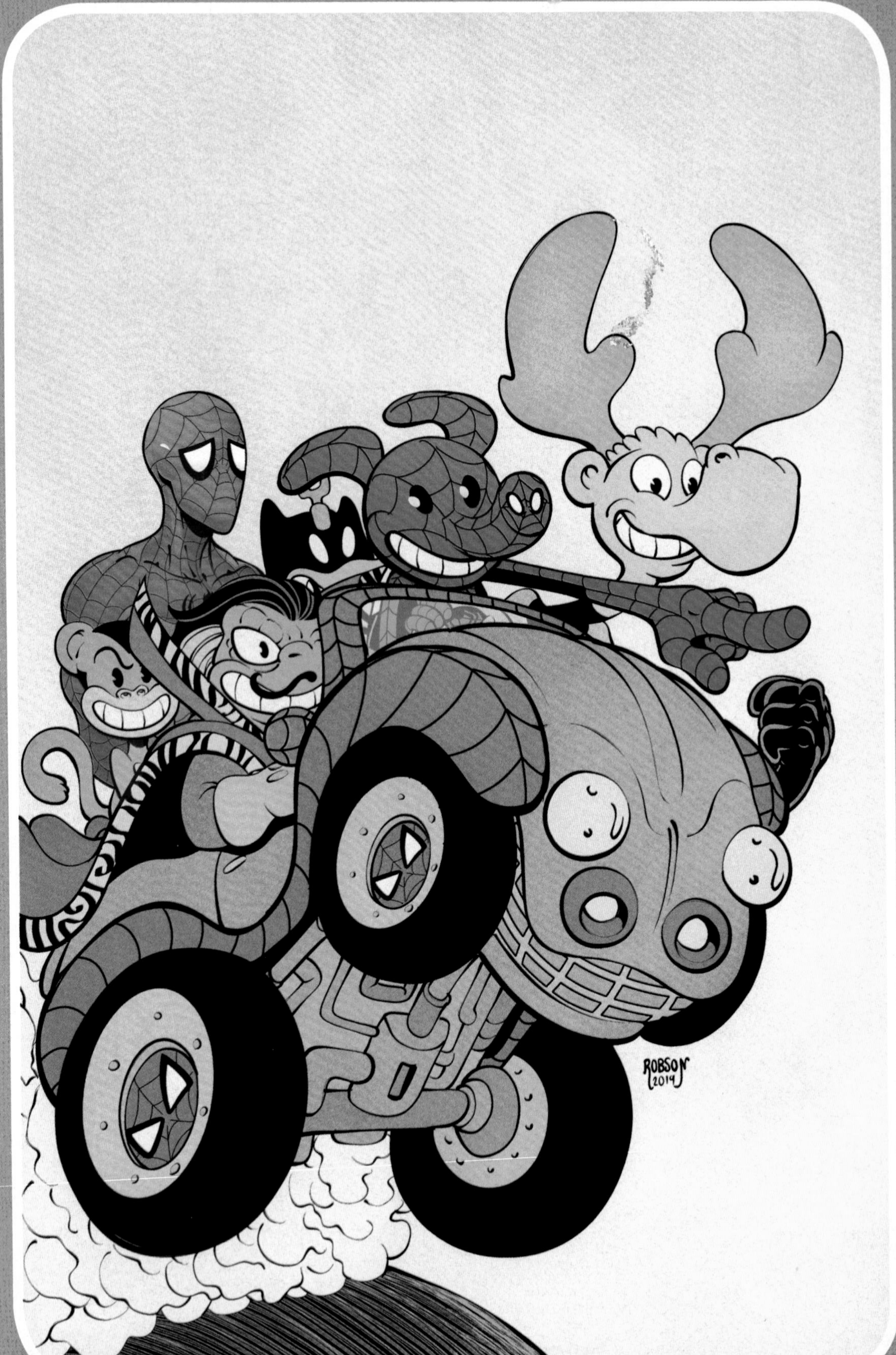
ROBSON
2019

3

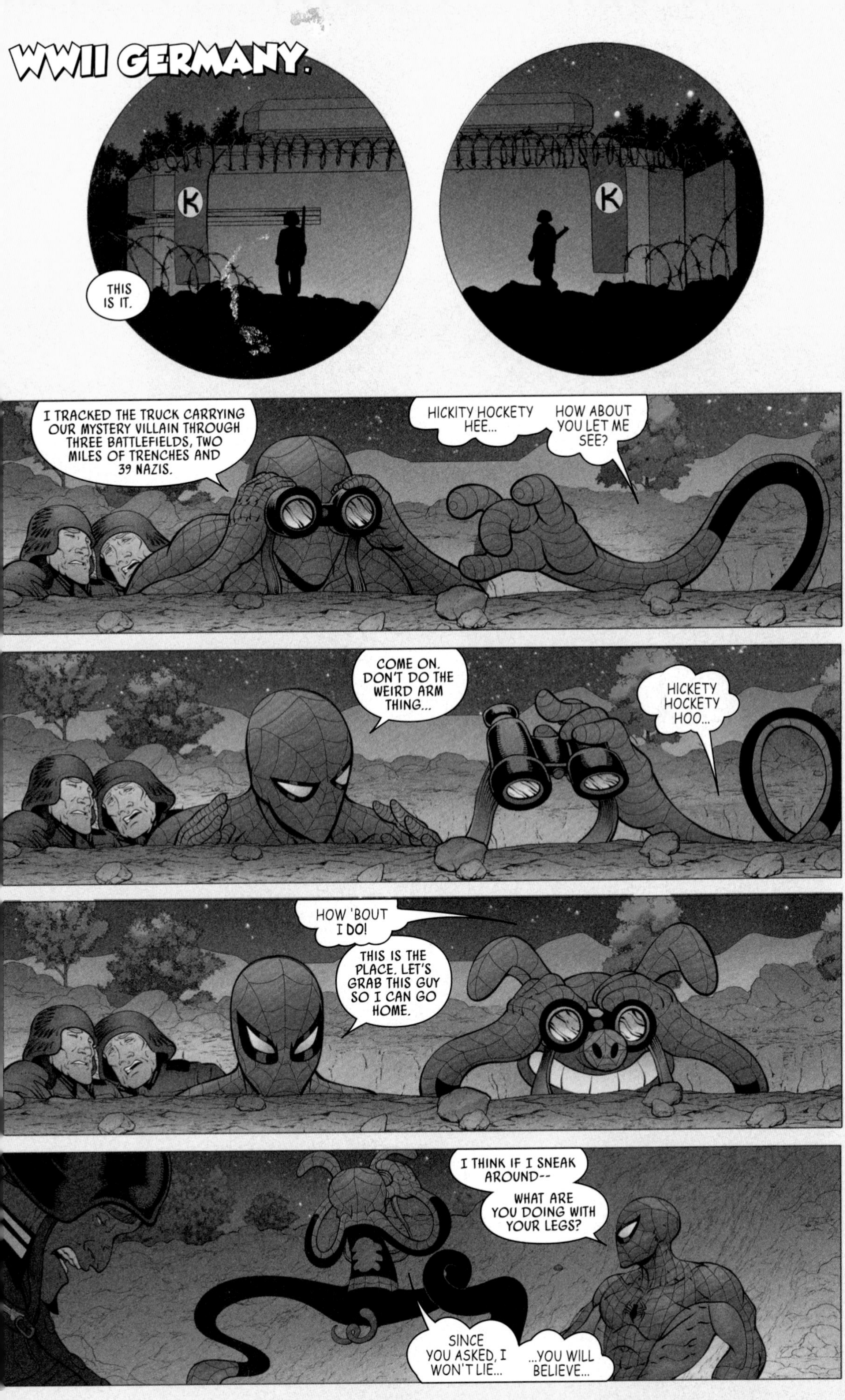
WWII GERMANY.
THIS IS IT.
K
K
I TRACKED THE TRUCK CARRYING OUR MYSTERY VILLAIN THROUGH THREE BATTLEFIELDS, TWO MILES OF TRENCHES AND 39 NAZIS.
HICKITY HOCKETY HEE...
HOW ABOUT YOU LET ME SEE?
COME ON. DON'T DO THE WEIRD ARM THING...
HICKETY HOCKETY HOO...
HOW 'BOUT I DO!
THIS IS THE PLACE. LET'S GRAB THIS GUY SO I CAN GO HOME.
I THINK IF I SNEAK AROUND--
WHAT ARE YOU DOING WITH YOUR LEGS?
SINCE YOU ASKED, I WON'T LIE...
...YOU WILL BELIEVE...

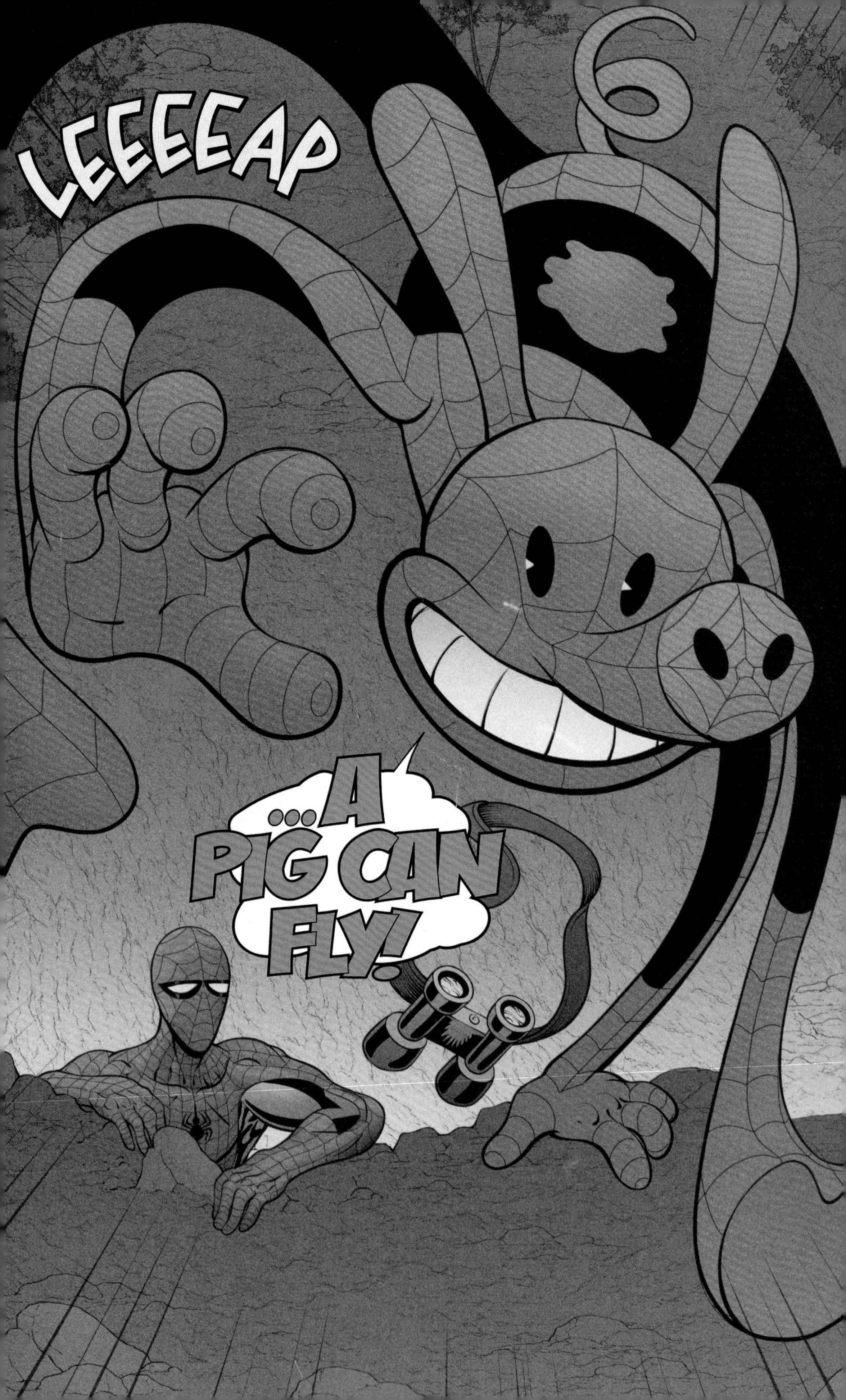
LEEEEAP
...A PIG CAN FLY!

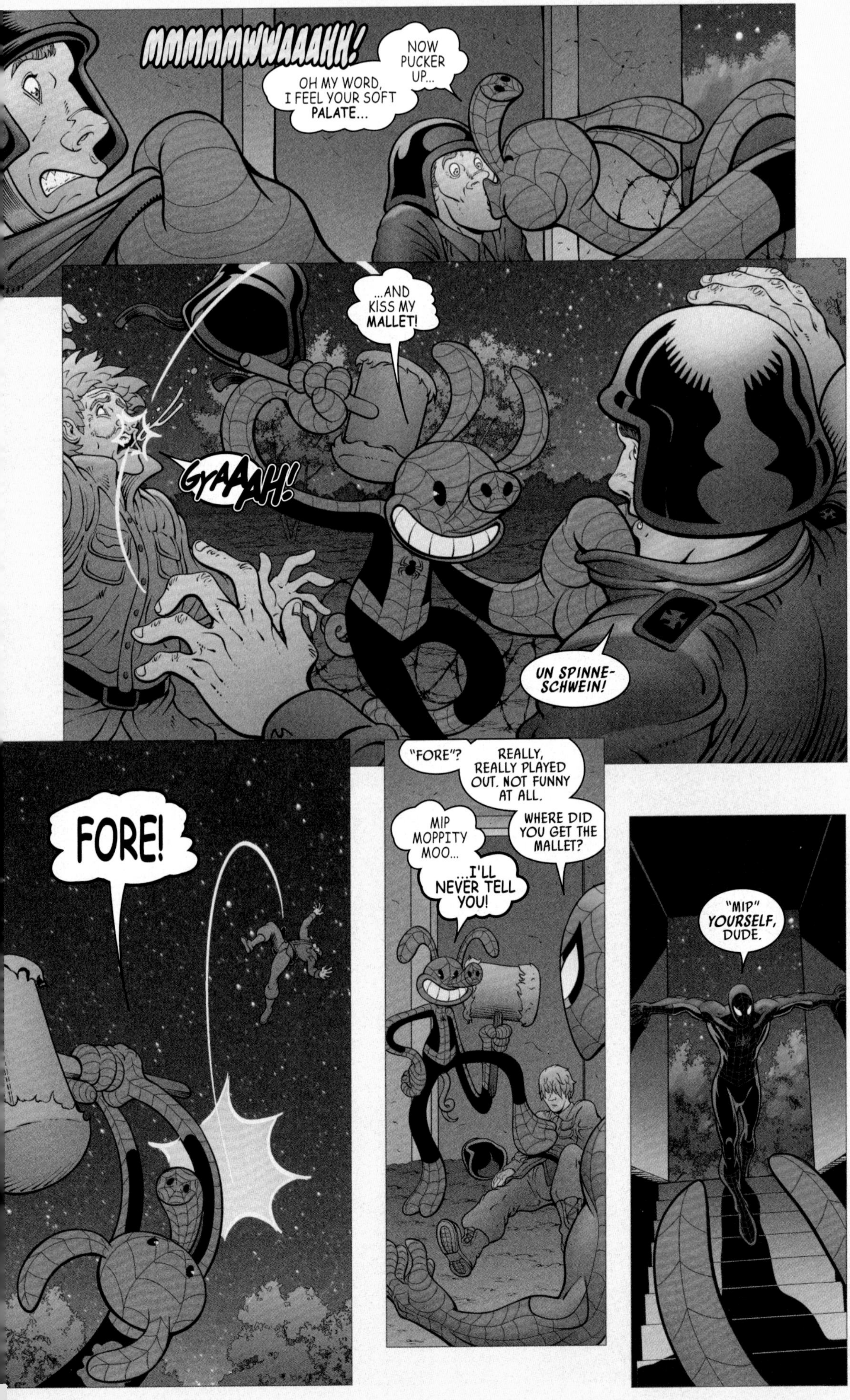
MMMMMWWAAAHH!
OH MY WORD, I FEEL YOUR SOFT PALATE...
NOW PUCKER UP...
...AND KISS MY MALLET!
GYAAAAH!
UN SPINNE-SCHWEIN!
FORE!
"FORE"?
REALLY, REALLY PLAYED OUT. NOT FUNNY AT ALL.
WHERE DID YOU GET THE MALLET?
MIP MOPPITY MOO...
...I'LL NEVER TELL YOU!
"MIP" YOURSELF, DUDE.

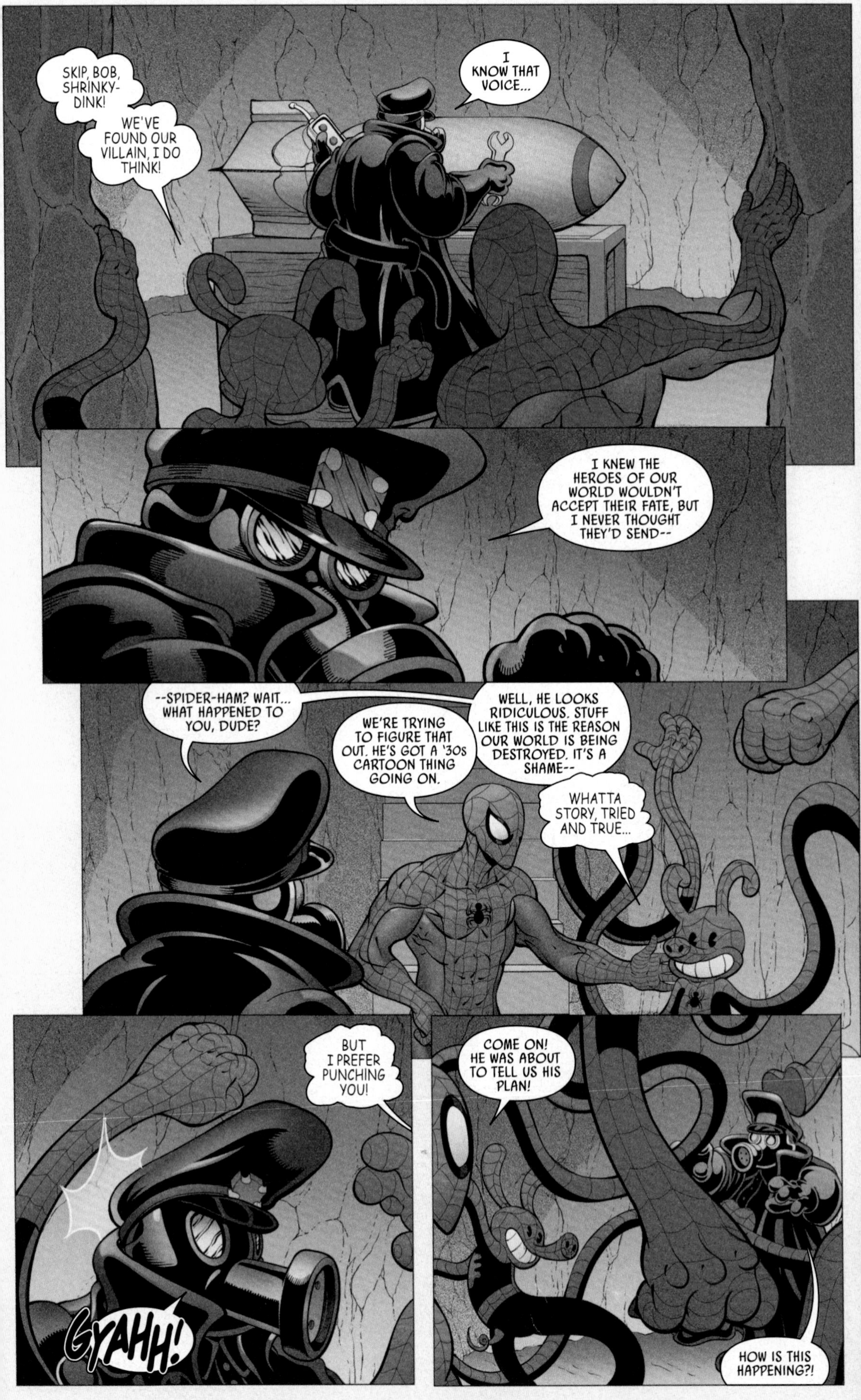
SKIP, BOB, SHRINKY-DINK!
WE'VE FOUND OUR VILLAIN, I DO THINK!
I KNOW THAT VOICE...
I KNEW THE HEROES OF OUR WORLD WOULDN'T ACCEPT THEIR FATE, BUT I NEVER THOUGHT THEY'D SEND--
--SPIDER-HAM? WAIT... WHAT HAPPENED TO YOU, DUDE?
WE'RE TRYING TO FIGURE THAT OUT. HE'S GOT A '30s CARTOON THING GOING ON.
WELL, HE LOOKS RIDICULOUS. STUFF LIKE THIS IS THE REASON OUR WORLD IS BEING DESTROYED. IT'S A SHAME--
WHATTA STORY, TRIED AND TRUE...
BUT I PREFER PUNCHING YOU!
GYAHH!
COME ON! HE WAS ABOUT TO TELL US HIS PLAN!
HOW IS THIS HAPPENING?!

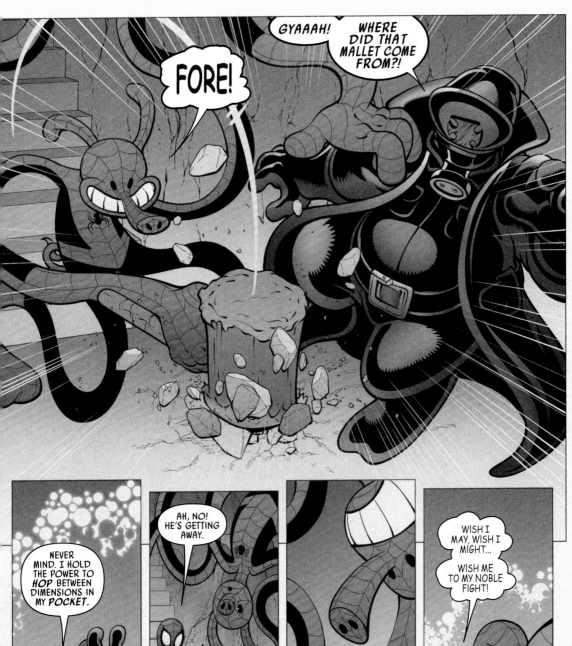

GYAAAH! WHERE DID THAT MALLET COME FROM?!

FORE!

NEVER MIND. I HOLD THE POWER TO *HOP* BETWEEN DIMENSIONS IN MY *POCKET.*

AH, NO! HE'S GETTING AWAY.

TOON TIMMY TINY TUM! I THINK YOU'RE RIGHT, AND NOW I'M BUMMED!

COME ON! MR. FANTASTIC'S GIZMO HAS THE COORDINATES OF HIS NEW LOCATION. DO THAT THING WHERE YOU WISH US THERE!

WISH I MAY, WISH I MIGHT...

WISH ME TO MY NOBLE FIGHT!

FINE, YEAH, HOWEVER YOU WANT TO SAY IT.

LET'S GO!

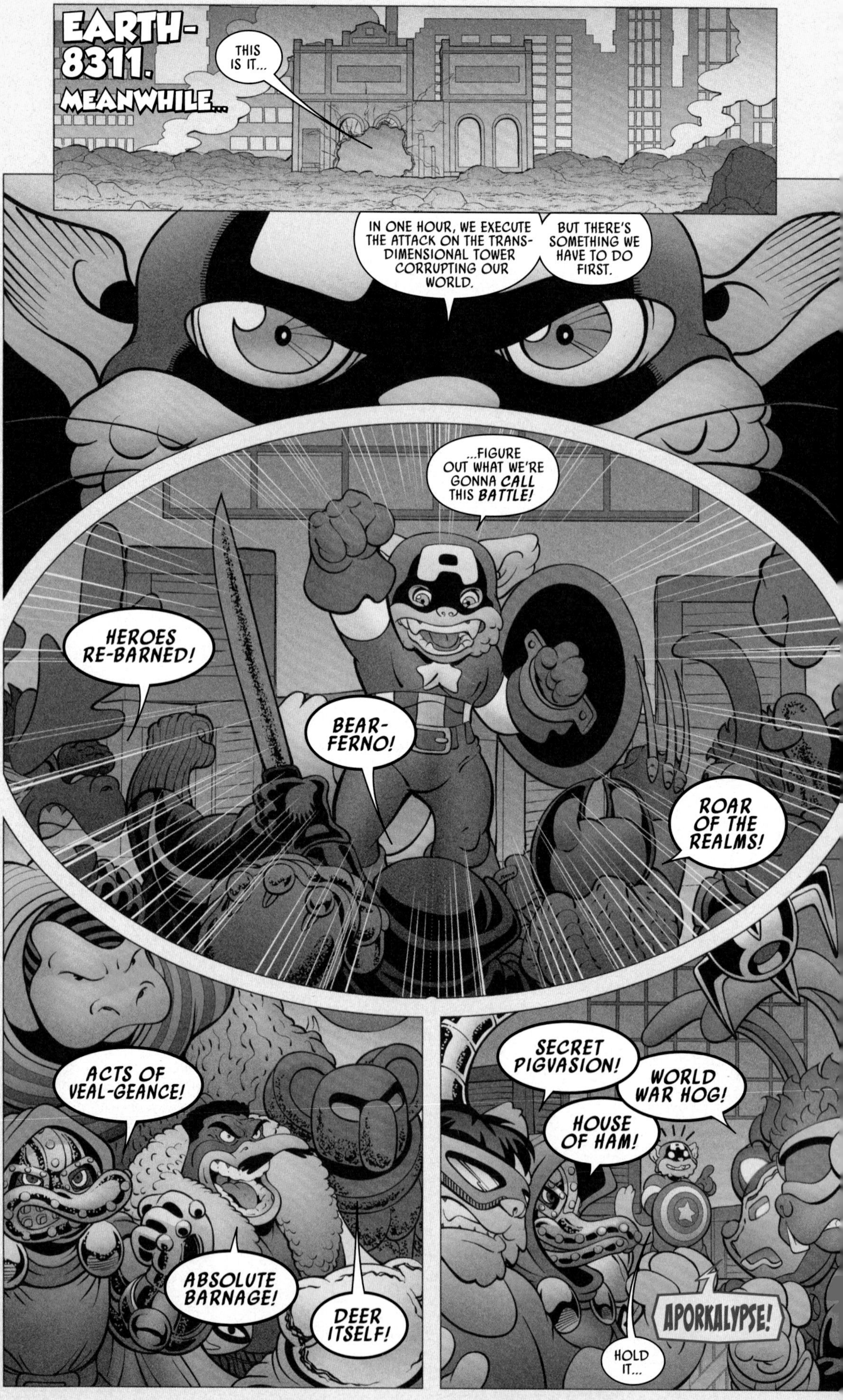
EARTH-8311. MEANWHILE...
THIS IS IT...
IN ONE HOUR, WE EXECUTE THE ATTACK ON THE TRANS-DIMENSIONAL TOWER CORRUPTING OUR WORLD.
BUT THERE'S SOMETHING WE HAVE TO DO FIRST.
...FIGURE OUT WHAT WE'RE GONNA CALL THIS BATTLE!
HEROES RE-BARNED!
BEAR-FERNO!
ROAR OF THE REALMS!
ACTS OF VEAL-GEANCE!
ABSOLUTE BARNAGE!
DEER ITSELF!
SECRET PIGVASION!
WORLD WAR HOG!
HOUSE OF HAM!
APORKALYPSE!
HOLD IT...

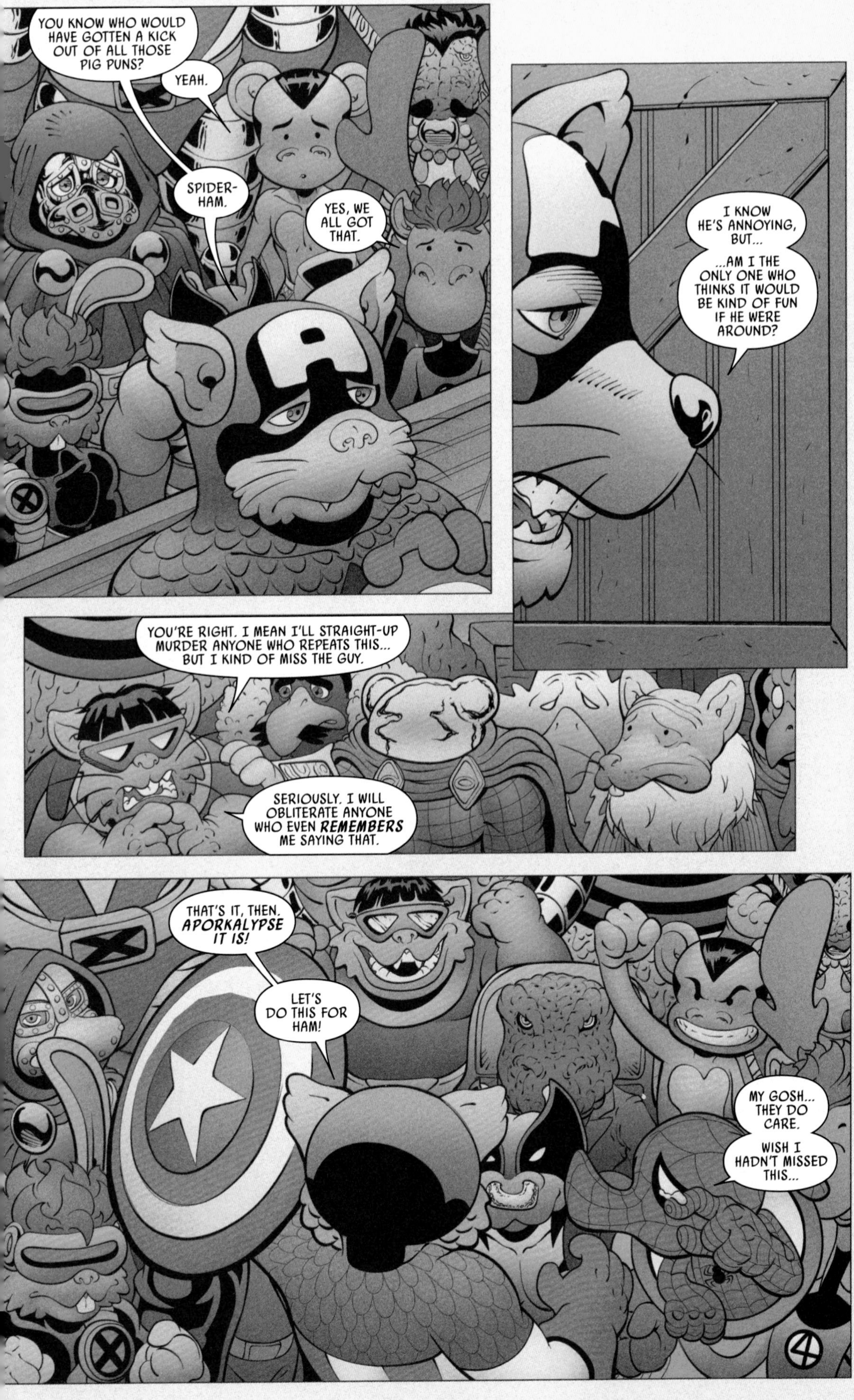
YOU KNOW WHO WOULD HAVE GOTTEN A KICK OUT OF ALL THOSE PIG PUNS?
YEAH.
SPIDER-HAM.
YES, WE ALL GOT THAT.
I KNOW HE'S ANNOYING, BUT...
...AM I THE ONLY ONE WHO THINKS IT WOULD BE KIND OF FUN IF HE WERE AROUND?
YOU'RE RIGHT. I MEAN I'LL STRAIGHT-UP MURDER ANYONE WHO REPEATS THIS... BUT I KIND OF MISS THE GUY.
SERIOUSLY. I WILL OBLITERATE ANYONE WHO EVEN **REMEMBERS** ME SAYING THAT.
THAT'S IT, THEN. ***APORKALYPSE* IT IS!**
LET'S DO THIS FOR HAM!
MY GOSH... THEY DO CARE.
WISH I HADN'T MISSED THIS...

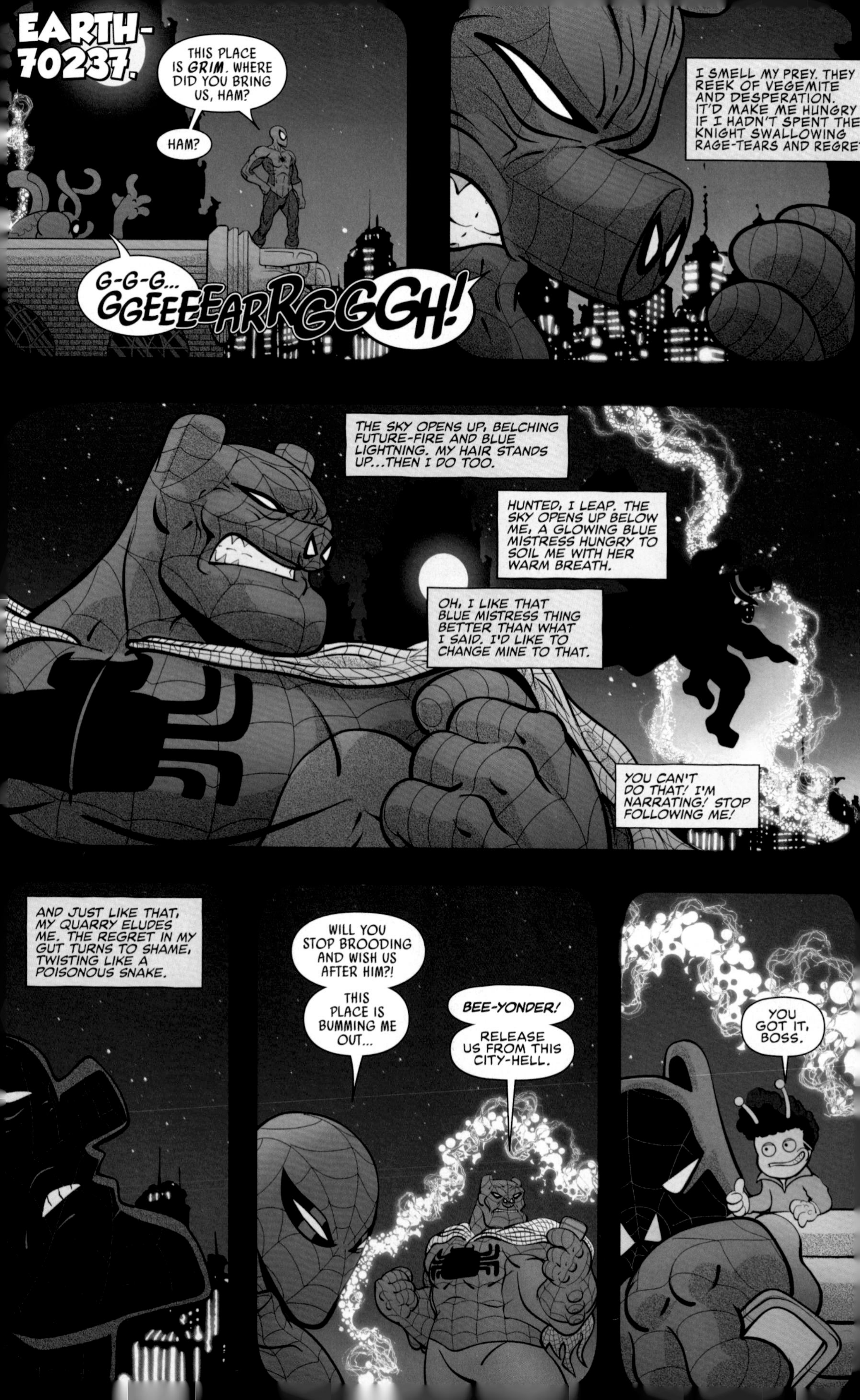
EARTH-70237.
THIS PLACE IS GRIM. WHERE DID YOU BRING US, HAM?
HAM?
G-G-G... GGEEEEARRGGGH!
I SMELL MY PREY. THEY REEK OF VEGEMITE AND DESPERATION. IT'D MAKE ME HUNGRY IF I HADN'T SPENT THE KNIGHT SWALLOWING RAGE-TEARS AND REGRE
THE SKY OPENS UP, BELCHING FUTURE-FIRE AND BLUE LIGHTNING. MY HAIR STANDS UP...THEN I DO TOO.
HUNTED, I LEAP. THE SKY OPENS UP BELOW ME, A GLOWING BLUE MISTRESS HUNGRY TO SOIL ME WITH HER WARM BREATH.
OH, I LIKE THAT BLUE MISTRESS THING BETTER THAN WHAT I SAID. I'D LIKE TO CHANGE MINE TO THAT.
YOU CAN'T DO THAT! I'M NARRATING! STOP FOLLOWING ME!
AND JUST LIKE THAT, MY QUARRY ELUDES ME. THE REGRET IN MY GUT TURNS TO SHAME, TWISTING LIKE A POISONOUS SNAKE.
WILL YOU STOP BROODING AND WISH US AFTER HIM?!
THIS PLACE IS BUMMING ME OUT...
BEE-YONDER!
RELEASE US FROM THIS CITY-HELL.
YOU GOT IT, BOSS.

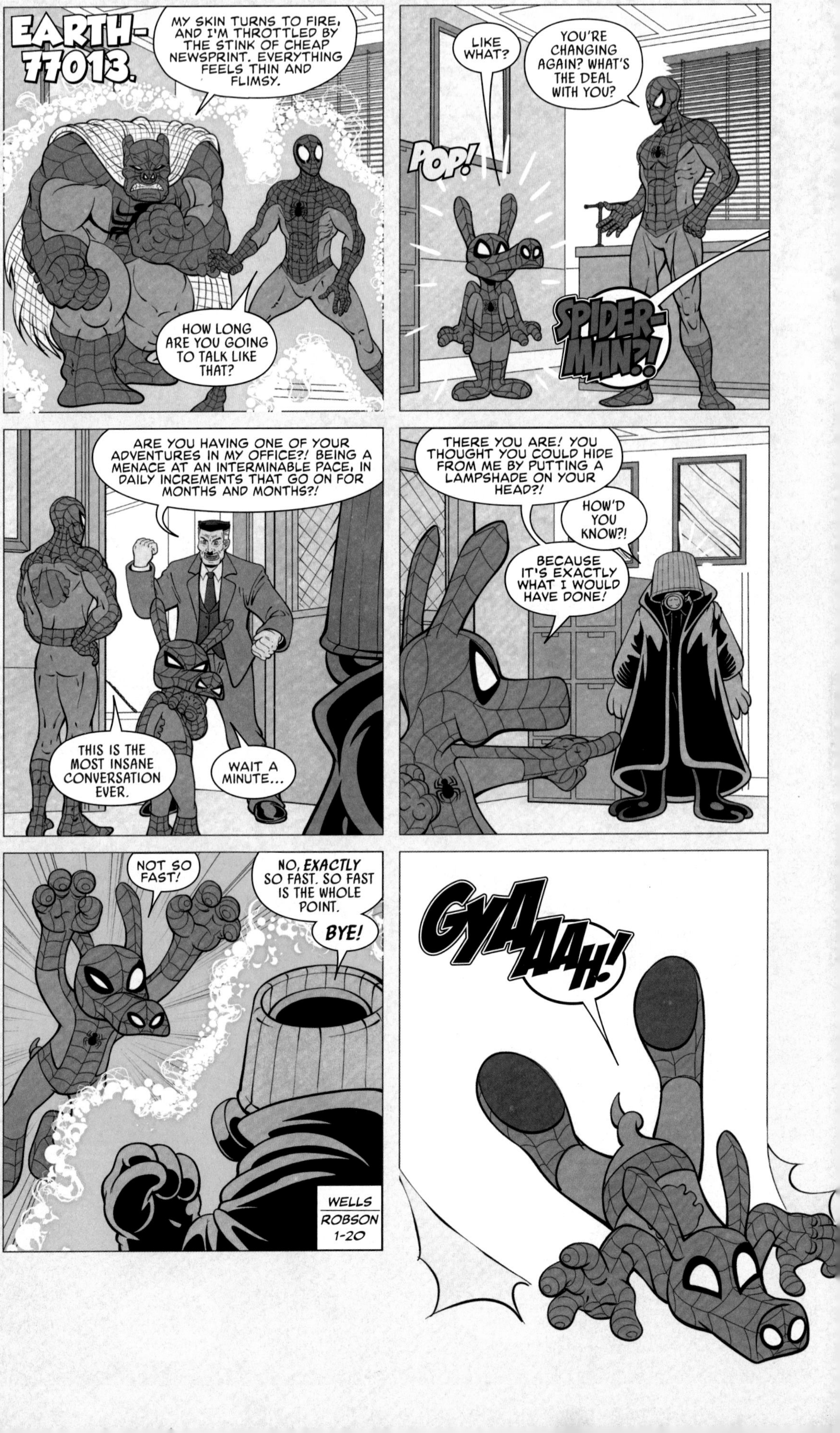
EARTH-77013.
MY SKIN TURNS TO FIRE, AND I'M THROTTLED BY THE STINK OF CHEAP NEWSPRINT. EVERYTHING FEELS THIN AND FLIMSY.
HOW LONG ARE YOU GOING TO TALK LIKE THAT?
LIKE WHAT?
YOU'RE CHANGING AGAIN? WHAT'S THE DEAL WITH YOU?
POP!
SPIDER-MAN?!
ARE YOU HAVING ONE OF YOUR ADVENTURES IN MY OFFICE?! BEING A MENACE AT AN INTERMINABLE PACE, IN DAILY INCREMENTS THAT GO ON FOR MONTHS AND MONTHS?!
THIS IS THE MOST INSANE CONVERSATION EVER.
WAIT A MINUTE...
THERE YOU ARE! YOU THOUGHT YOU COULD HIDE FROM ME BY PUTTING A LAMPSHADE ON YOUR HEAD?!
HOW'D YOU KNOW?!
BECAUSE IT'S EXACTLY WHAT I WOULD HAVE DONE!
NOT SO FAST!
NO, EXACTLY SO FAST. SO FAST IS THE WHOLE POINT.
BYE!
WELLS ROBSON 1-20
GYAAAAH!

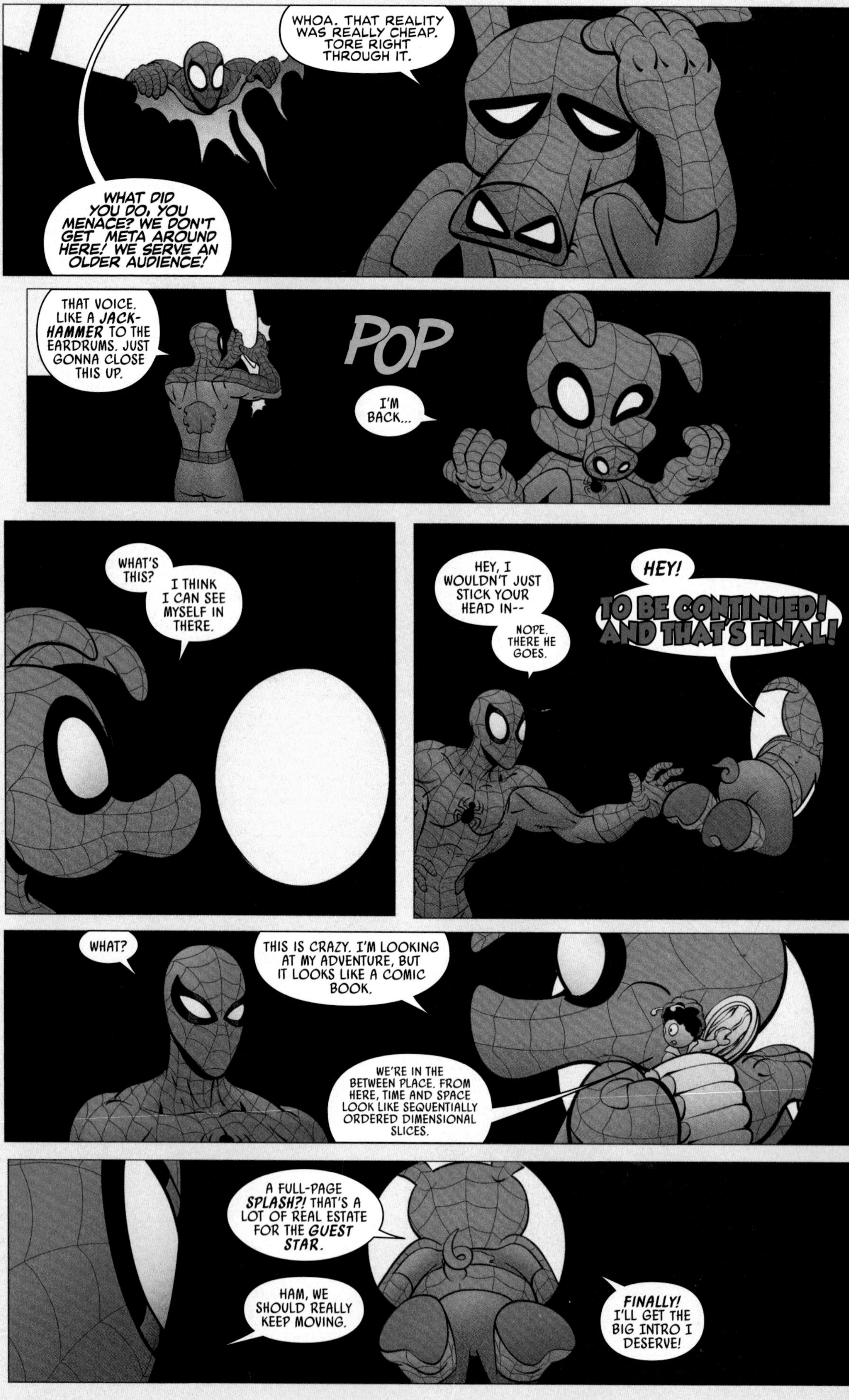
WHOA. THAT REALITY WAS REALLY CHEAP. TORE RIGHT THROUGH IT.
WHAT DID YOU DO, YOU MENACE? WE DON'T GET META AROUND HERE! WE SERVE AN OLDER AUDIENCE!
THAT VOICE. LIKE A JACK-HAMMER TO THE EARDRUMS. JUST GONNA CLOSE THIS UP.
POP
I'M BACK...
WHAT'S THIS?
I THINK I CAN SEE MYSELF IN THERE.
HEY, I WOULDN'T JUST STICK YOUR HEAD IN--
NOPE. THERE HE GOES.
HEY!
TO BE CONTINUED! AND THAT'S FINAL!
WHAT?
THIS IS CRAZY. I'M LOOKING AT MY ADVENTURE, BUT IT LOOKS LIKE A COMIC BOOK.
WE'RE IN THE BETWEEN PLACE. FROM HERE, TIME AND SPACE LOOK LIKE SEQUENTIALLY ORDERED DIMENSIONAL SLICES.
A FULL-PAGE SPLASH?! THAT'S A LOT OF REAL ESTATE FOR THE GUEST STAR.
HAM, WE SHOULD REALLY KEEP MOVING.
FINALLY! I'LL GET THE BIG INTRO I DESERVE!

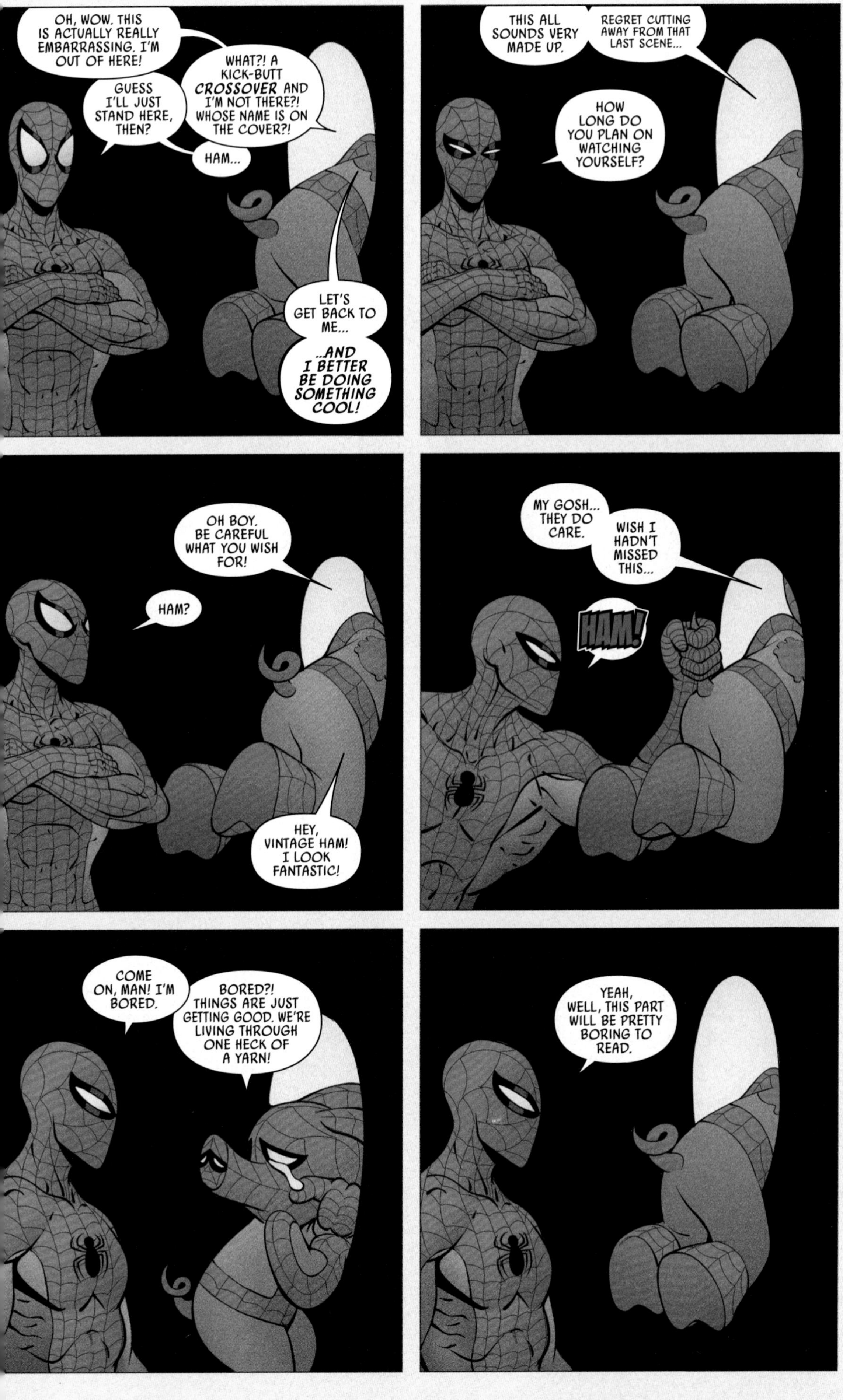
OH, WOW. THIS IS ACTUALLY REALLY EMBARRASSING. I'M OUT OF HERE!
GUESS I'LL JUST STAND HERE, THEN?
WHAT?! A KICK-BUTT CROSSOVER AND I'M NOT THERE?! WHOSE NAME IS ON THE COVER?!
HAM...
LET'S GET BACK TO ME...
...AND I BETTER BE DOING SOMETHING COOL!
THIS ALL SOUNDS VERY MADE UP.
REGRET CUTTING AWAY FROM THAT LAST SCENE...
HOW LONG DO YOU PLAN ON WATCHING YOURSELF?
OH BOY. BE CAREFUL WHAT YOU WISH FOR!
HAM?
HEY, VINTAGE HAM! I LOOK FANTASTIC!
MY GOSH... THEY DO CARE.
WISH I HADN'T MISSED THIS...
HAM!
COME ON, MAN! I'M BORED.
BORED?! THINGS ARE JUST GETTING GOOD. WE'RE LIVING THROUGH ONE HECK OF A YARN!
YEAH, WELL, THIS PART WILL BE PRETTY BORING TO READ.

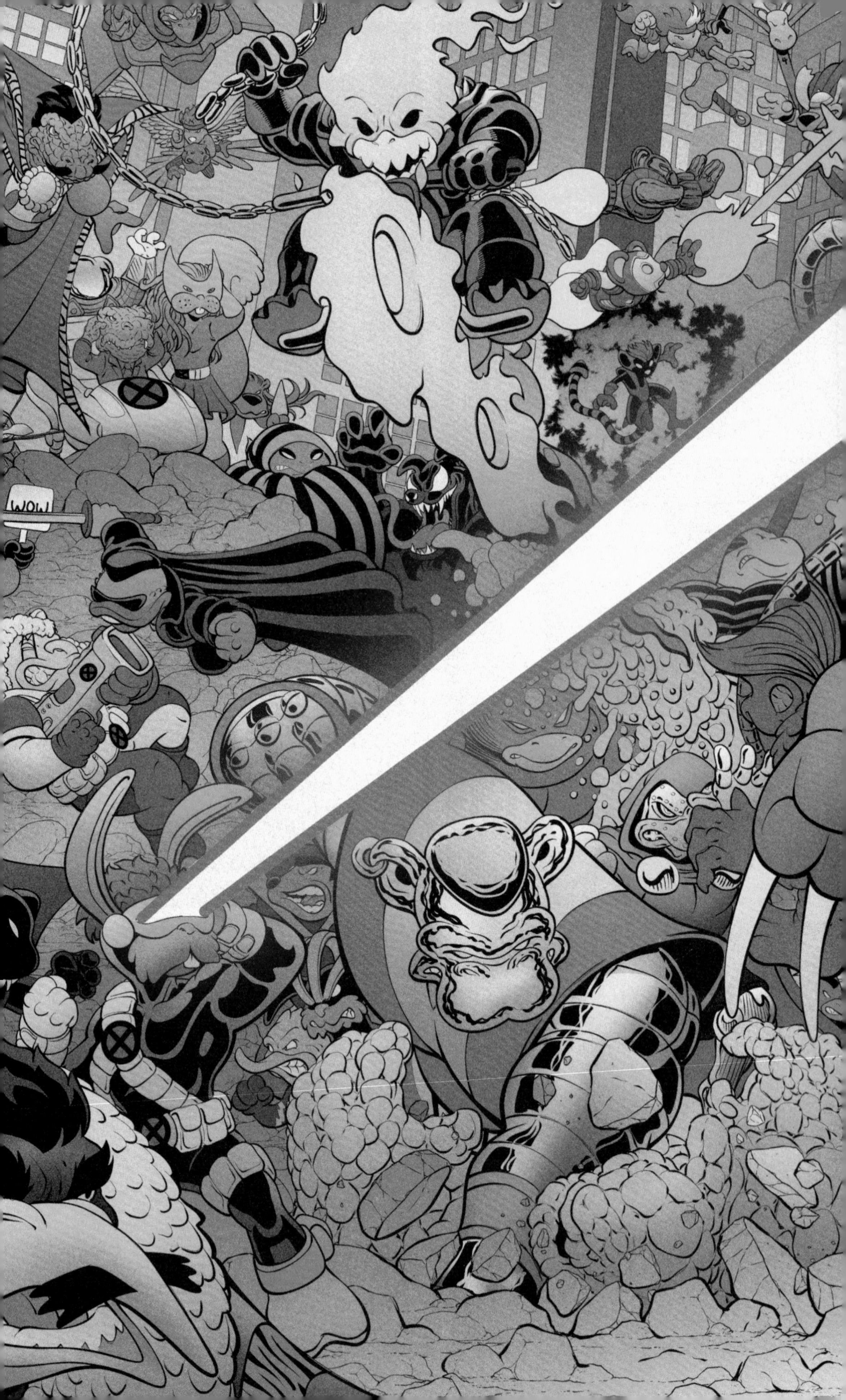
WOW

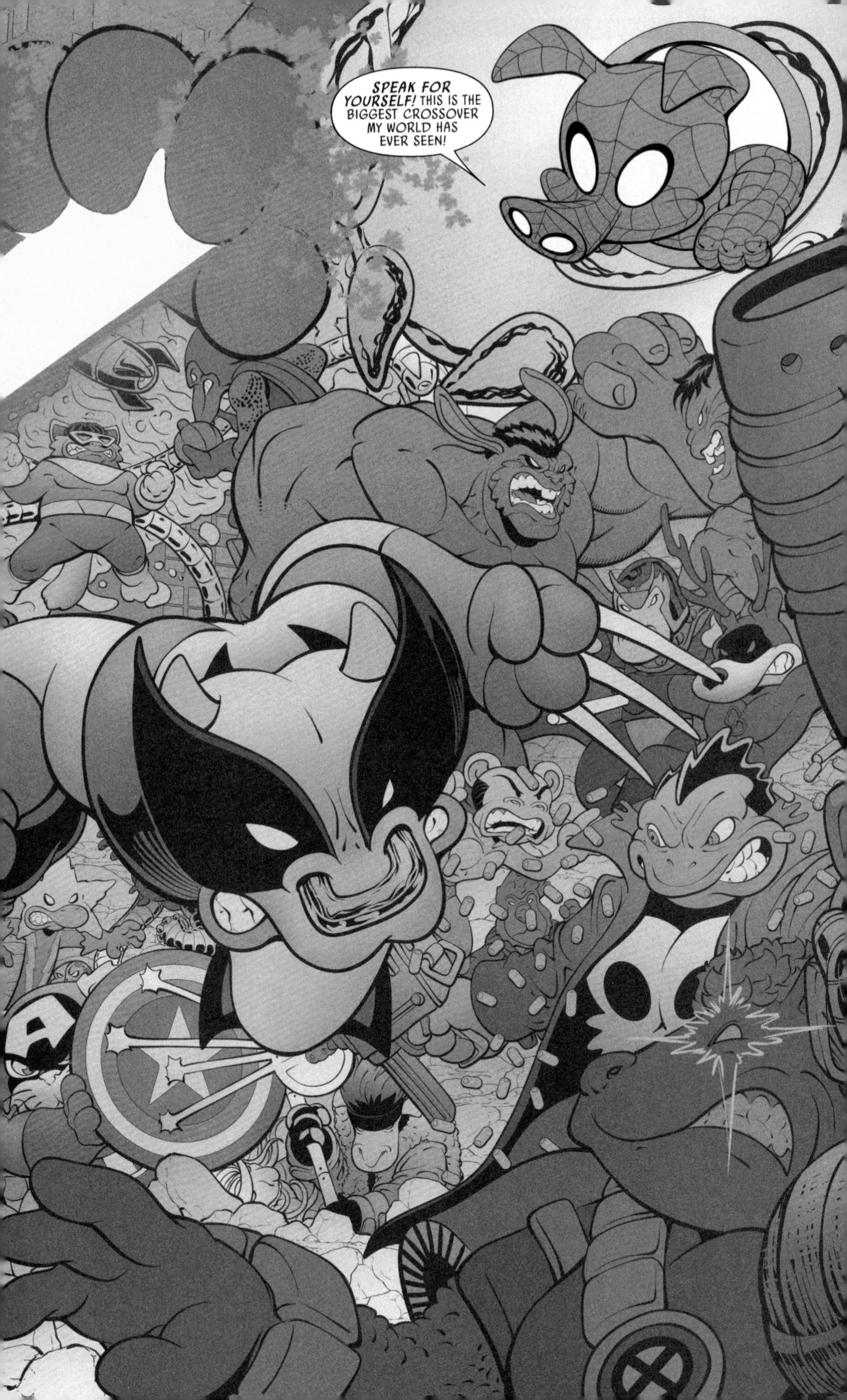
SPEAK FOR YOURSELF! THIS IS THE BIGGEST CROSSOVER MY WORLD HAS EVER SEEN!

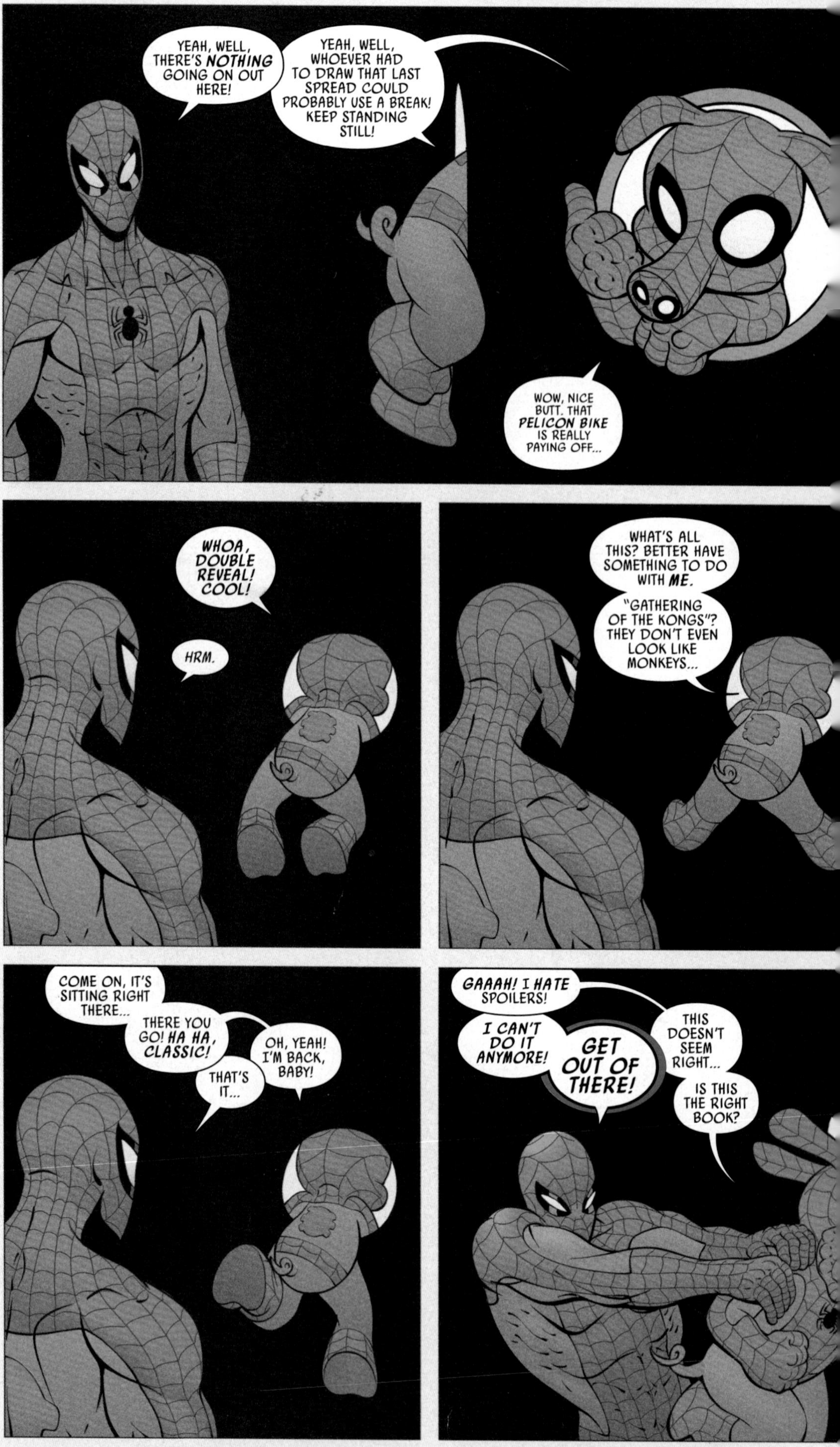
YEAH, WELL, THERE'S NOTHING GOING ON OUT HERE!
YEAH, WELL, WHOEVER HAD TO DRAW THAT LAST SPREAD COULD PROBABLY USE A BREAK! KEEP STANDING STILL!
WOW, NICE BUTT. THAT PELICON BIKE IS REALLY PAYING OFF...
WHOA, DOUBLE REVEAL! COOL!
HRM.
WHAT'S ALL THIS? BETTER HAVE SOMETHING TO DO WITH ME.
"GATHERING OF THE KONGS"? THEY DON'T EVEN LOOK LIKE MONKEYS...
COME ON, IT'S SITTING RIGHT THERE...
THERE YOU GO! HA HA, CLASSIC!
THAT'S IT...
OH, YEAH! I'M BACK, BABY!
GAAAH! I HATE SPOILERS!
I CAN'T DO IT ANYMORE!
GET OUT OF THERE!
THIS DOESN'T SEEM RIGHT...
IS THIS THE RIGHT BOOK?

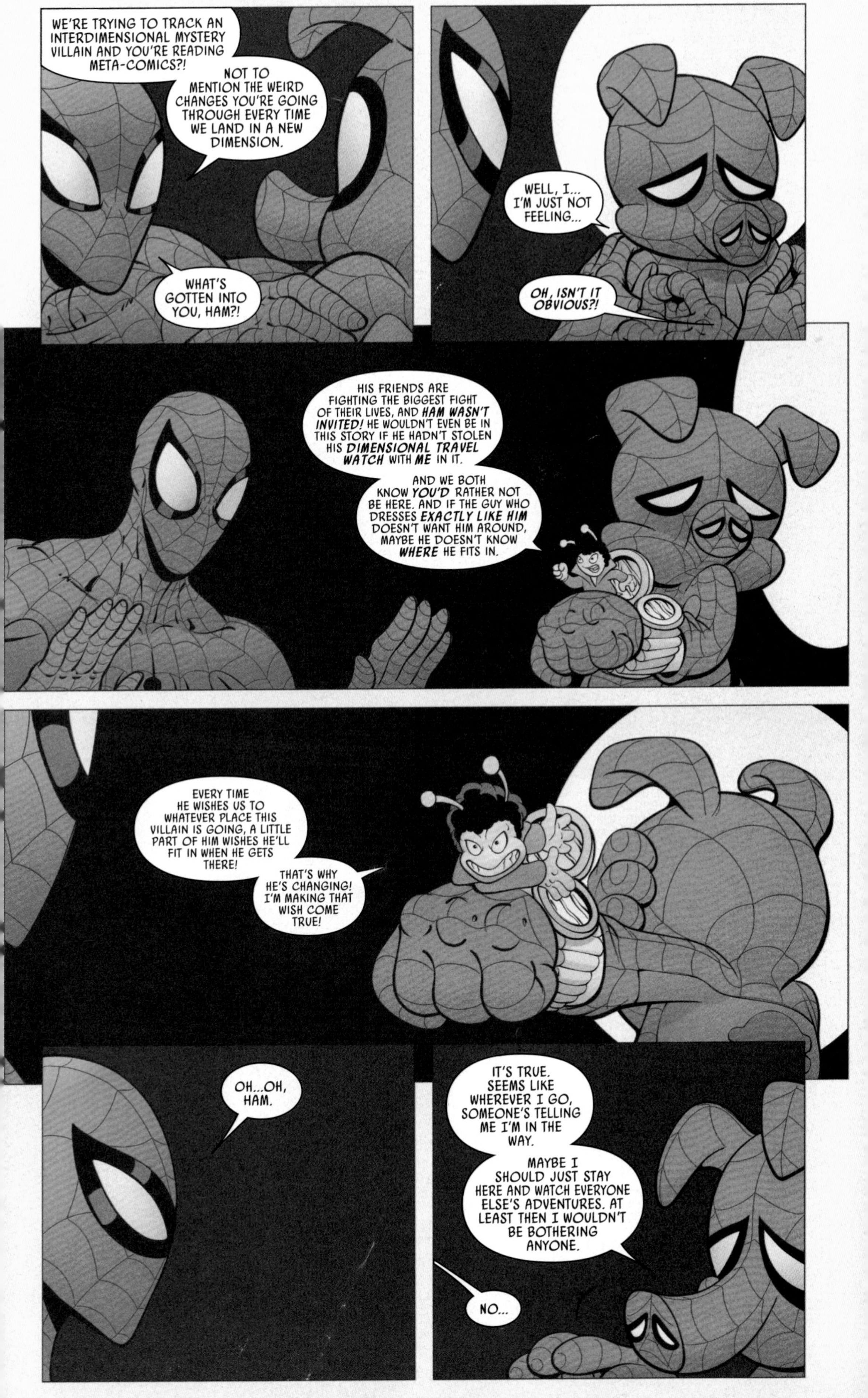
WE'RE TRYING TO TRACK AN INTERDIMENSIONAL MYSTERY VILLAIN AND YOU'RE READING META-COMICS?!
NOT TO MENTION THE WEIRD CHANGES YOU'RE GOING THROUGH EVERY TIME WE LAND IN A NEW DIMENSION.
WHAT'S GOTTEN INTO YOU, HAM?!
WELL, I... I'M JUST NOT FEELING...
OH, ISN'T IT OBVIOUS?!
HIS FRIENDS ARE FIGHTING THE BIGGEST FIGHT OF THEIR LIVES, AND HAM WASN'T INVITED! HE WOULDN'T EVEN BE IN THIS STORY IF HE HADN'T STOLEN HIS DIMENSIONAL TRAVEL WATCH WITH ME IN IT.
AND WE BOTH KNOW YOU'D RATHER NOT BE HERE. AND IF THE GUY WHO DRESSES EXACTLY LIKE HIM DOESN'T WANT HIM AROUND, MAYBE HE DOESN'T KNOW WHERE HE FITS IN.
EVERY TIME HE WISHES US TO WHATEVER PLACE THIS VILLAIN IS GOING, A LITTLE PART OF HIM WISHES HE'LL FIT IN WHEN HE GETS THERE!
THAT'S WHY HE'S CHANGING! I'M MAKING THAT WISH COME TRUE!
OH...OH, HAM.
IT'S TRUE. SEEMS LIKE WHEREVER I GO, SOMEONE'S TELLING ME I'M IN THE WAY.
MAYBE I SHOULD JUST STAY HERE AND WATCH EVERYONE ELSE'S ADVENTURES. AT LEAST THEN I WOULDN'T BE BOTHERING ANYONE.
NO...

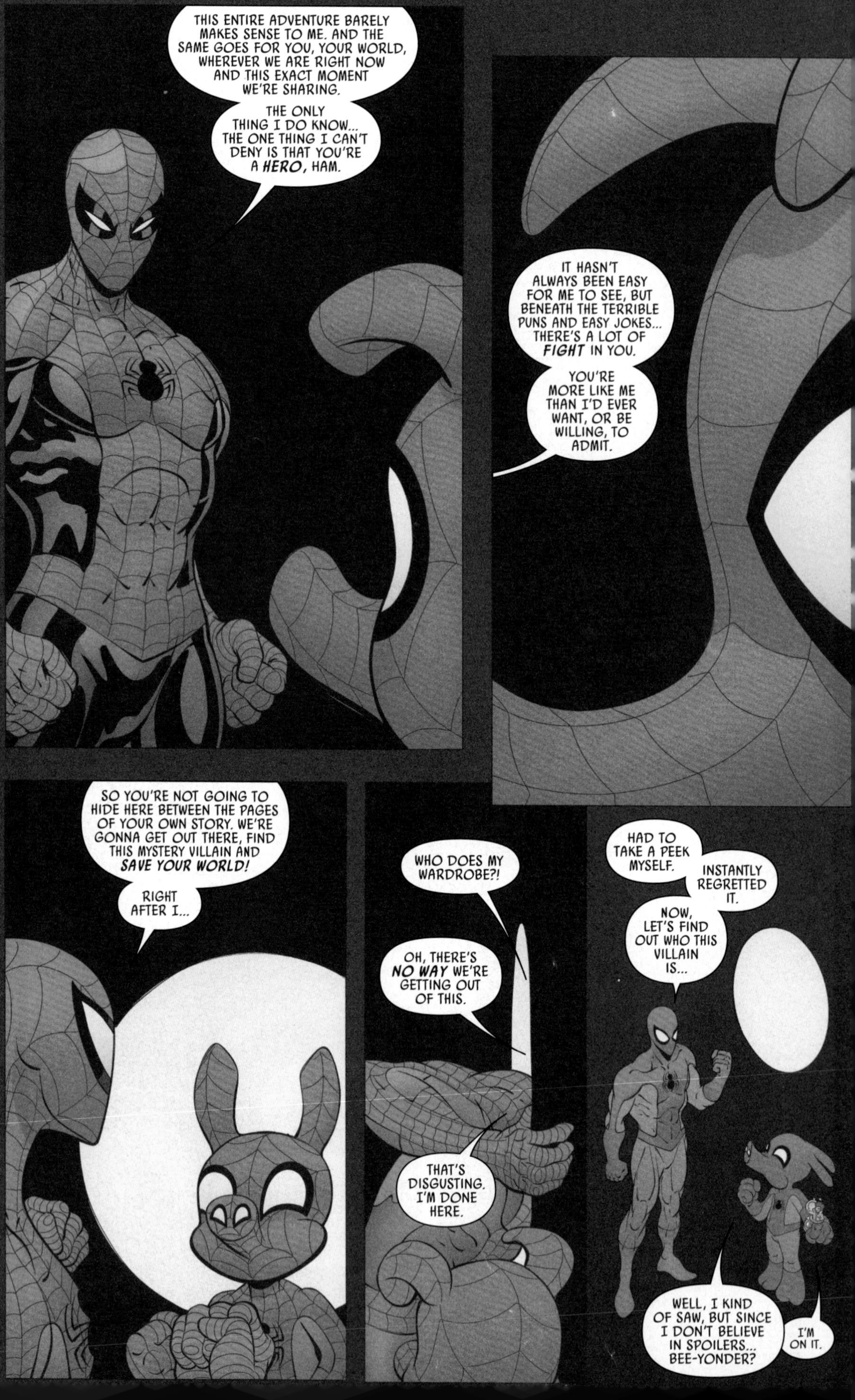

THIS ENTIRE ADVENTURE BARELY MAKES SENSE TO ME. AND THE SAME GOES FOR YOU, YOUR WORLD, WHEREVER WE ARE RIGHT NOW AND THIS EXACT MOMENT WE'RE SHARING.
THE ONLY THING I DO KNOW... THE ONE THING I CAN'T DENY IS THAT YOU'RE A ***HERO,*** HAM.
IT HASN'T ALWAYS BEEN EASY FOR ME TO SEE, BUT BENEATH THE TERRIBLE PUNS AND EASY JOKES... THERE'S A LOT OF ***FIGHT*** IN YOU.
YOU'RE MORE LIKE ME THAN I'D EVER WANT, OR BE WILLING, TO ADMIT.
SO YOU'RE NOT GOING TO HIDE HERE BETWEEN THE PAGES OF YOUR OWN STORY. WE'RE GONNA GET OUT THERE, FIND THIS MYSTERY VILLAIN AND ***SAVE YOUR WORLD!***
RIGHT AFTER I...
WHO DOES MY WARDROBE?!
OH, THERE'S ***NO WAY*** WE'RE GETTING OUT OF THIS.
THAT'S DISGUSTING. I'M DONE HERE.
HAD TO TAKE A PEEK MYSELF.
INSTANTLY REGRETTED IT.
NOW, LET'S FIND OUT WHO THIS VILLAIN IS...
WELL, I KIND OF SAW, BUT SINCE I DON'T BELIEVE IN SPOILERS... BEE-YONDER?
I'M ON IT.

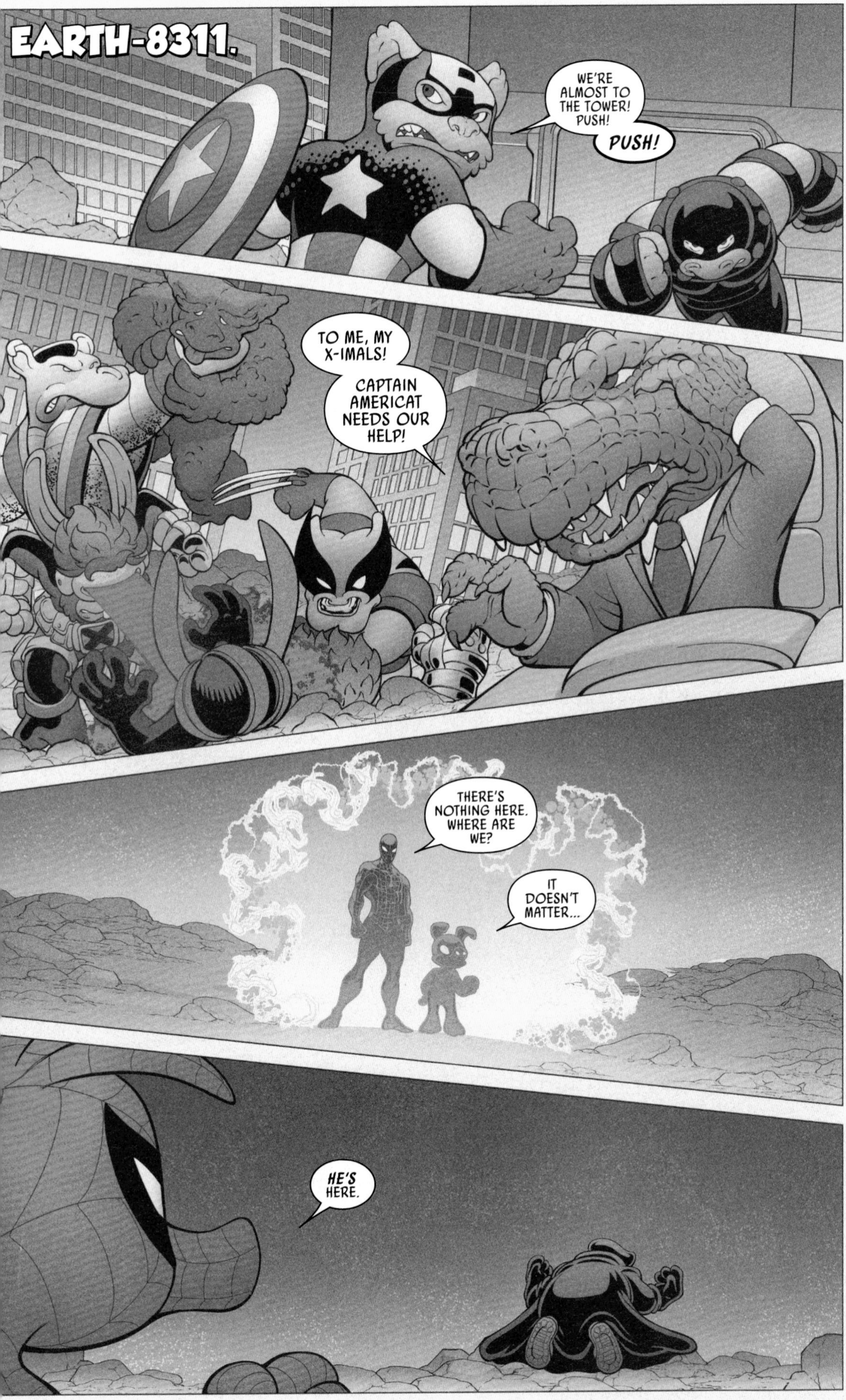
EARTH-8311.
WE'RE ALMOST TO THE TOWER! PUSH!
PUSH!
TO ME, MY X-IMALS!
CAPTAIN AMERICAT NEEDS OUR HELP!
THERE'S NOTHING HERE. WHERE ARE WE?
IT DOESN'T MATTER...
HE'S HERE.

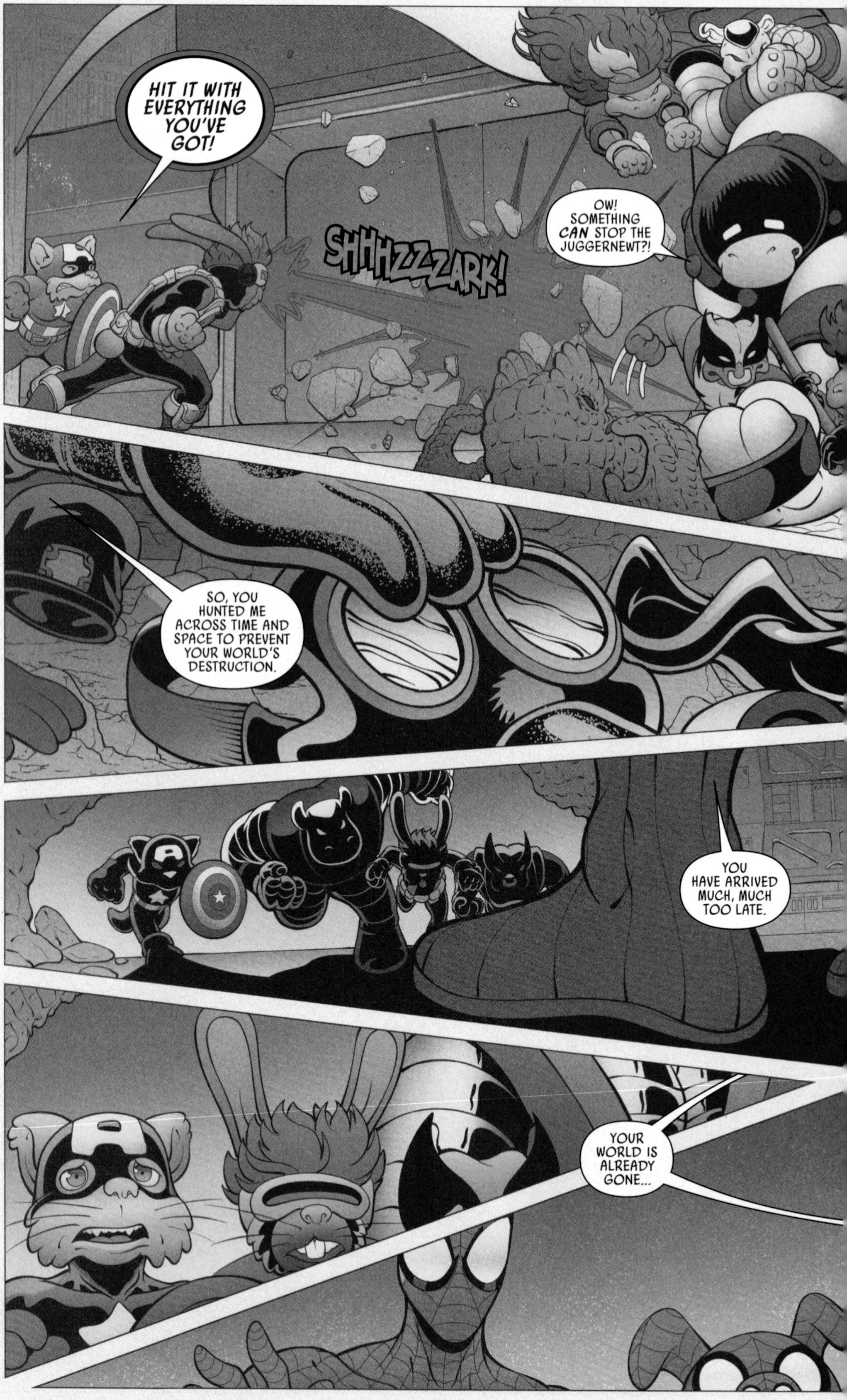
HIT IT WITH EVERYTHING YOU'VE GOT!
SHHHZZZZARK!
OW! SOMETHING CAN STOP THE JUGGERNEWT?!
SO, YOU HUNTED ME ACROSS TIME AND SPACE TO PREVENT YOUR WORLD'S DESTRUCTION.
YOU HAVE ARRIVED MUCH, MUCH TOO LATE.
YOUR WORLD IS ALREADY GONE...

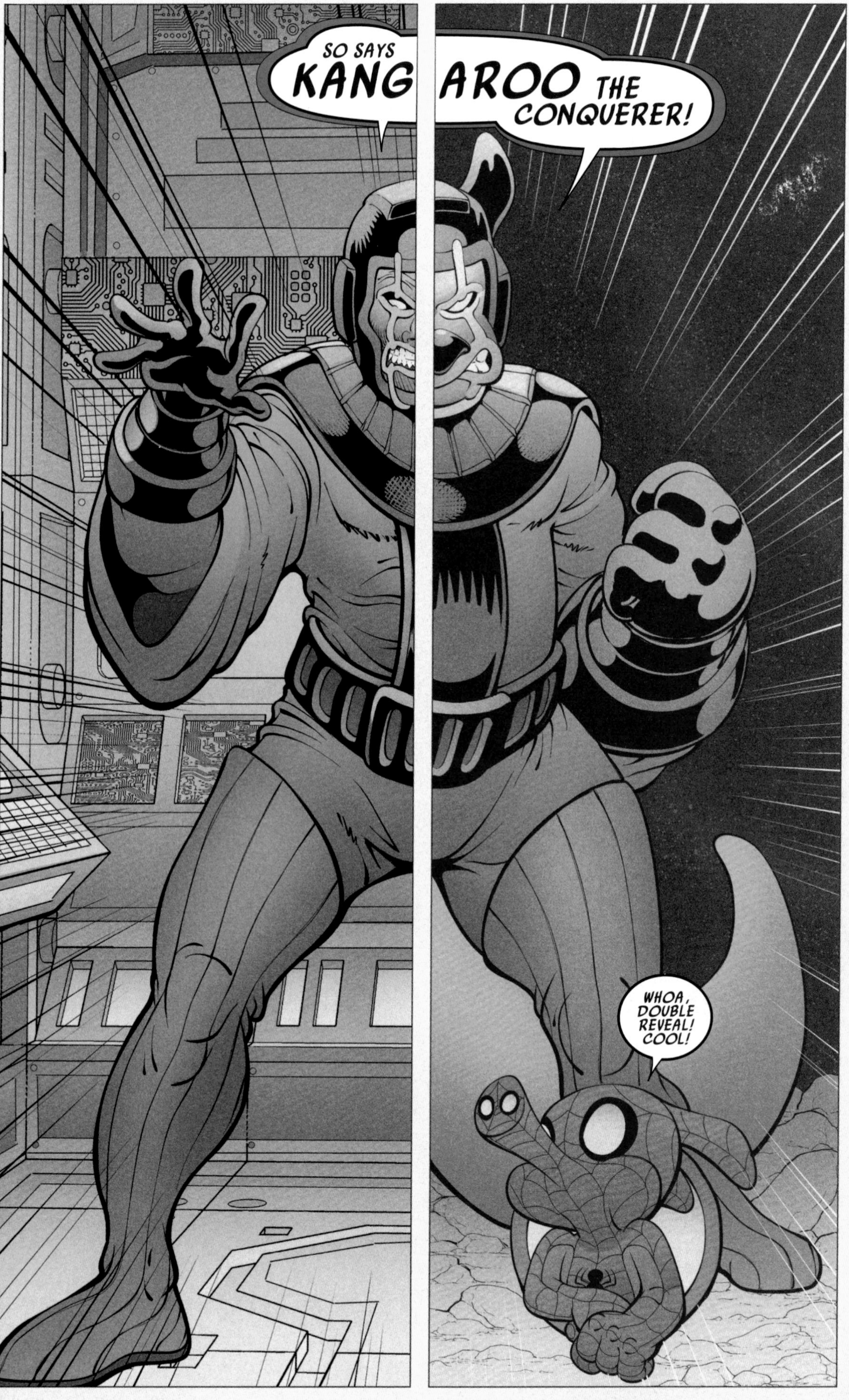
SO SAYS KANGAROO THE CONQUERER!
WHOA, DOUBLE REVEAL! COOL!

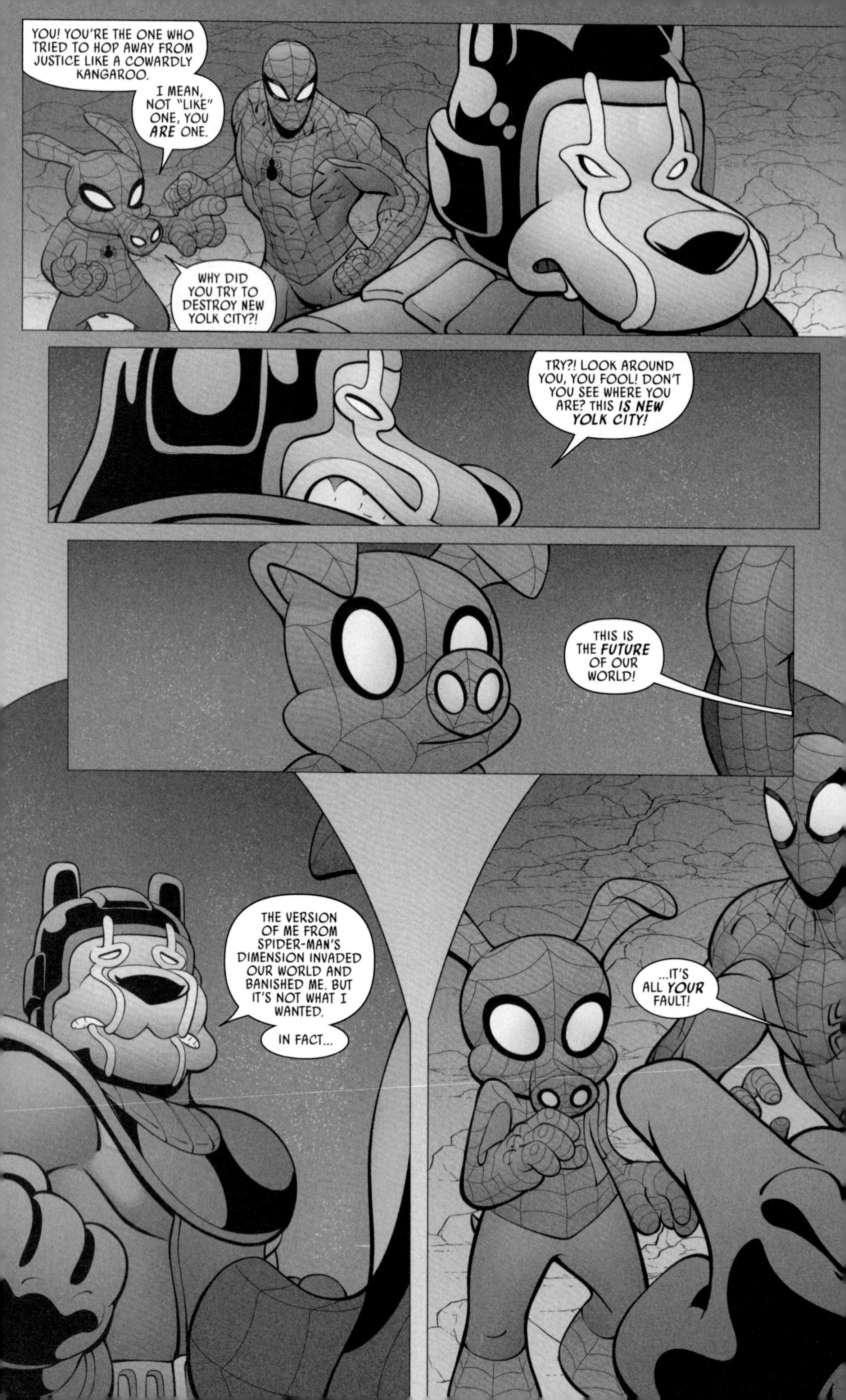
YOU! YOU'RE THE ONE WHO TRIED TO HOP AWAY FROM JUSTICE LIKE A COWARDLY KANGAROO.
I MEAN, NOT "LIKE" ONE, YOU ARE ONE.
WHY DID YOU TRY TO DESTROY NEW YOLK CITY?!
TRY?! LOOK AROUND YOU, YOU FOOL! DON'T YOU SEE WHERE YOU ARE? THIS IS NEW YOLK CITY!
THIS IS THE FUTURE OF OUR WORLD!
THE VERSION OF ME FROM SPIDER-MAN'S DIMENSION INVADED OUR WORLD AND BANISHED ME. BUT IT'S NOT WHAT I WANTED.
IN FACT...
...IT'S ALL YOUR FAULT!

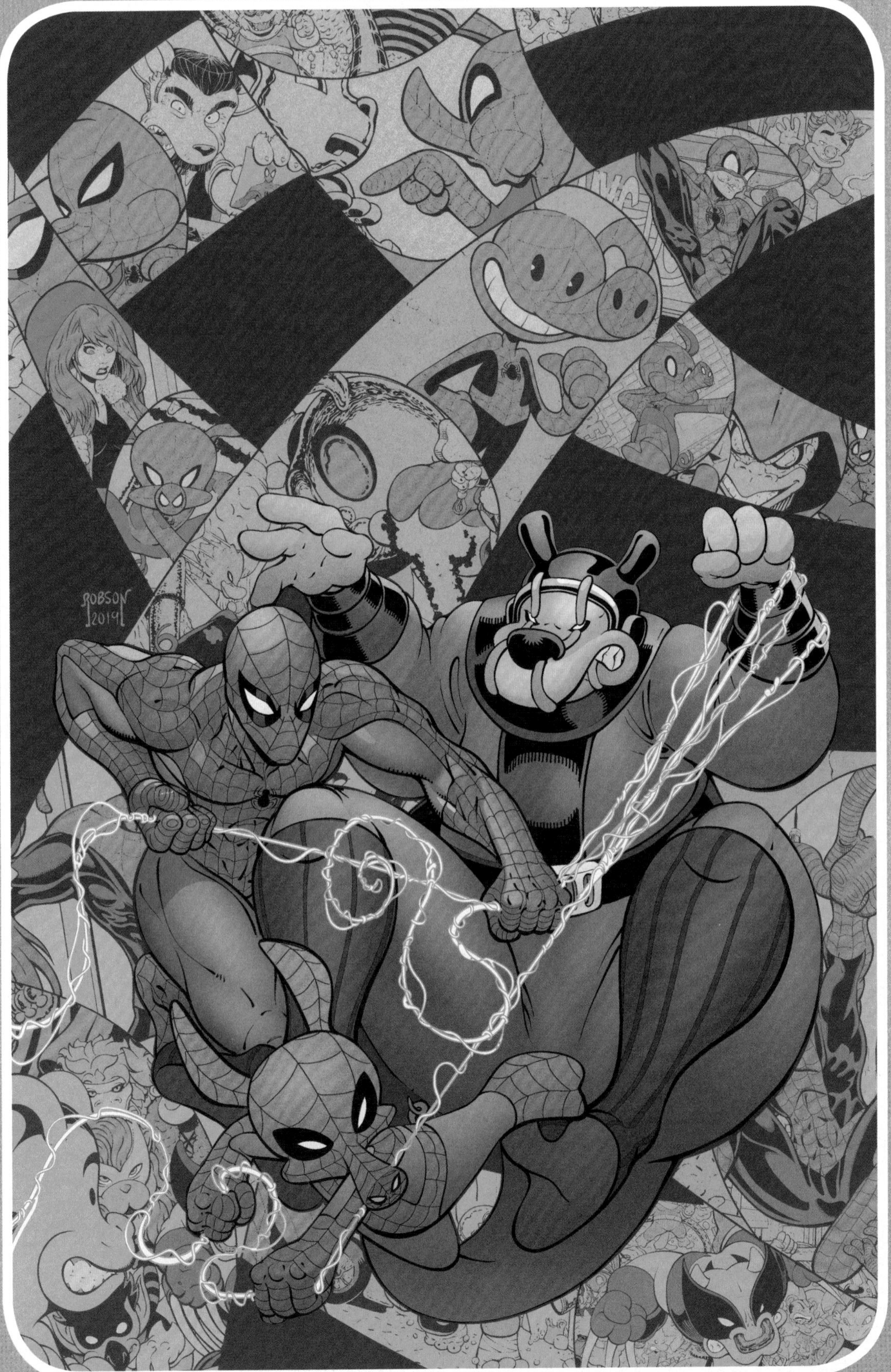
ROBSON
2019

4

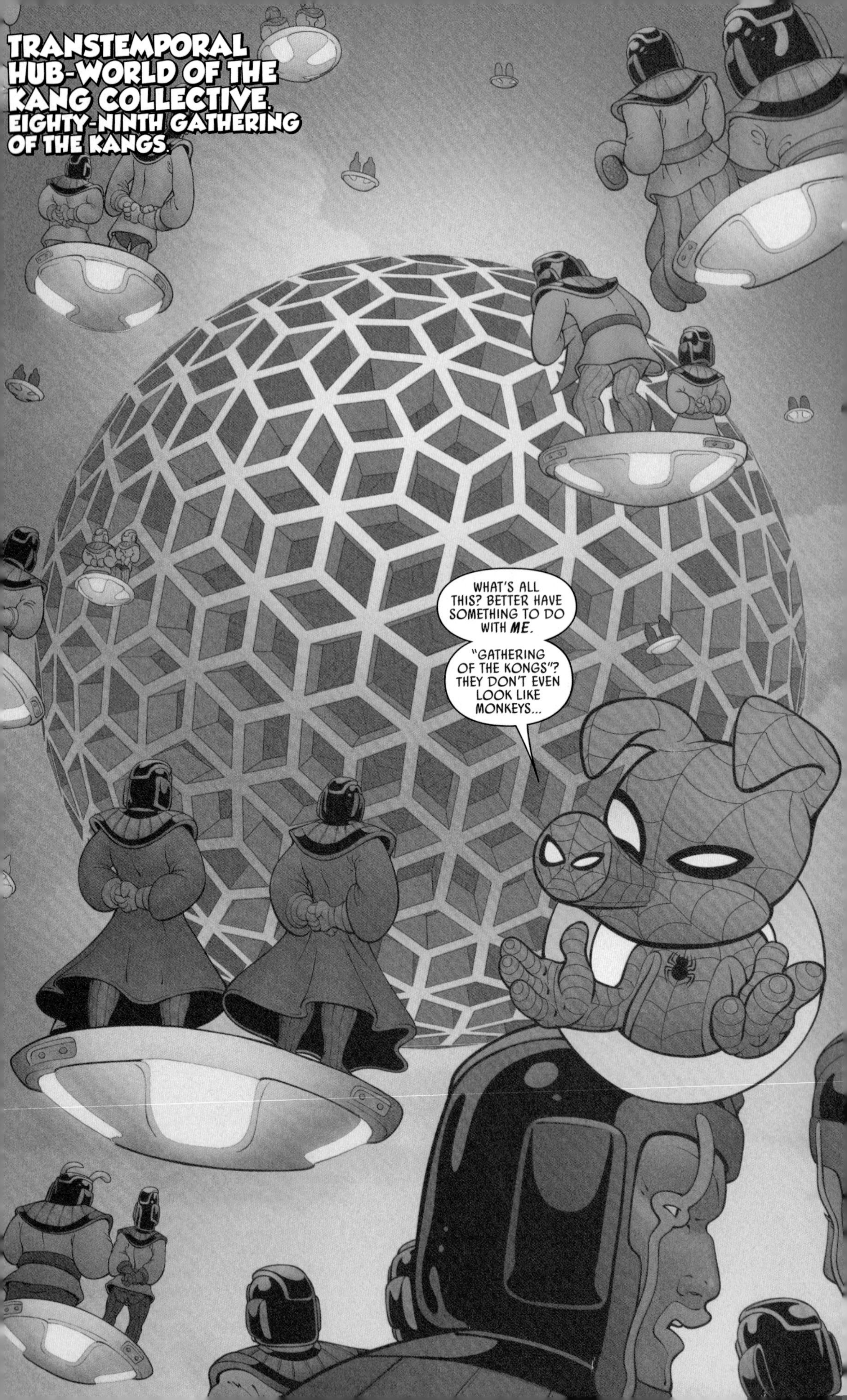
TRANSTEMPORAL HUB-WORLD OF THE KANG COLLECTIVE.
EIGHTY-NINTH GATHERING OF THE KANGS.
WHAT'S ALL THIS? BETTER HAVE SOMETHING TO DO WITH *ME*.
"GATHERING OF THE KONGS"? THEY DON'T EVEN LOOK LIKE MONKEYS...

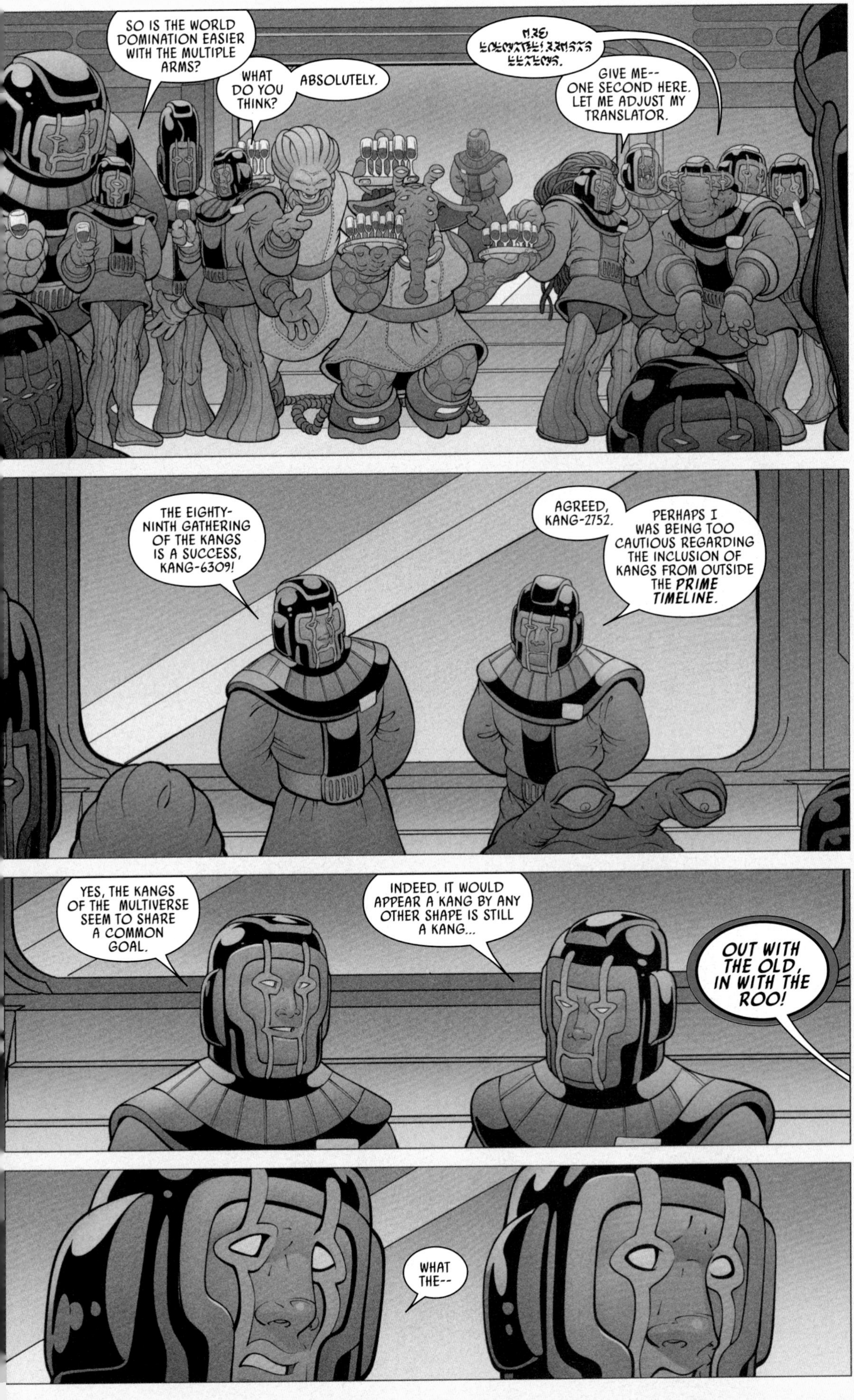
SO IS THE WORLD DOMINATION EASIER WITH THE MULTIPLE ARMS?
WHAT DO YOU THINK?
ABSOLUTELY.
GIVE ME-- ONE SECOND HERE. LET ME ADJUST MY TRANSLATOR.
THE EIGHTY-NINTH GATHERING OF THE KANGS IS A SUCCESS, KANG-6309!
AGREED, KANG-2752.
PERHAPS I WAS BEING TOO CAUTIOUS REGARDING THE INCLUSION OF KANGS FROM OUTSIDE THE *PRIME TIMELINE.*
YES, THE KANGS OF THE MULTIVERSE SEEM TO SHARE A COMMON GOAL.
INDEED. IT WOULD APPEAR A KANG BY ANY OTHER SHAPE IS STILL A KANG...
OUT WITH THE OLD, IN WITH THE ROO!
WHAT THE--

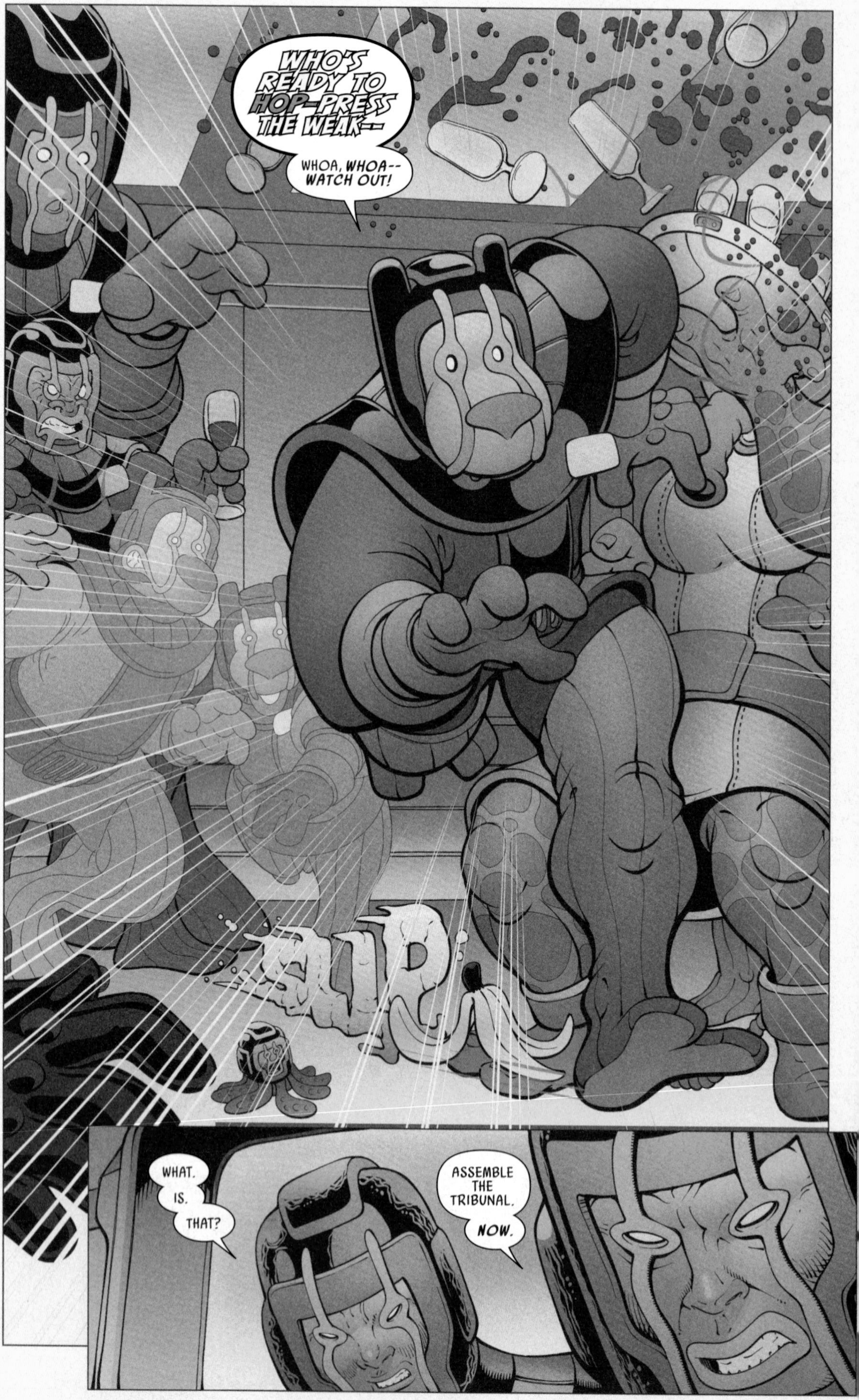
WHO'S READY TO HOP-PRESS THE WEAK--
WHOA, WHOA-- WATCH OUT!
WHAT. IS. THAT?
ASSEMBLE THE TRIBUNAL. NOW.

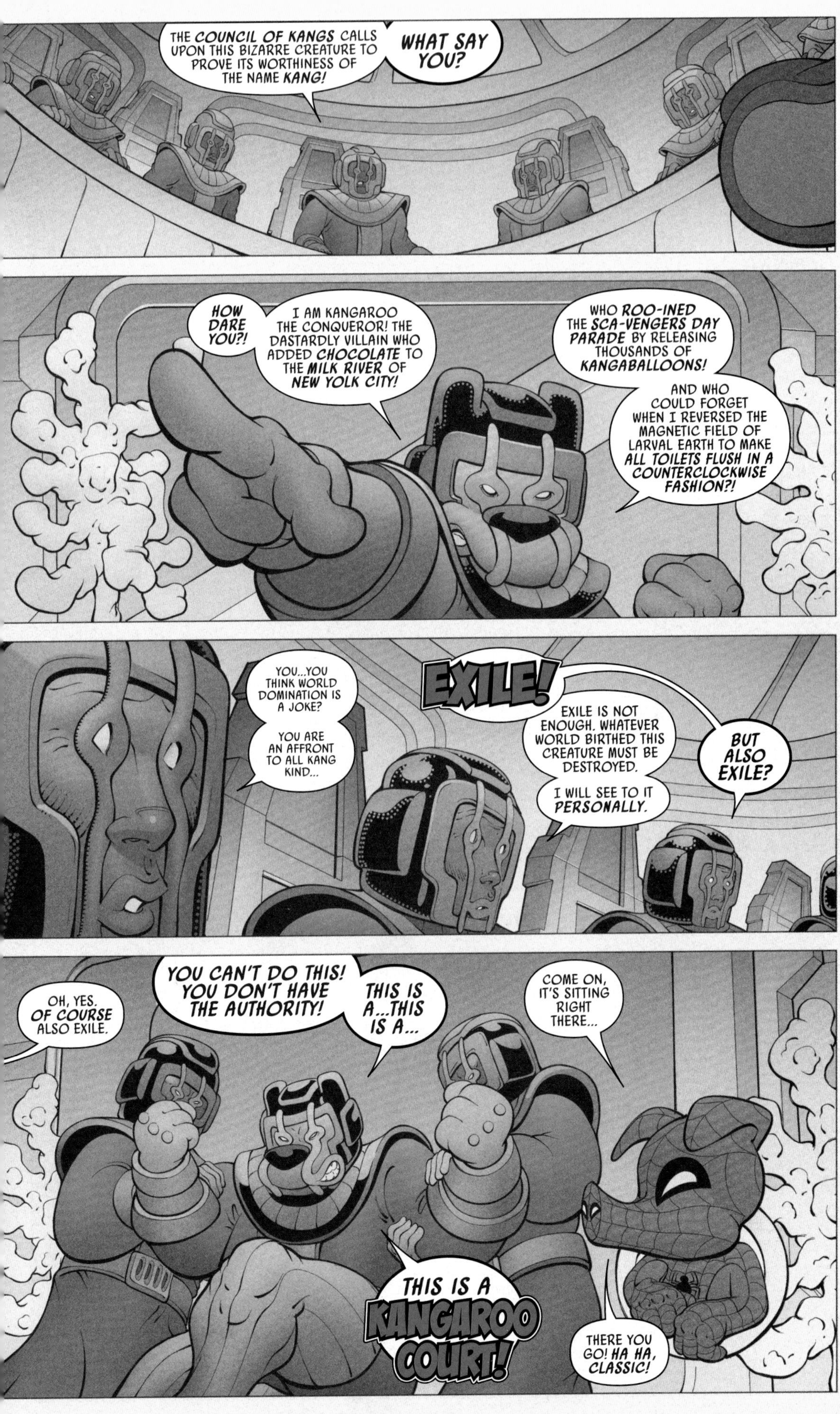
THE COUNCIL OF KANGS CALLS UPON THIS BIZARRE CREATURE TO PROVE ITS WORTHINESS OF THE NAME KANG!
WHAT SAY YOU?
HOW DARE YOU?!
I AM KANGAROO THE CONQUEROR! THE DASTARDLY VILLAIN WHO ADDED CHOCOLATE TO THE MILK RIVER OF NEW YOLK CITY!
WHO ROO-INED THE SCA-VENGERS DAY PARADE BY RELEASING THOUSANDS OF KANGABALLOONS!
AND WHO COULD FORGET WHEN I REVERSED THE MAGNETIC FIELD OF LARVAL EARTH TO MAKE ALL TOILETS FLUSH IN A COUNTERCLOCKWISE FASHION?!
YOU...YOU THINK WORLD DOMINATION IS A JOKE?
YOU ARE AN AFFRONT TO ALL KANG KIND...
EXILE!
EXILE IS NOT ENOUGH. WHATEVER WORLD BIRTHED THIS CREATURE MUST BE DESTROYED.
I WILL SEE TO IT PERSONALLY.
BUT ALSO EXILE?
OH, YES. OF COURSE ALSO EXILE.
YOU CAN'T DO THIS! YOU DON'T HAVE THE AUTHORITY!
THIS IS A...THIS IS A...
COME ON, IT'S SITTING RIGHT THERE...
THIS IS A KANGAROO COURT!
THERE YOU GO! HA HA, CLASSIC!

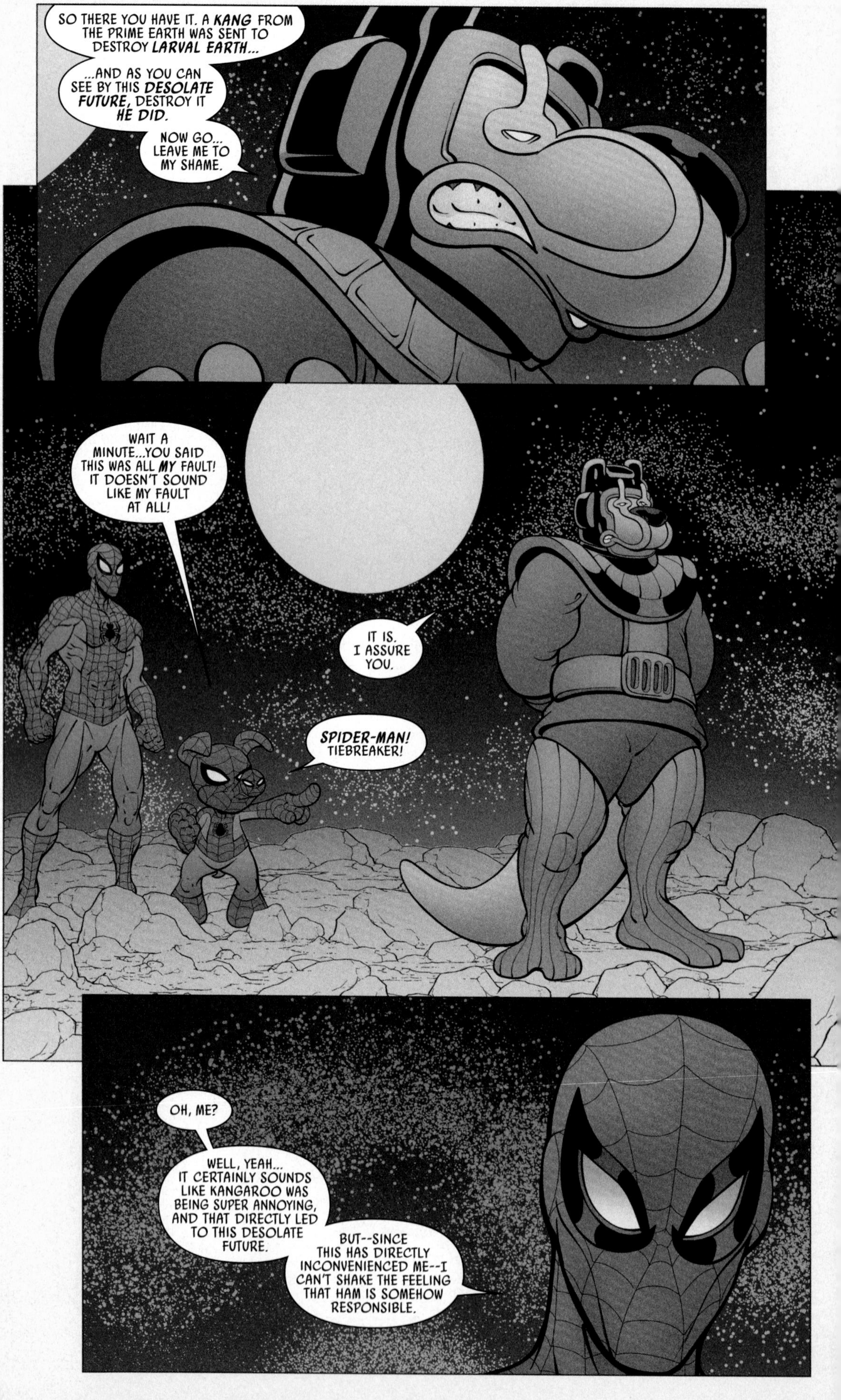
SO THERE YOU HAVE IT. A KANG FROM THE PRIME EARTH WAS SENT TO DESTROY LARVAL EARTH...
...AND AS YOU CAN SEE BY THIS DESOLATE FUTURE, DESTROY IT HE DID.
NOW GO... LEAVE ME TO MY SHAME.
WAIT A MINUTE...YOU SAID THIS WAS ALL MY FAULT! IT DOESN'T SOUND LIKE MY FAULT AT ALL!
IT IS. I ASSURE YOU.
SPIDER-MAN! TIEBREAKER!
OH, ME?
WELL, YEAH... IT CERTAINLY SOUNDS LIKE KANGAROO WAS BEING SUPER ANNOYING, AND THAT DIRECTLY LED TO THIS DESOLATE FUTURE.
BUT--SINCE THIS HAS DIRECTLY INCONVENIENCED ME--I CAN'T SHAKE THE FEELING THAT HAM IS SOMEHOW RESPONSIBLE.

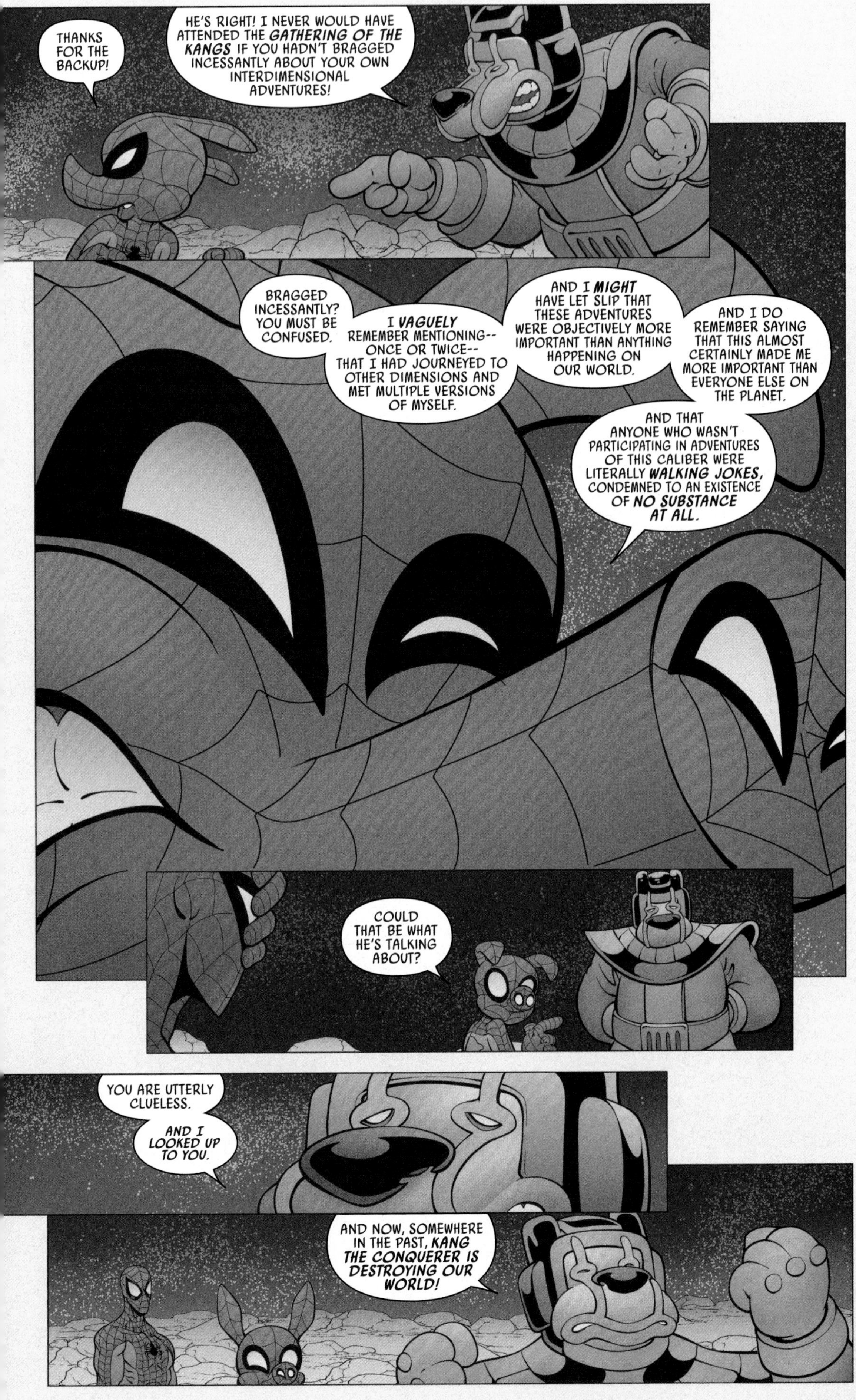
THANKS FOR THE BACKUP!
HE'S RIGHT! I NEVER WOULD HAVE ATTENDED THE GATHERING OF THE KANGS IF YOU HADN'T BRAGGED INCESSANTLY ABOUT YOUR OWN INTERDIMENSIONAL ADVENTURES!
BRAGGED INCESSANTLY? YOU MUST BE CONFUSED.
I VAGUELY REMEMBER MENTIONING-- ONCE OR TWICE-- THAT I HAD JOURNEYED TO OTHER DIMENSIONS AND MET MULTIPLE VERSIONS OF MYSELF.
AND I MIGHT HAVE LET SLIP THAT THESE ADVENTURES WERE OBJECTIVELY MORE IMPORTANT THAN ANYTHING HAPPENING ON OUR WORLD.
AND I DO REMEMBER SAYING THAT THIS ALMOST CERTAINLY MADE ME MORE IMPORTANT THAN EVERYONE ELSE ON THE PLANET.
AND THAT ANYONE WHO WASN'T PARTICIPATING IN ADVENTURES OF THIS CALIBER WERE LITERALLY WALKING JOKES, CONDEMNED TO AN EXISTENCE OF NO SUBSTANCE AT ALL.
COULD THAT BE WHAT HE'S TALKING ABOUT?
YOU ARE UTTERLY CLUELESS.
AND I LOOKED UP TO YOU.
AND NOW, SOMEWHERE IN THE PAST, KANG THE CONQUERER IS DESTROYING OUR WORLD!

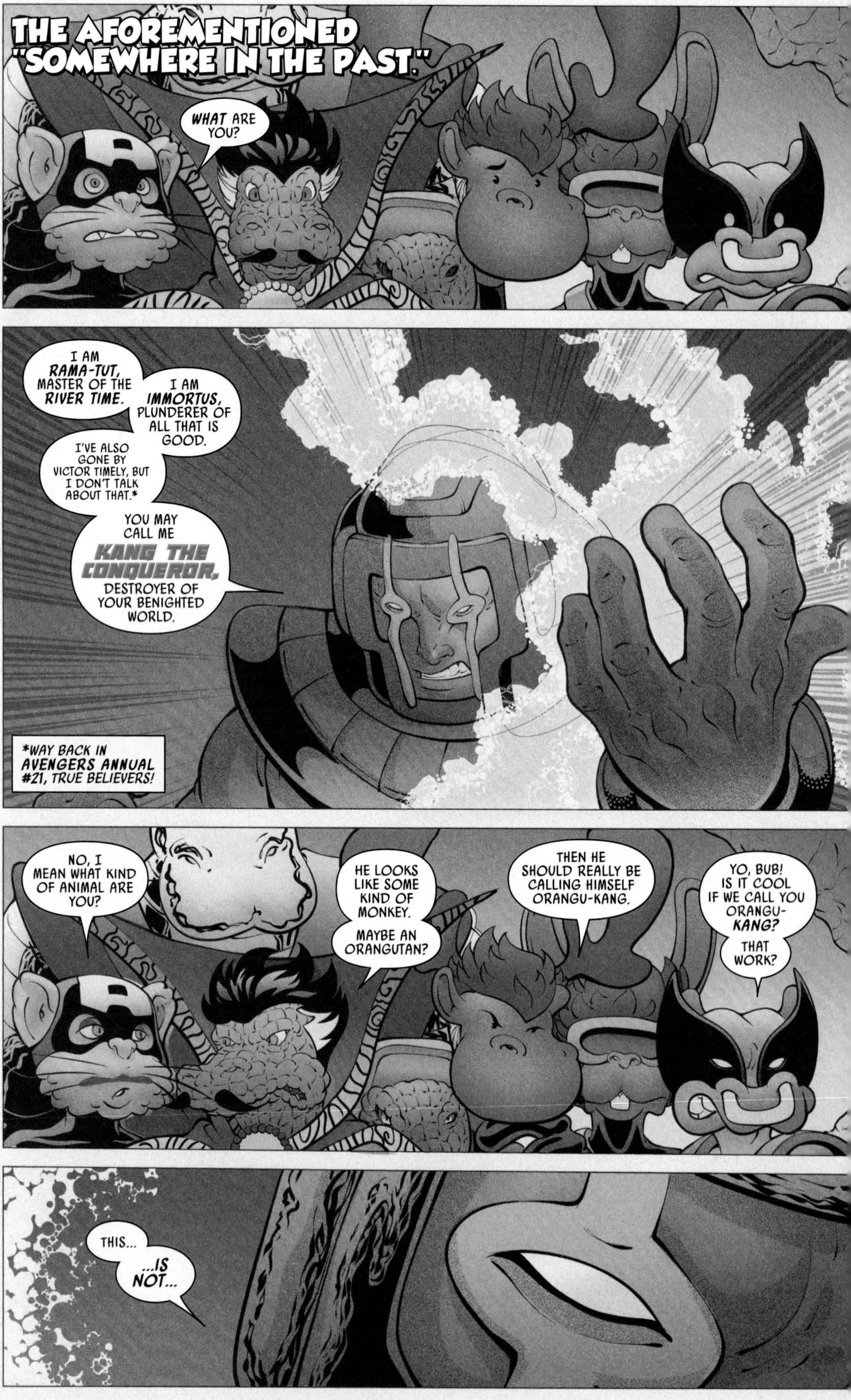
THE AFOREMENTIONED "SOMEWHERE IN THE PAST."
WHAT ARE YOU?
I AM RAMA-TUT, MASTER OF THE RIVER TIME.
I AM IMMORTUS, PLUNDERER OF ALL THAT IS GOOD.
I'VE ALSO GONE BY VICTOR TIMELY, BUT I DON'T TALK ABOUT THAT.*
YOU MAY CALL ME KANG THE CONQUEROR, DESTROYER OF YOUR BENIGHTED WORLD.
*WAY BACK IN AVENGERS ANNUAL #21, TRUE BELIEVERS!
NO, I MEAN WHAT KIND OF ANIMAL ARE YOU?
HE LOOKS LIKE SOME KIND OF MONKEY.
MAYBE AN ORANGUTAN?
THEN HE SHOULD REALLY BE CALLING HIMSELF ORANGU-KANG.
YO, BUB! IS IT COOL IF WE CALL YOU ORANGU-KANG?
THAT WORK?
THIS...
...IS NOT...

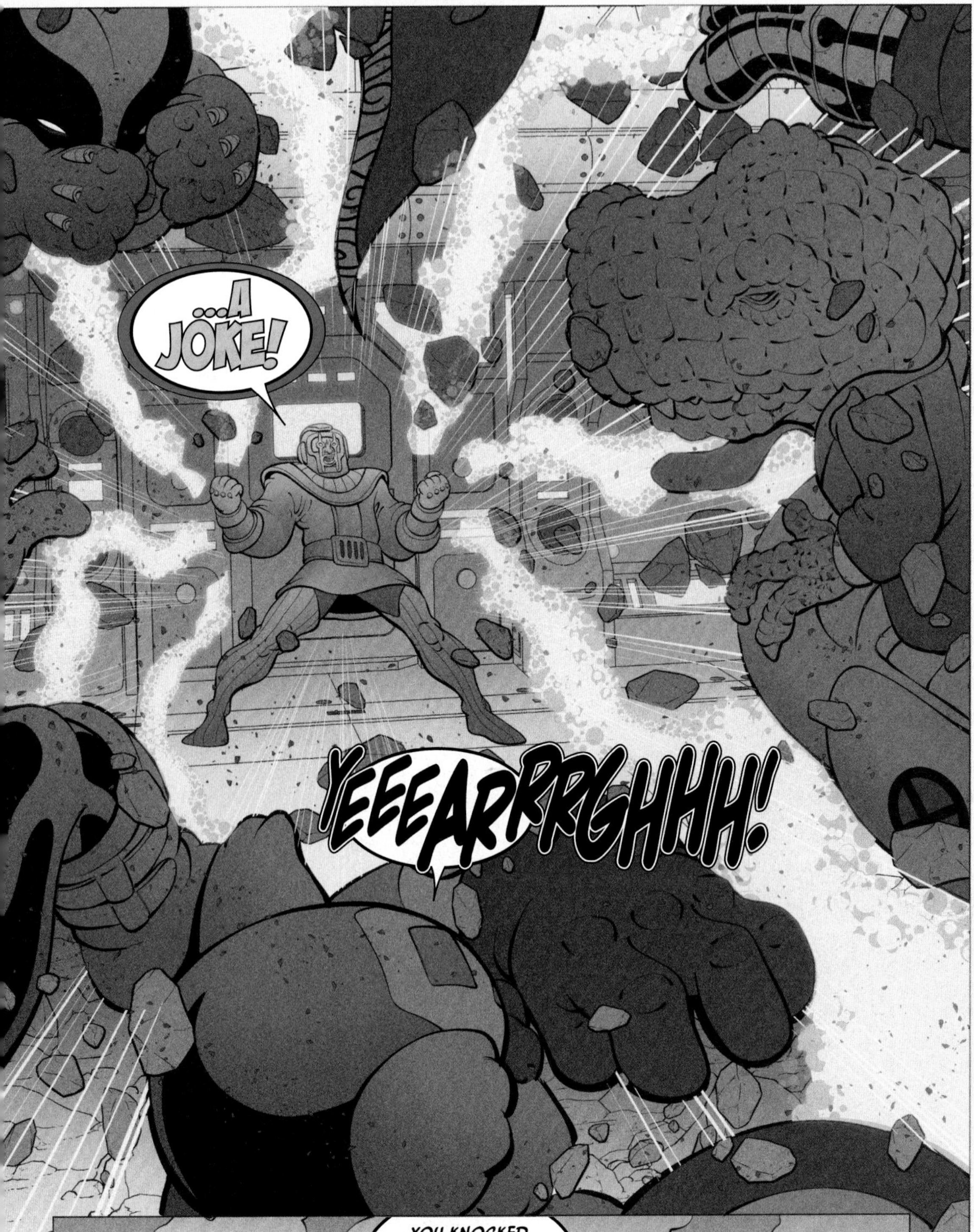
...A JOKE!
YEEEARRRGHHH!

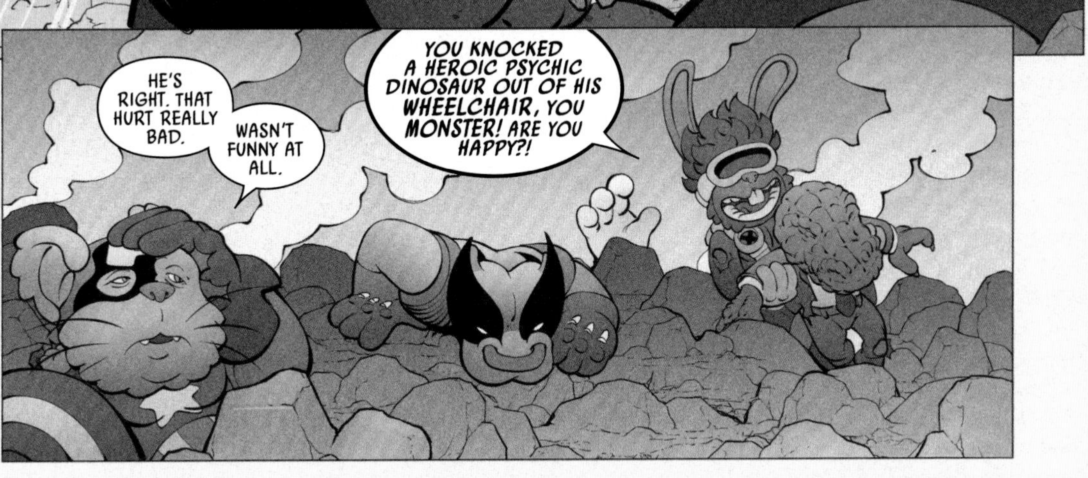
HE'S RIGHT. THAT HURT REALLY BAD.
WASN'T FUNNY AT ALL.
YOU KNOCKED A HEROIC PSYCHIC DINOSAUR OUT OF HIS WHEELCHAIR, YOU MONSTER! ARE YOU HAPPY?!

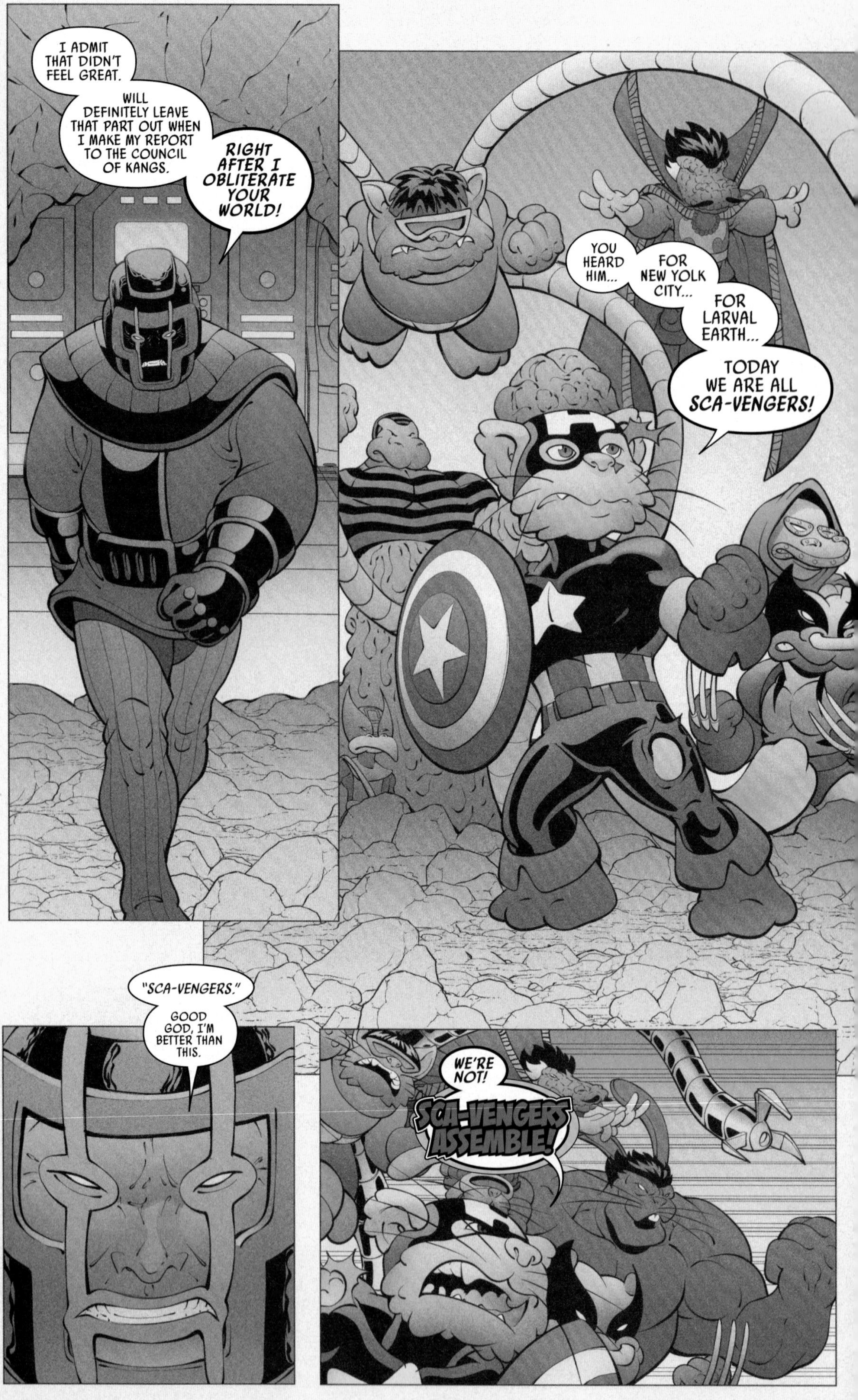
I ADMIT THAT DIDN'T FEEL GREAT.
WILL DEFINITELY LEAVE THAT PART OUT WHEN I MAKE MY REPORT TO THE COUNCIL OF KANGS.
RIGHT AFTER I OBLITERATE YOUR WORLD!
YOU HEARD HIM...
FOR NEW YOLK CITY...
FOR LARVAL EARTH...
TODAY WE ARE ALL SCA-VENGERS!
"SCA-VENGERS."
GOOD GOD, I'M BETTER THAN THIS.
WE'RE NOT!
SCA-VENGERS ASSEMBLE!

WAIT, YOU'RE JUST GONNA SIT HERE WHILE A *HUMAN KANG* DESTROYS YOUR PLANET FOR *YOU?!*

THAT ISN'T THE KANGAROO THE CONQUEROR I KNOW!

MAYBE IT'S FOR THE BEST.

PERHAPS WE *ARE* ALL JUST *ONE-NOTE JOKES.*

HEY, WE NEED TO HAVE A LITTLE TALK, JUST YOU AND ME.

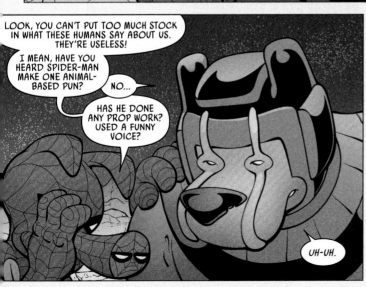

LOOK, YOU CAN'T PUT TOO MUCH STOCK IN WHAT THESE HUMANS SAY ABOUT US. THEY'RE USELESS!

I MEAN, HAVE YOU HEARD SPIDER-MAN MAKE ONE ANIMAL-BASED PUN?

NO...

HAS HE DONE ANY PROP WORK? USED A FUNNY VOICE?

UH-UH.

RIGHT! THE HUMAN BRAIN *BARELY WORKS.* THE WORDS THAT SPILL OUT OF THEIR MOUTHS ARE UTTERLY POINTLESS!

THEY HAVE NOTHING TO OFFER ANYONE, ANYWHERE, AT ANY TIME!

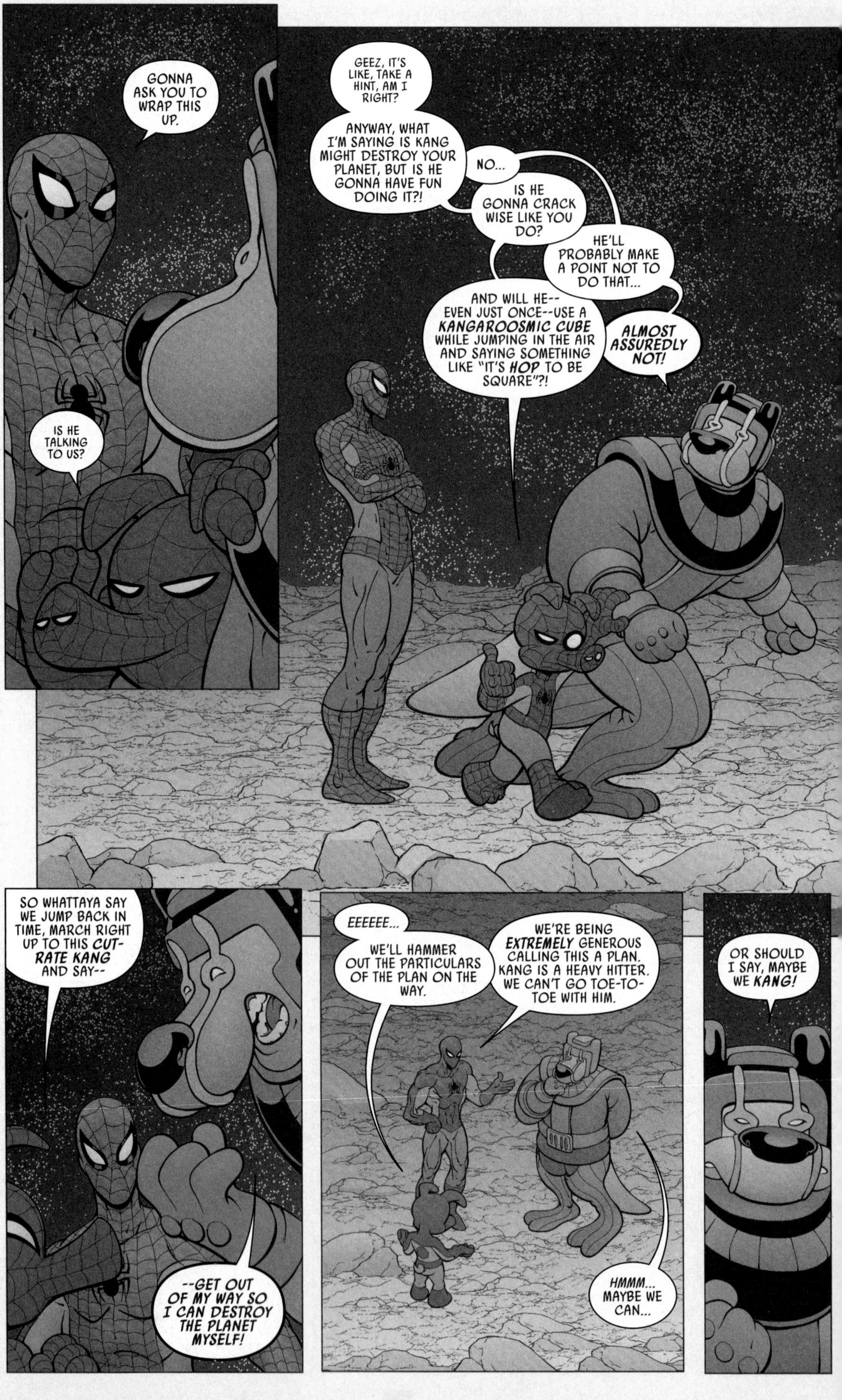

GONNA ASK YOU TO WRAP THIS UP.
IS HE TALKING TO US?
GEEZ, IT'S LIKE, TAKE A HINT, AM I RIGHT?
ANYWAY, WHAT I'M SAYING IS KANG MIGHT DESTROY YOUR PLANET, BUT IS HE GONNA HAVE FUN DOING IT?!
NO...
IS HE GONNA CRACK WISE LIKE YOU DO?
HE'LL PROBABLY MAKE A POINT NOT TO DO THAT...
AND WILL HE-- EVEN JUST ONCE--USE A KANGAROOSMIC CUBE WHILE JUMPING IN THE AIR AND SAYING SOMETHING LIKE "IT'S HOP TO BE SQUARE"?!
ALMOST ASSUREDLY NOT!
SO WHATTAYA SAY WE JUMP BACK IN TIME, MARCH RIGHT UP TO THIS CUT-RATE KANG AND SAY--
--GET OUT OF MY WAY SO I CAN DESTROY THE PLANET MYSELF!
EEEEEE...
WE'LL HAMMER OUT THE PARTICULARS OF THE PLAN ON THE WAY.
WE'RE BEING EXTREMELY GENEROUS CALLING THIS A PLAN. KANG IS A HEAVY HITTER. WE CAN'T GO TOE-TO-TOE WITH HIM.
HMMM... MAYBE WE CAN...
OR SHOULD I SAY, MAYBE WE KANG!

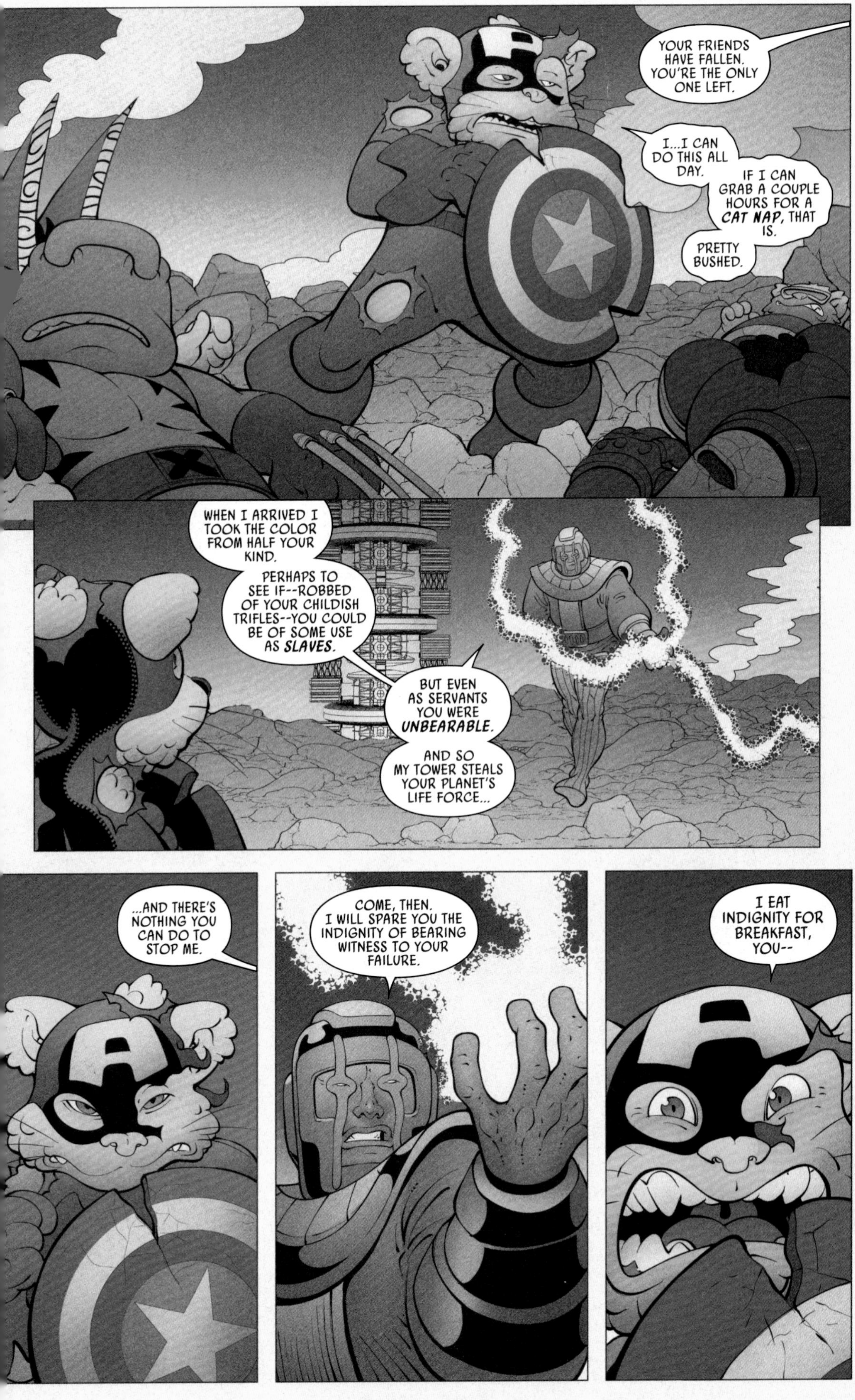
YOUR FRIENDS HAVE FALLEN. YOU'RE THE ONLY ONE LEFT.
I...I CAN DO THIS ALL DAY.
IF I CAN GRAB A COUPLE HOURS FOR A CAT NAP, THAT IS.
PRETTY BUSHED.
WHEN I ARRIVED I TOOK THE COLOR FROM HALF YOUR KIND.
PERHAPS TO SEE IF--ROBBED OF YOUR CHILDISH TRIFLES--YOU COULD BE OF SOME USE AS SLAVES.
BUT EVEN AS SERVANTS YOU WERE UNBEARABLE.
AND SO MY TOWER STEALS YOUR PLANET'S LIFE FORCE...
...AND THERE'S NOTHING YOU CAN DO TO STOP ME.
COME, THEN. I WILL SPARE YOU THE INDIGNITY OF BEARING WITNESS TO YOUR FAILURE.
I EAT INDIGNITY FOR BREAKFAST, YOU--

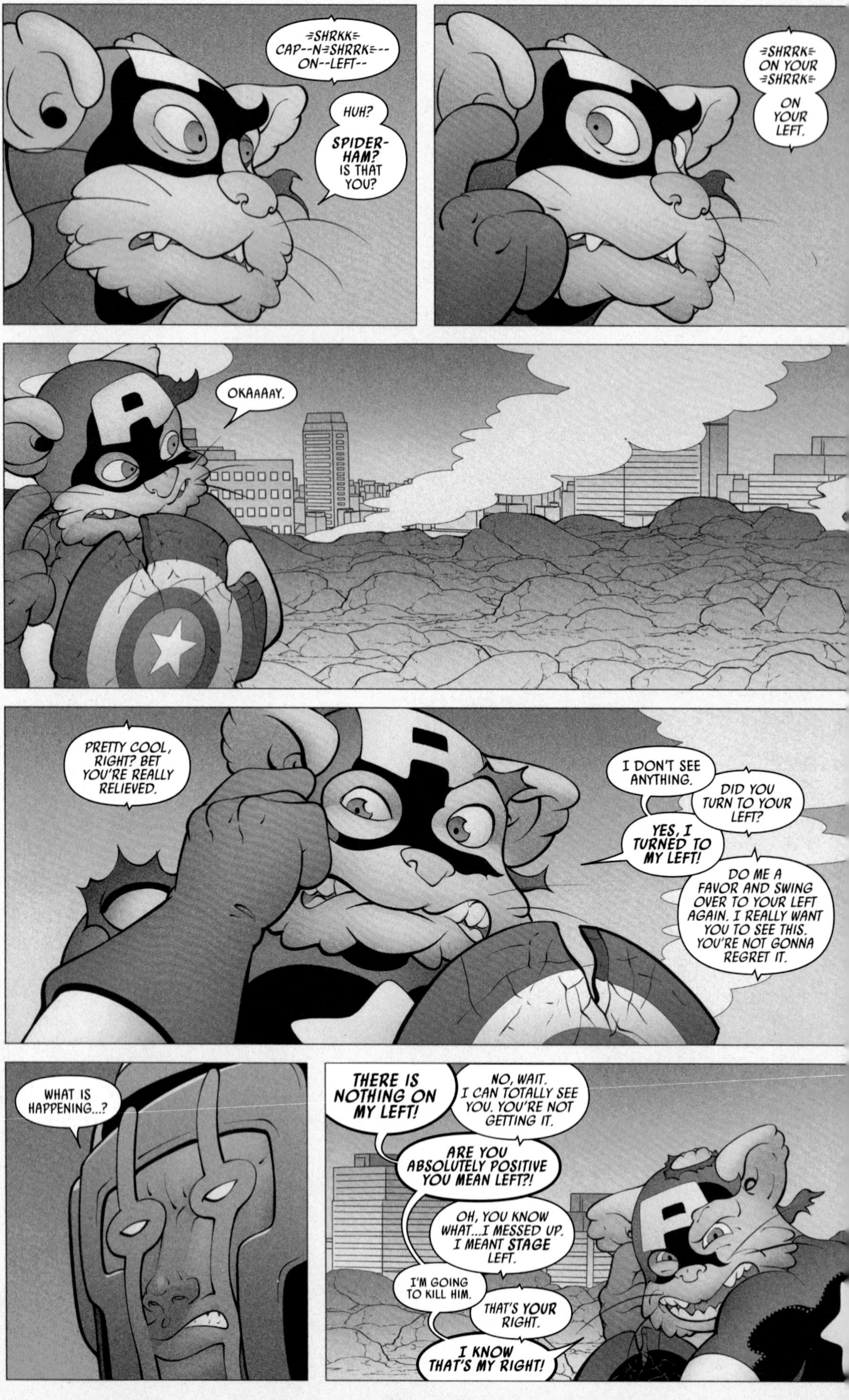

≡SHRKK≡ CAP--N≡SHRRK≡-- ON--LEFT--
HUH?
SPIDER-HAM? IS THAT YOU?
≡SHRRK≡ ON YOUR ≡SHRRK≡
ON YOUR LEFT.
OKAAAAY.
PRETTY COOL, RIGHT? BET YOU'RE REALLY RELIEVED.
I DON'T SEE ANYTHING.
DID YOU TURN TO YOUR LEFT?
YES, I TURNED TO MY LEFT!
DO ME A FAVOR AND SWING OVER TO YOUR LEFT AGAIN. I REALLY WANT YOU TO SEE THIS. YOU'RE NOT GONNA REGRET IT.
WHAT IS HAPPENING...?
THERE IS NOTHING ON MY LEFT!
NO, WAIT. I CAN TOTALLY SEE YOU. YOU'RE NOT GETTING IT.
ARE YOU ABSOLUTELY POSITIVE YOU MEAN LEFT?!
OH, YOU KNOW WHAT...I MESSED UP. I MEANT STAGE LEFT.
I'M GOING TO KILL HIM.
THAT'S YOUR RIGHT.
I KNOW THAT'S MY RIGHT!

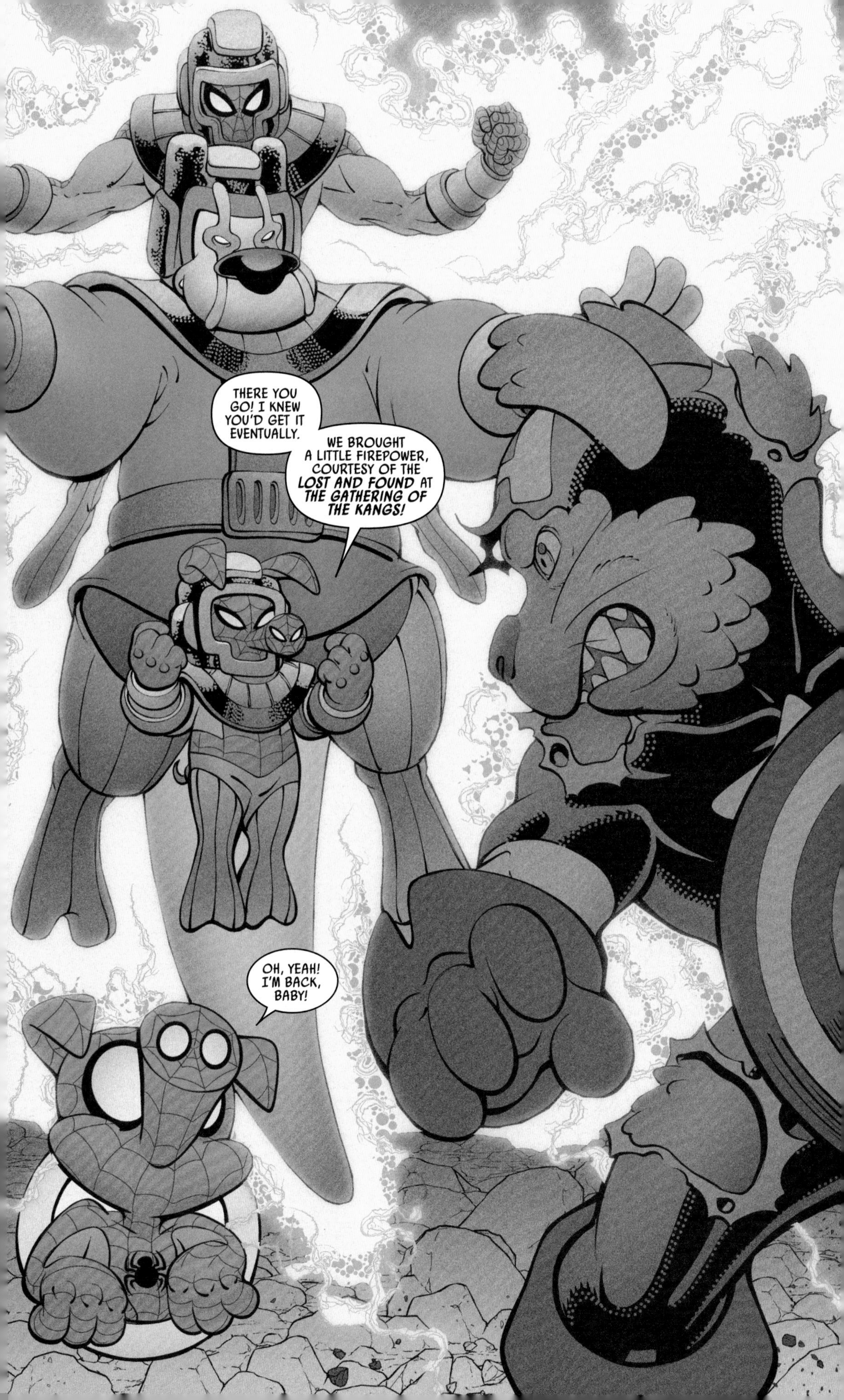
THERE YOU GO! I KNEW YOU'D GET IT EVENTUALLY.
WE BROUGHT A LITTLE FIREPOWER, COURTESY OF THE *LOST AND FOUND* AT *THE GATHERING OF THE KANGS!*
OH, YEAH! I'M BACK, BABY!

THOSE SUITS ARE PROPERTY OF THE KANG COLLECTIVE!

HAVE YOU NO RESPECT?!

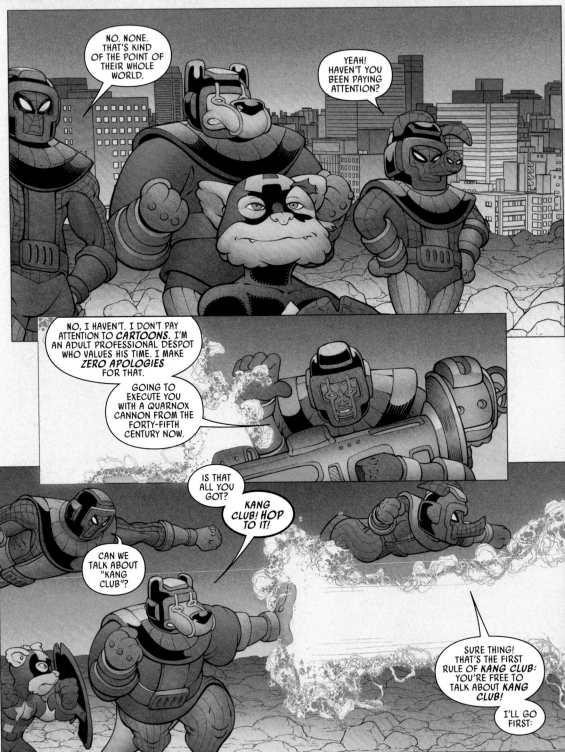

NO. NONE. THAT'S KIND OF THE POINT OF THEIR WHOLE WORLD.

YEAH! HAVEN'T YOU BEEN PAYING ATTENTION?

NO, I HAVEN'T. I DON'T PAY ATTENTION TO *CARTOONS*. I'M AN ADULT PROFESSIONAL DESPOT WHO VALUES HIS TIME. I MAKE *ZERO APOLOGIES* FOR THAT.

GOING TO EXECUTE YOU WITH A QUARNOX CANNON FROM THE FORTY-FIFTH CENTURY NOW.

IS THAT ALL YOU GOT?

KANG CLUB! HOP TO IT!

CAN WE TALK ABOUT "KANG CLUB"?

SURE THING! THAT'S THE FIRST RULE OF *KANG CLUB*: YOU'RE FREE TO TALK ABOUT *KANG CLUB*!

I'LL GO FIRST:

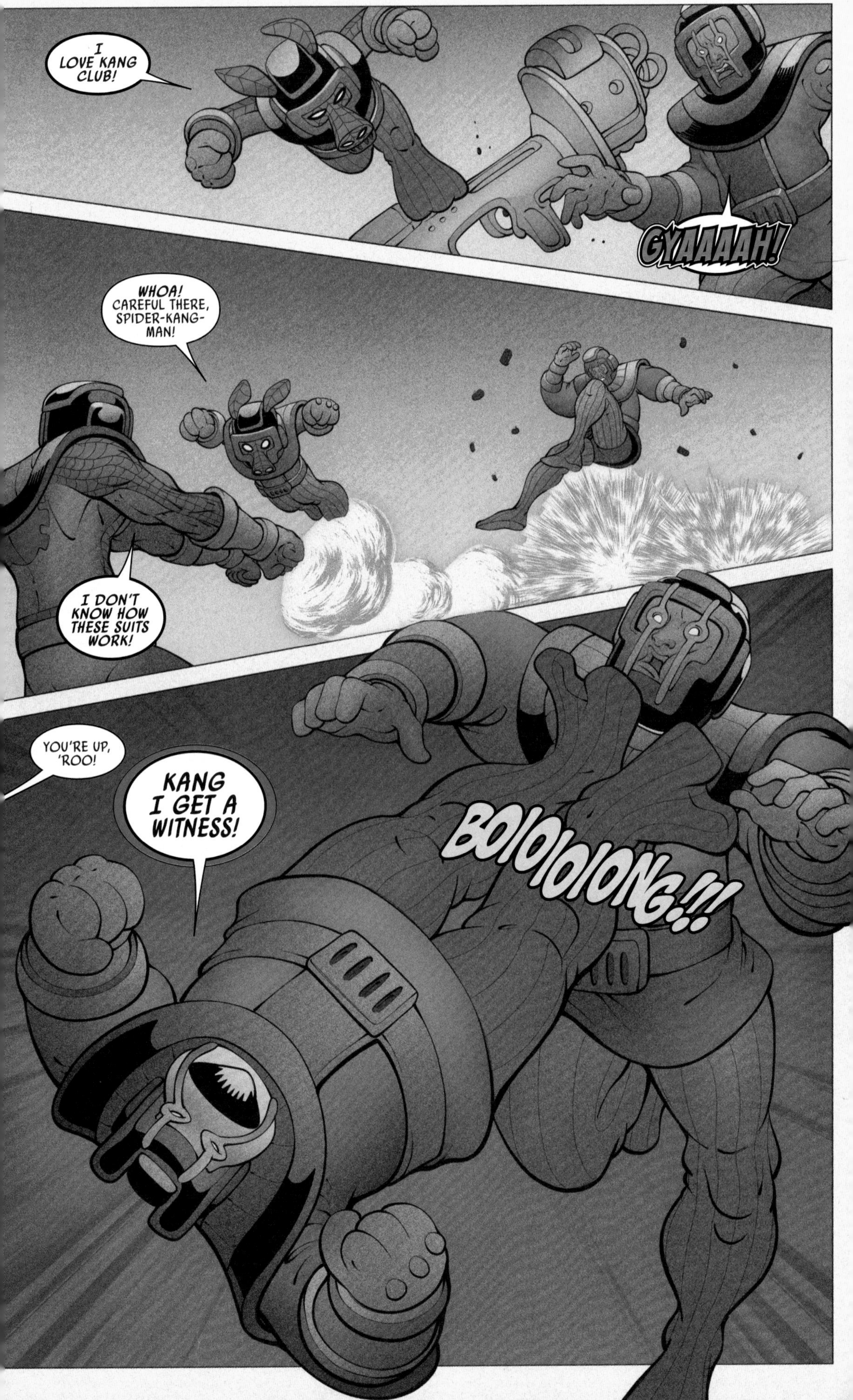
I LOVE KANG CLUB!
GYAAAAH!
WHOA! CAREFUL THERE, SPIDER-KANG-MAN!
I DON'T KNOW HOW THESE SUITS WORK!
YOU'RE UP, 'ROO!
KANG I GET A WITNESS!
BOIOIOIOING!!!

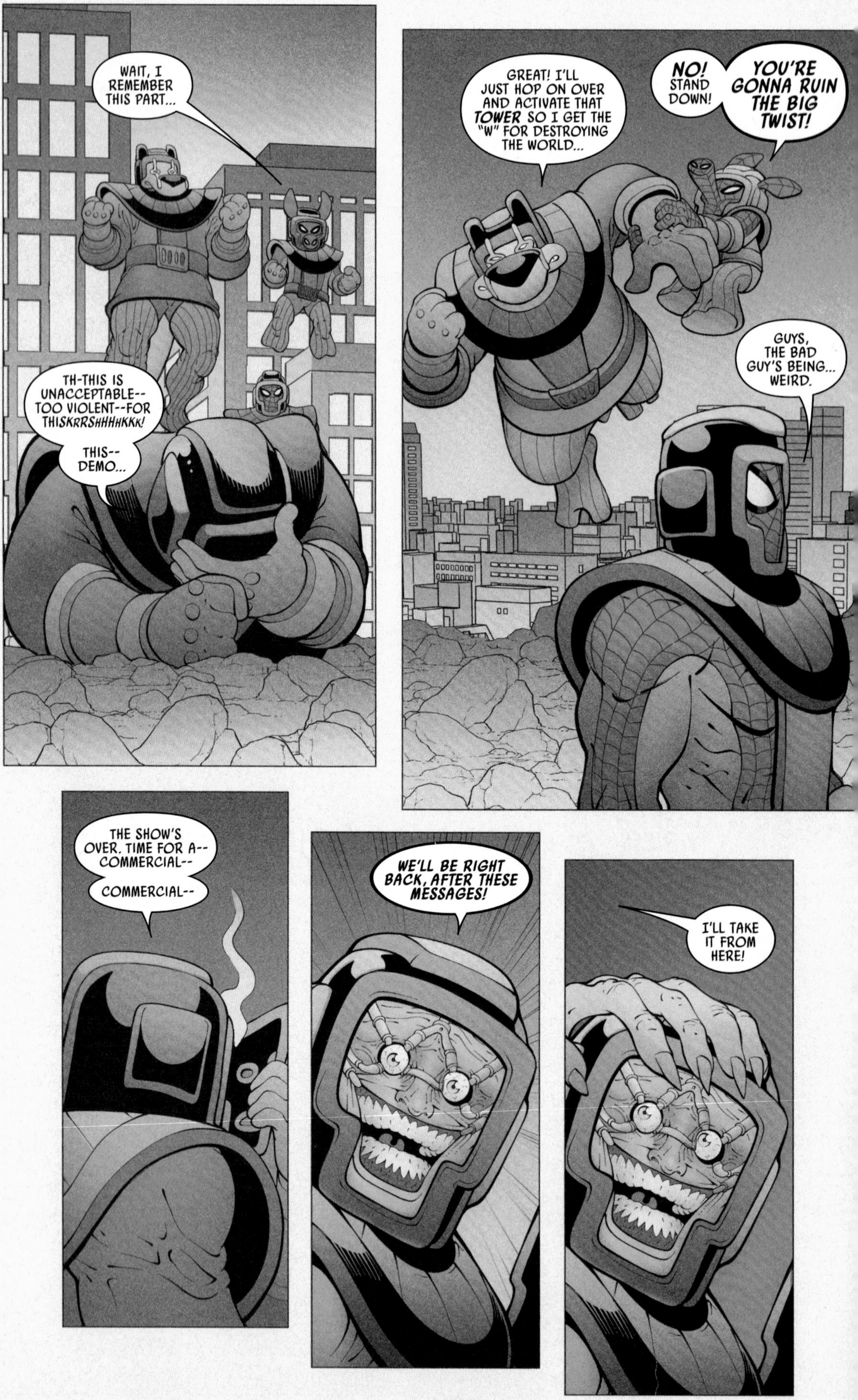
WAIT, I REMEMBER THIS PART...
TH-THIS IS UNACCEPTABLE-- TOO VIOLENT--FOR THISKRRSHHHHKKK!
THIS-- DEMO...
GREAT! I'LL JUST HOP ON OVER AND ACTIVATE THAT TOWER SO I GET THE "W" FOR DESTROYING THE WORLD...
NO! STAND DOWN!
YOU'RE GONNA RUIN THE BIG TWIST!
GUYS, THE BAD GUY'S BEING... WEIRD.
THE SHOW'S OVER. TIME FOR A-- COMMERCIAL--
COMMERCIAL--
WE'LL BE RIGHT BACK, AFTER THESE MESSAGES!
I'LL TAKE IT FROM HERE!

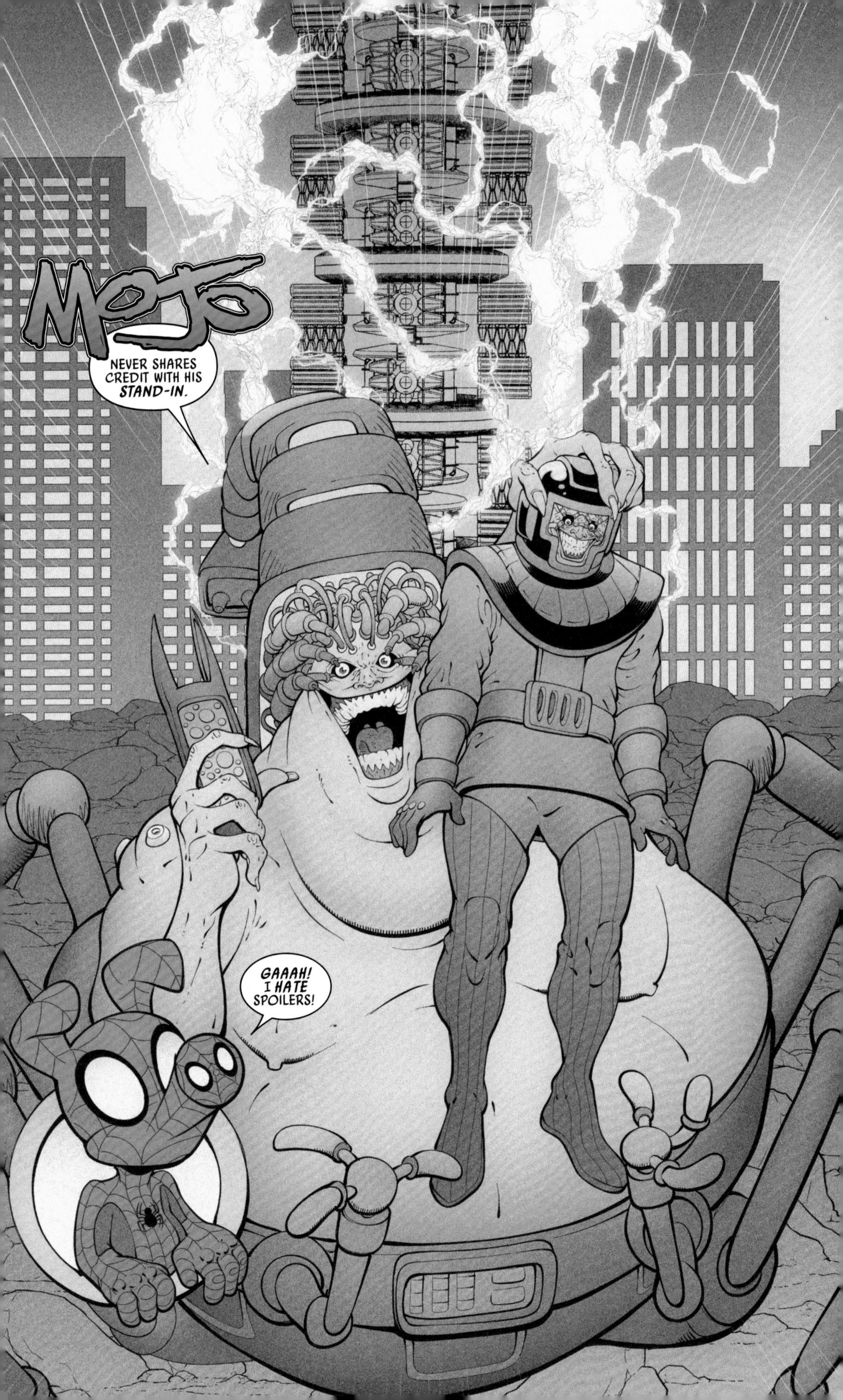
MOJO
NEVER SHARES CREDIT WITH HIS STAND-IN.
GAAAH! I HATE SPOILERS!

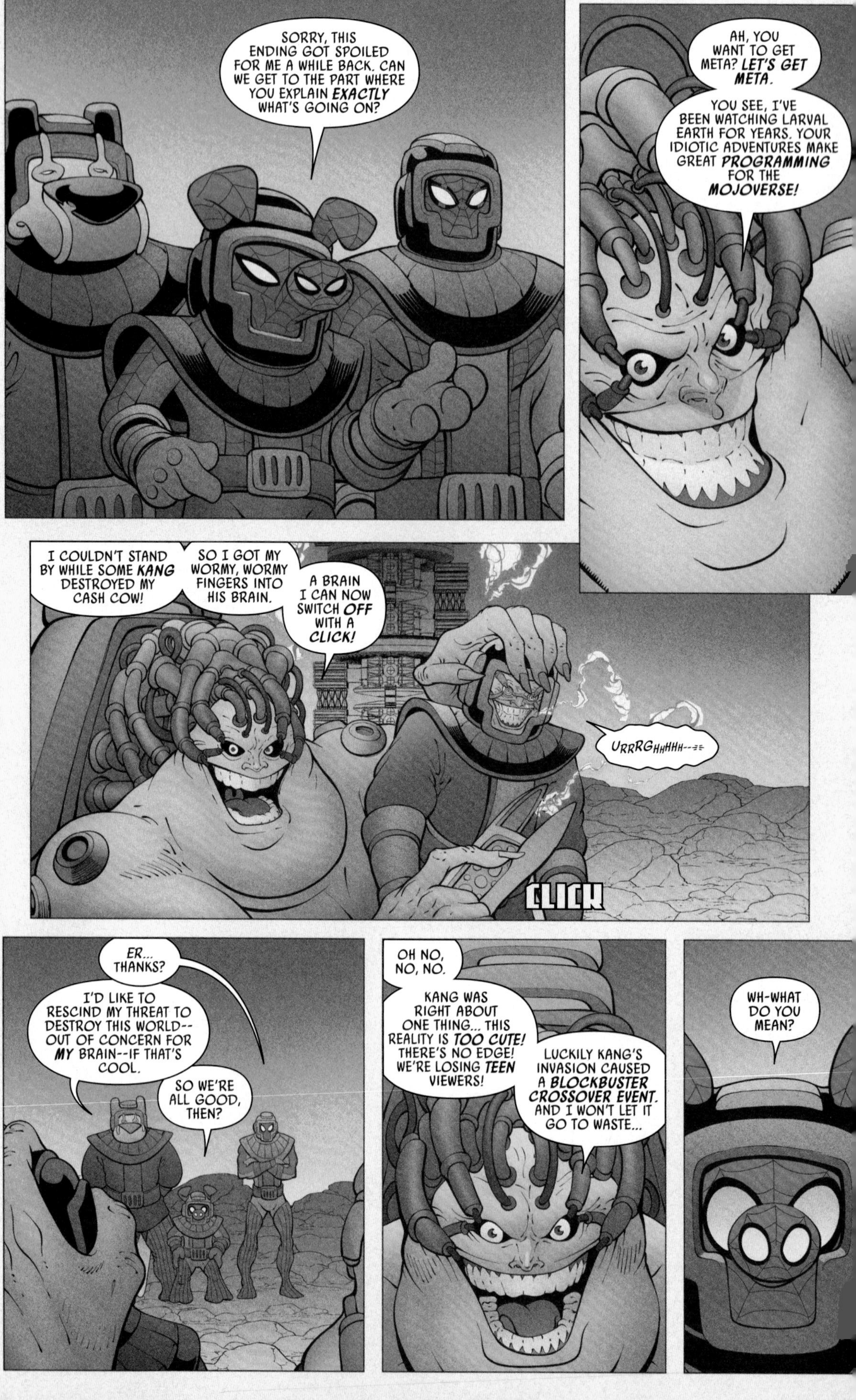

SORRY, THIS ENDING GOT SPOILED FOR ME A WHILE BACK. CAN WE GET TO THE PART WHERE YOU EXPLAIN EXACTLY WHAT'S GOING ON?
AH, YOU WANT TO GET META? LET'S GET META.
YOU SEE, I'VE BEEN WATCHING LARVAL EARTH FOR YEARS. YOUR IDIOTIC ADVENTURES MAKE GREAT PROGRAMMING FOR THE MOJOVERSE!
I COULDN'T STAND BY WHILE SOME KANG DESTROYED MY CASH COW!
SO I GOT MY WORMY, WORMY FINGERS INTO HIS BRAIN.
A BRAIN I CAN NOW SWITCH OFF WITH A CLICK!
URRRGHHHHH--
CLICK
ER... THANKS?
I'D LIKE TO RESCIND MY THREAT TO DESTROY THIS WORLD--OUT OF CONCERN FOR MY BRAIN--IF THAT'S COOL.
SO WE'RE ALL GOOD, THEN?
OH NO, NO, NO.
KANG WAS RIGHT ABOUT ONE THING... THIS REALITY IS TOO CUTE! THERE'S NO EDGE! WE'RE LOSING TEEN VIEWERS!
LUCKILY KANG'S INVASION CAUSED A BLOCKBUSTER CROSSOVER EVENT. AND I WON'T LET IT GO TO WASTE...
WH-WHAT DO YOU MEAN?

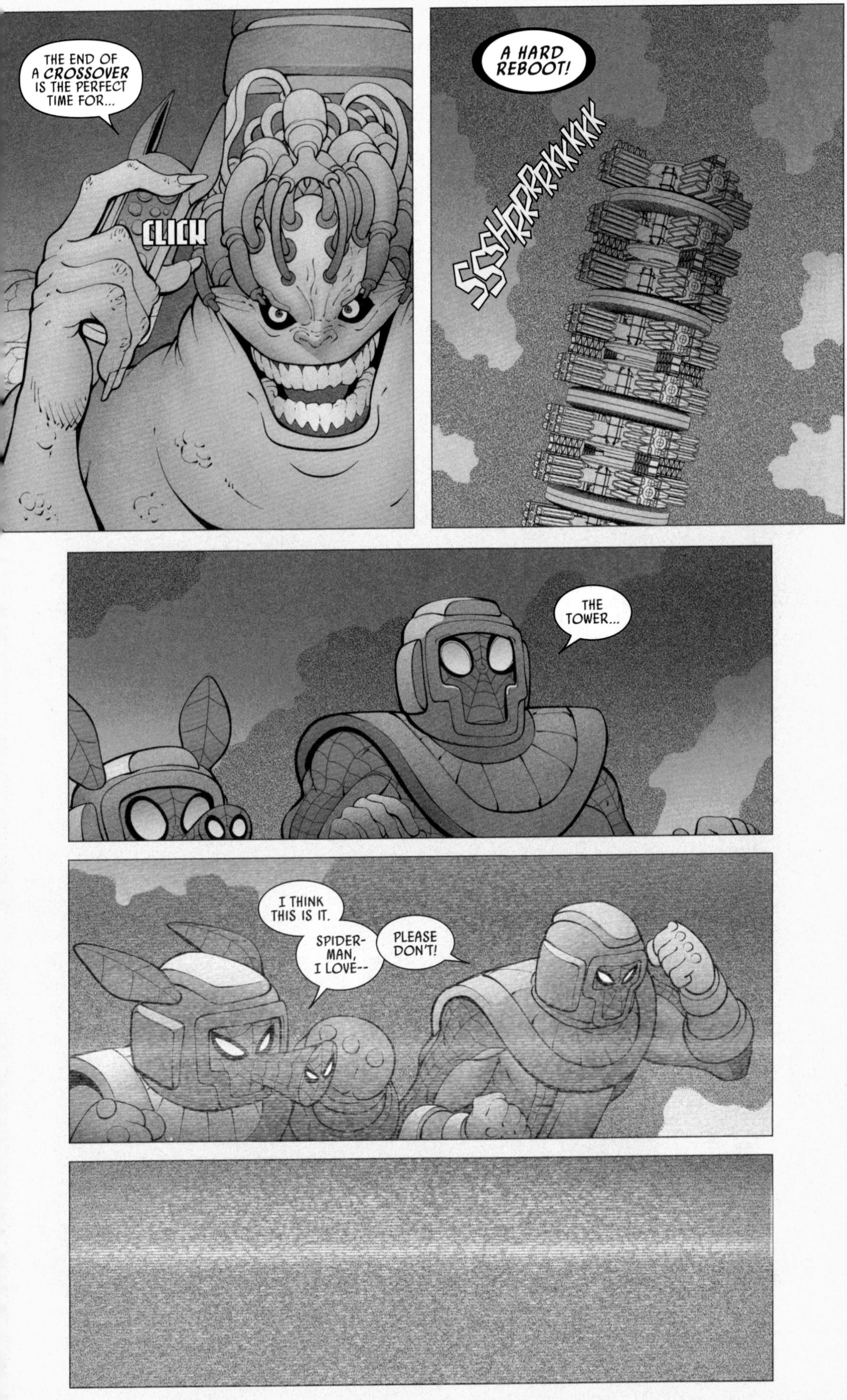
THE END OF A CROSSOVER IS THE PERFECT TIME FOR...
CLICK
A HARD REBOOT!
SSSHRRRKKKKK
THE TOWER...
I THINK THIS IS IT.
SPIDER-MAN, I LOVE--
PLEASE DON'T!

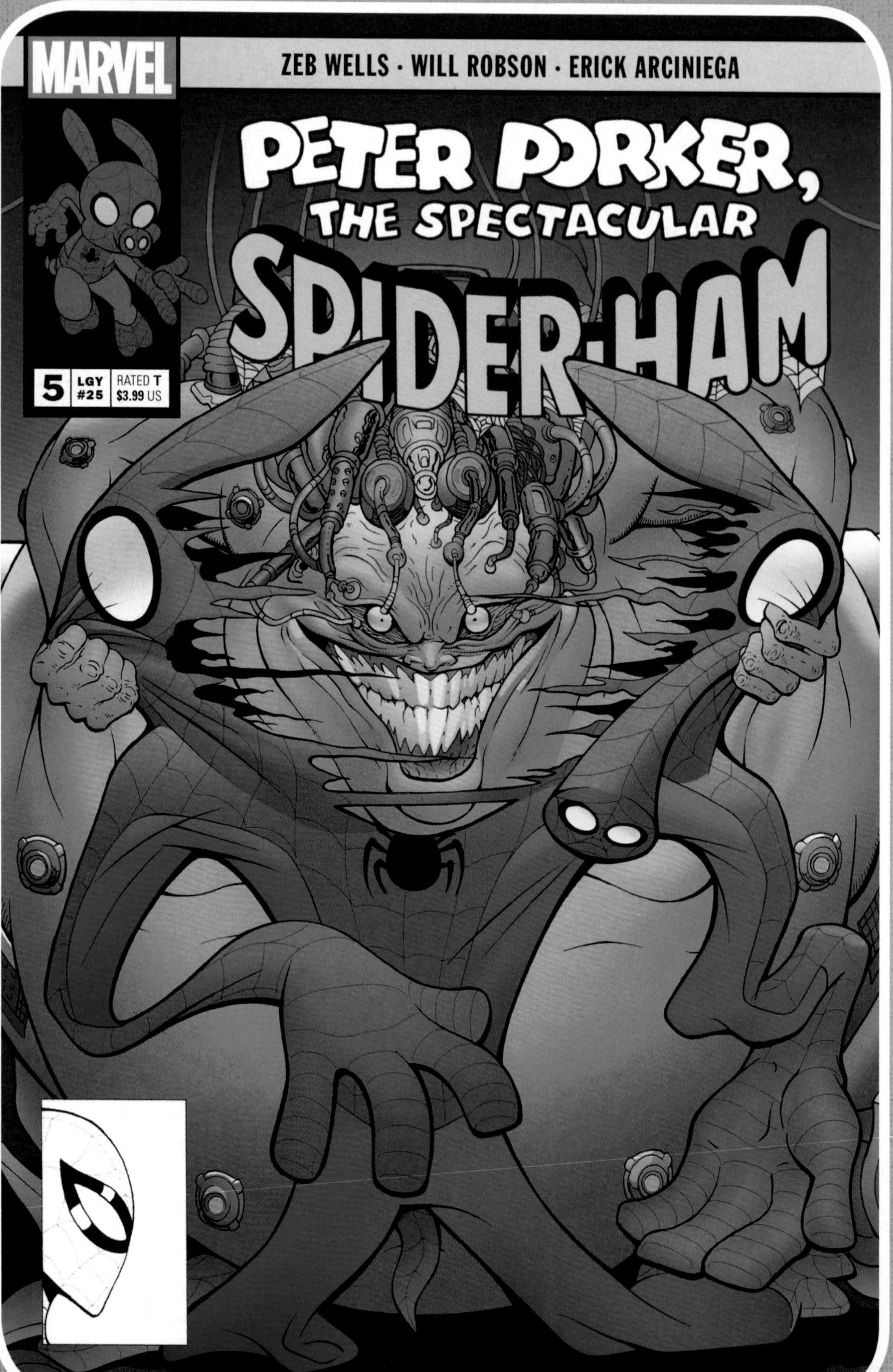
MARVEL
ZEB WELLS · WILL ROBSON · ERICK ARCINIEGA
PETER PORKER, THE SPECTACULAR SPIDER-HAM
5 LGY #25 RATED T $3.99 US

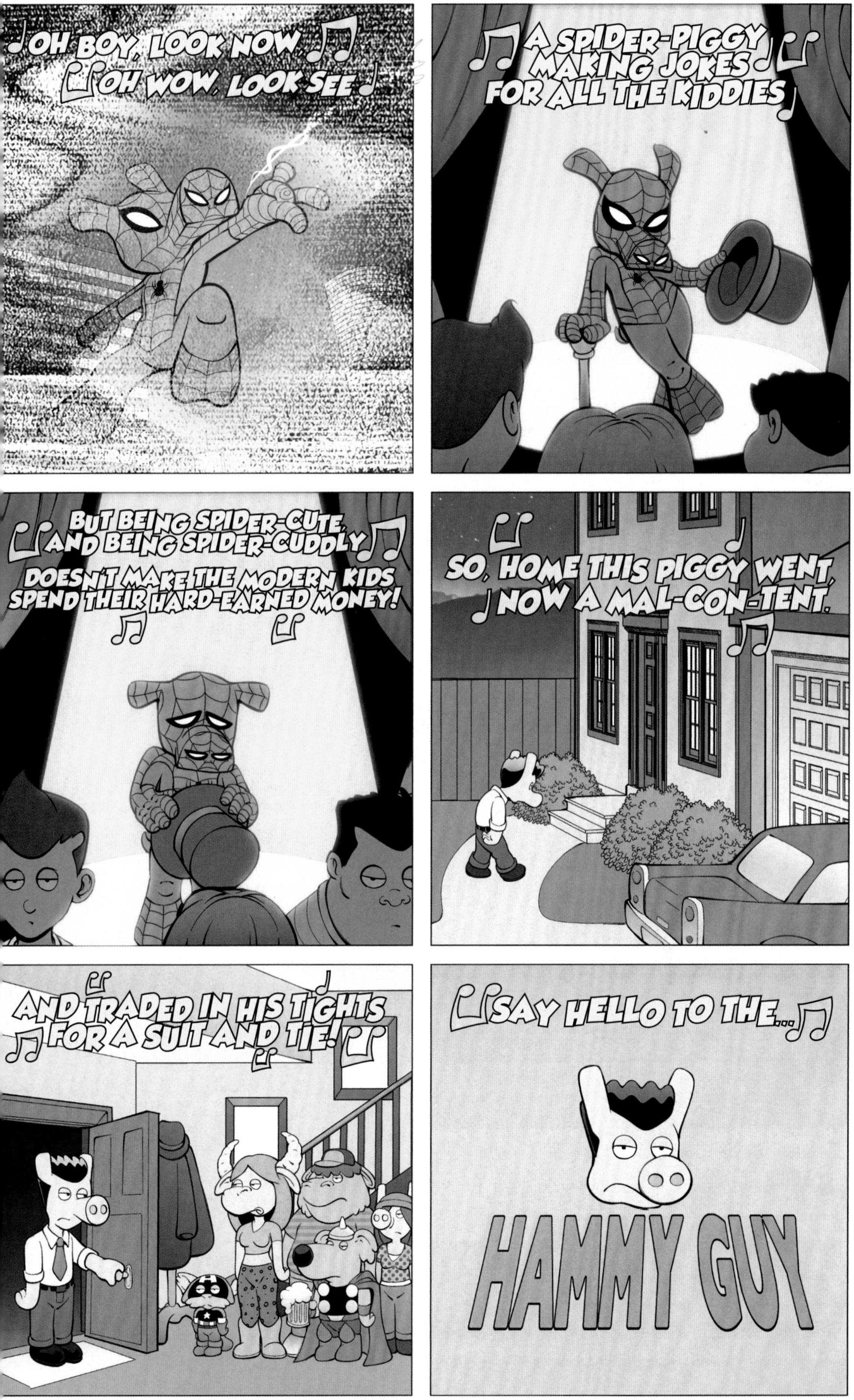
OH BOY, LOOK NOW,
OH WOW, LOOK SEE
A SPIDER-PIGGY MAKING JOKES FOR ALL THE KIDDIES
BUT BEING SPIDER-CUTE, AND BEING SPIDER-CUDDLY
DOESN'T MAKE THE MODERN KIDS SPEND THEIR HARD-EARNED MONEY!
SO, HOME THIS PIGGY WENT, NOW A MAL-CON-TENT,
AND TRADED IN HIS TIGHTS FOR A SUIT AND TIE!
SAY HELLO TO THE...
HAMMY GUY

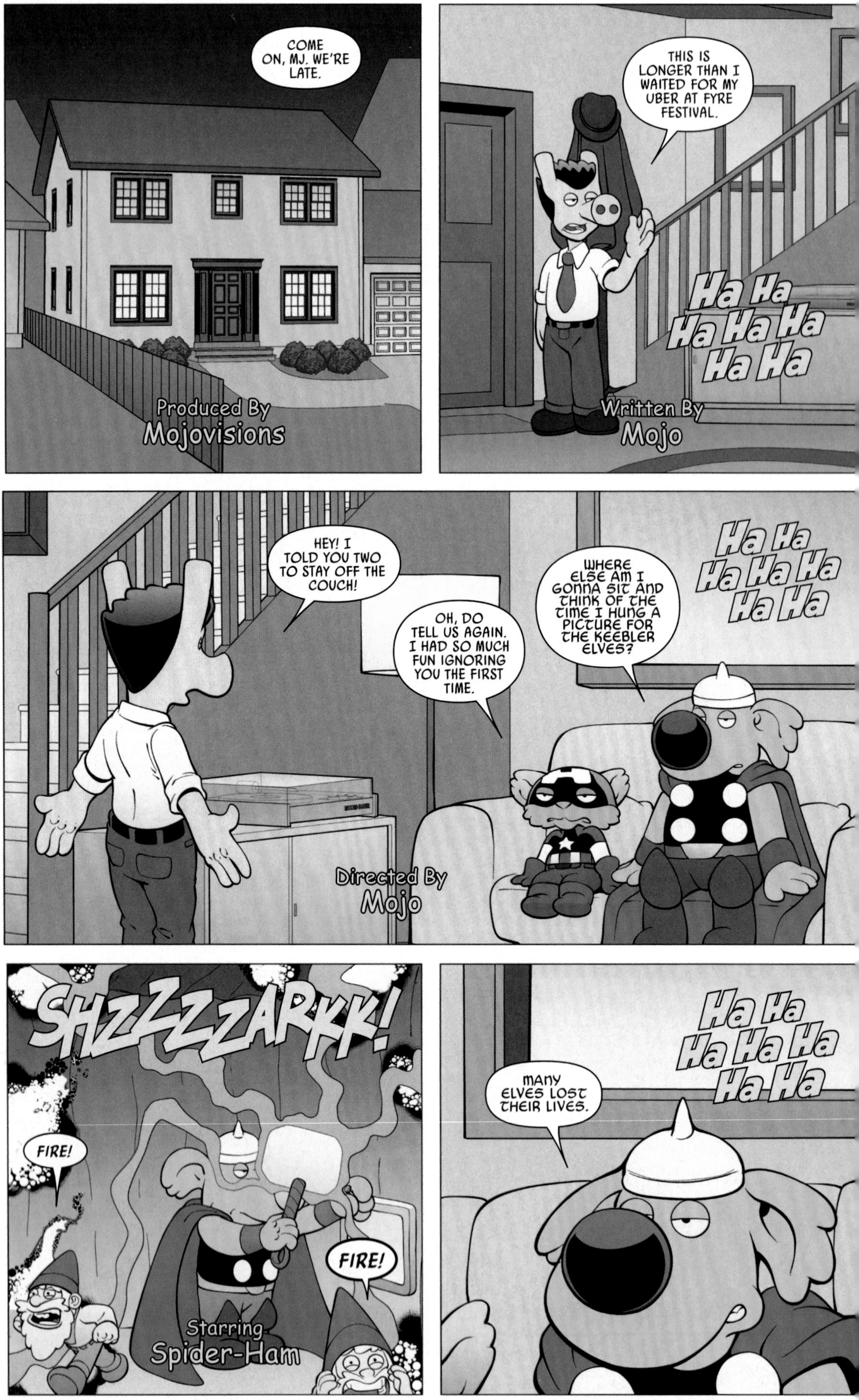

COME ON, MJ. WE'RE LATE.
Produced By Mojovisions
THIS IS LONGER THAN I WAITED FOR MY UBER AT FYRE FESTIVAL.
Ha Ha Ha Ha Ha Ha Ha
Written By Mojo
HEY! I TOLD YOU TWO TO STAY OFF THE COUCH!
OH, DO TELL US AGAIN. I HAD SO MUCH FUN IGNORING YOU THE FIRST TIME.
WHERE ELSE AM I GONNA SIT AND THINK OF THE TIME I HUNG A PICTURE FOR THE KEEBLER ELVES?
Ha Ha Ha Ha Ha Ha Ha
Directed By Mojo
SHZZZZZARKK!
FIRE!
FIRE!
Starring Spider-Ham
MANY ELVES LOST THEIR LIVES.
Ha Ha Ha Ha Ha Ha Ha

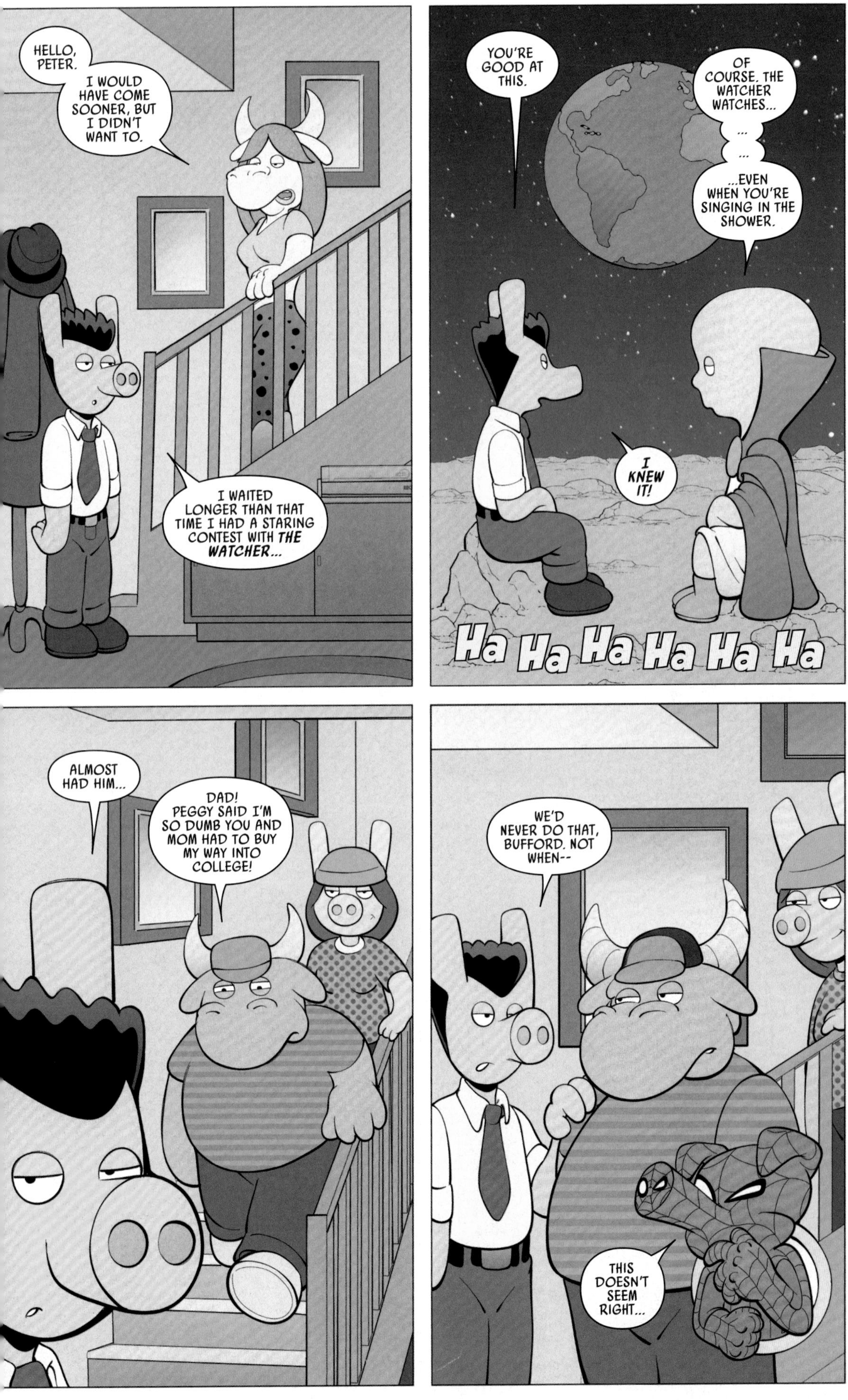
HELLO, PETER.
I WOULD HAVE COME SOONER, BUT I DIDN'T WANT TO.
I WAITED LONGER THAN THAT TIME I HAD A STARING CONTEST WITH THE WATCHER...
YOU'RE GOOD AT THIS.
OF COURSE. THE WATCHER WATCHES...
...
...
...EVEN WHEN YOU'RE SINGING IN THE SHOWER.
I KNEW IT!
Ha Ha Ha Ha Ha Ha
ALMOST HAD HIM...
DAD! PEGGY SAID I'M SO DUMB YOU AND MOM HAD TO BUY MY WAY INTO COLLEGE!
WE'D NEVER DO THAT, BUFFORD. NOT WHEN--
THIS DOESN'T SEEM RIGHT...

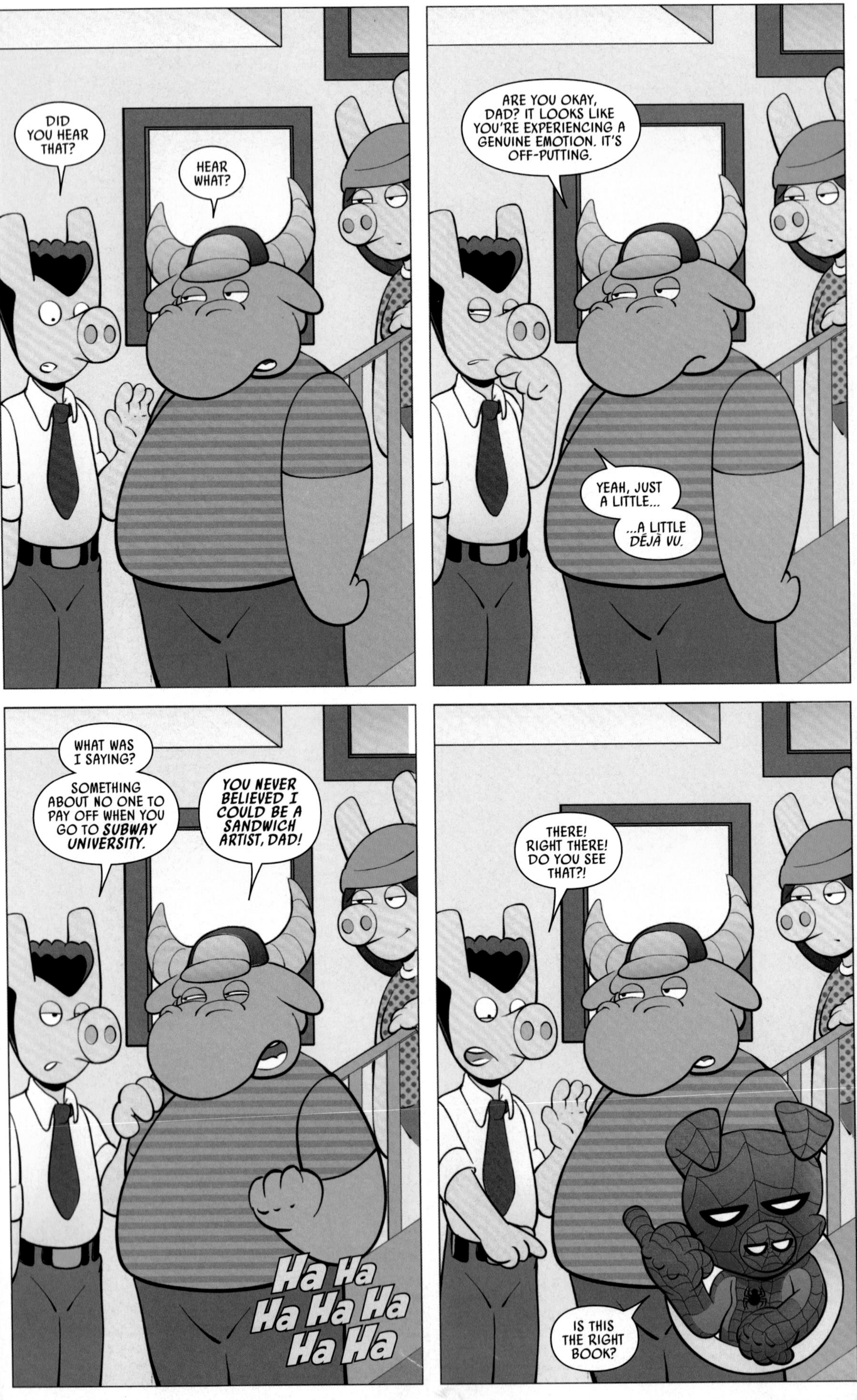
DID YOU HEAR THAT?
HEAR WHAT?
ARE YOU OKAY, DAD? IT LOOKS LIKE YOU'RE EXPERIENCING A GENUINE EMOTION. IT'S OFF-PUTTING.
YEAH, JUST A LITTLE...
...A LITTLE DÉJÀ VU.
WHAT WAS I SAYING?
SOMETHING ABOUT NO ONE TO PAY OFF WHEN YOU GO TO SUBWAY UNIVERSITY.
YOU NEVER BELIEVED I COULD BE A SANDWICH ARTIST, DAD!
Ha Ha Ha Ha Ha Ha Ha
THERE! RIGHT THERE! DO YOU SEE THAT?!
IS THIS THE RIGHT BOOK?

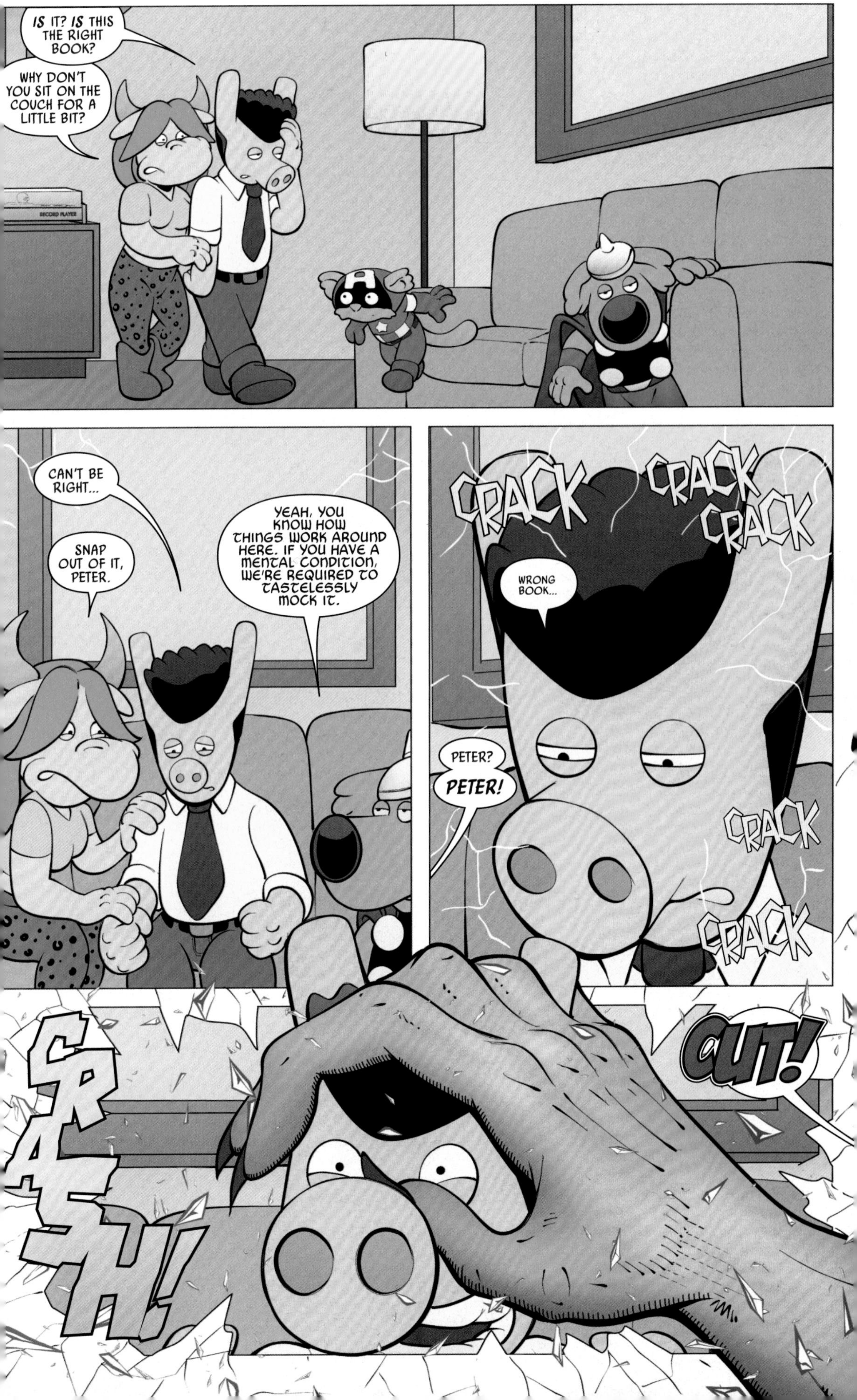

IS IT? IS THIS THE RIGHT BOOK?
WHY DON'T YOU SIT ON THE COUCH FOR A LITTLE BIT?
RECORD PLAYER
CAN'T BE RIGHT...
SNAP OUT OF IT, PETER.
YEAH, YOU KNOW HOW THINGS WORK AROUND HERE. IF YOU HAVE A MENTAL CONDITION, WE'RE REQUIRED TO TASTELESSLY MOCK IT.
CRACK
CRACK
CRACK
WRONG BOOK...
PETER? PETER!
CRACK
CRACK
CRASH!
CUT!

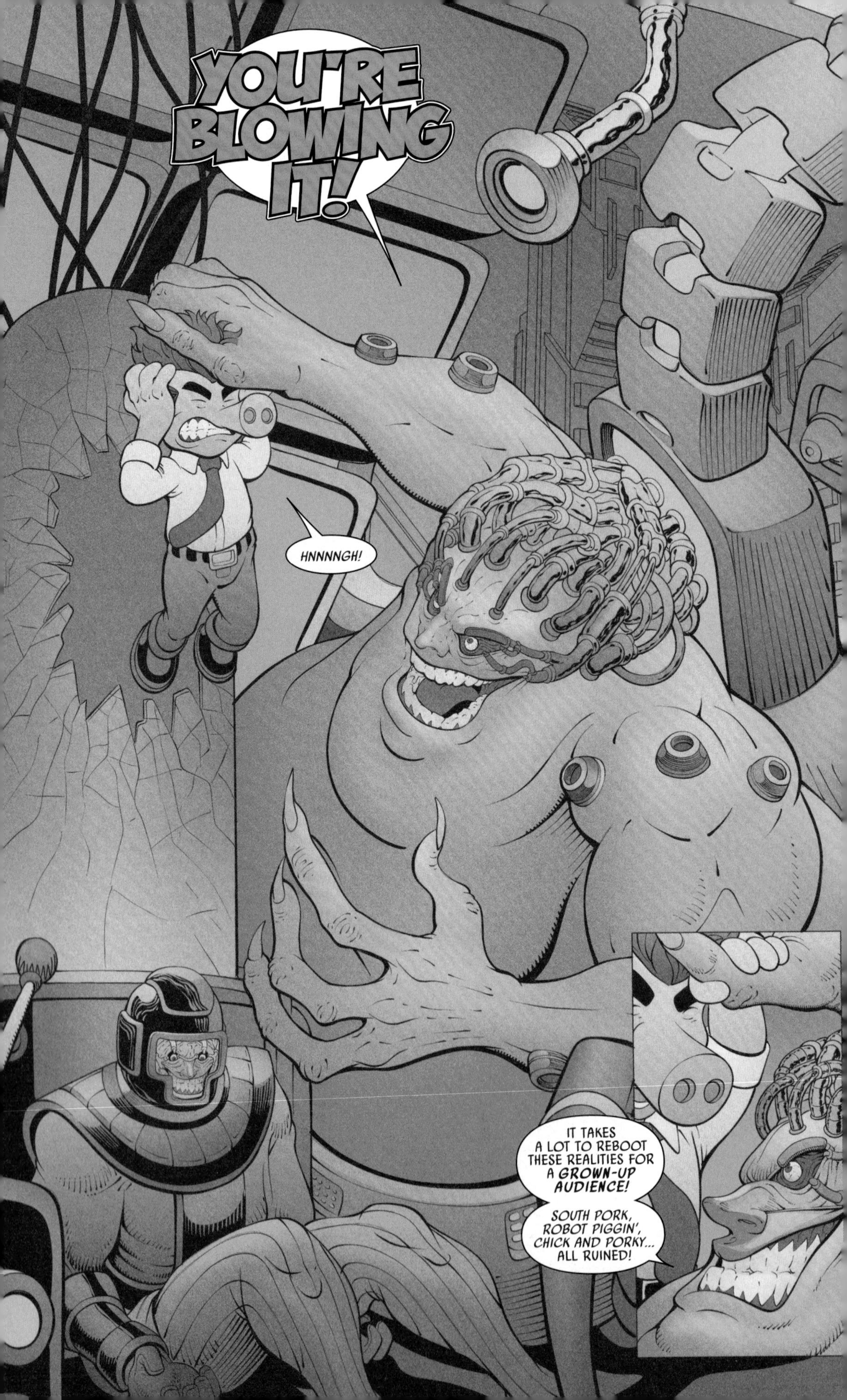
YOU'RE BLOWING IT!
HNNNNGH!
IT TAKES A LOT TO REBOOT THESE REALITIES FOR A GROWN-UP AUDIENCE!
SOUTH PORK, ROBOT PIGGIN', CHICK AND PORKY... ALL RUINED!

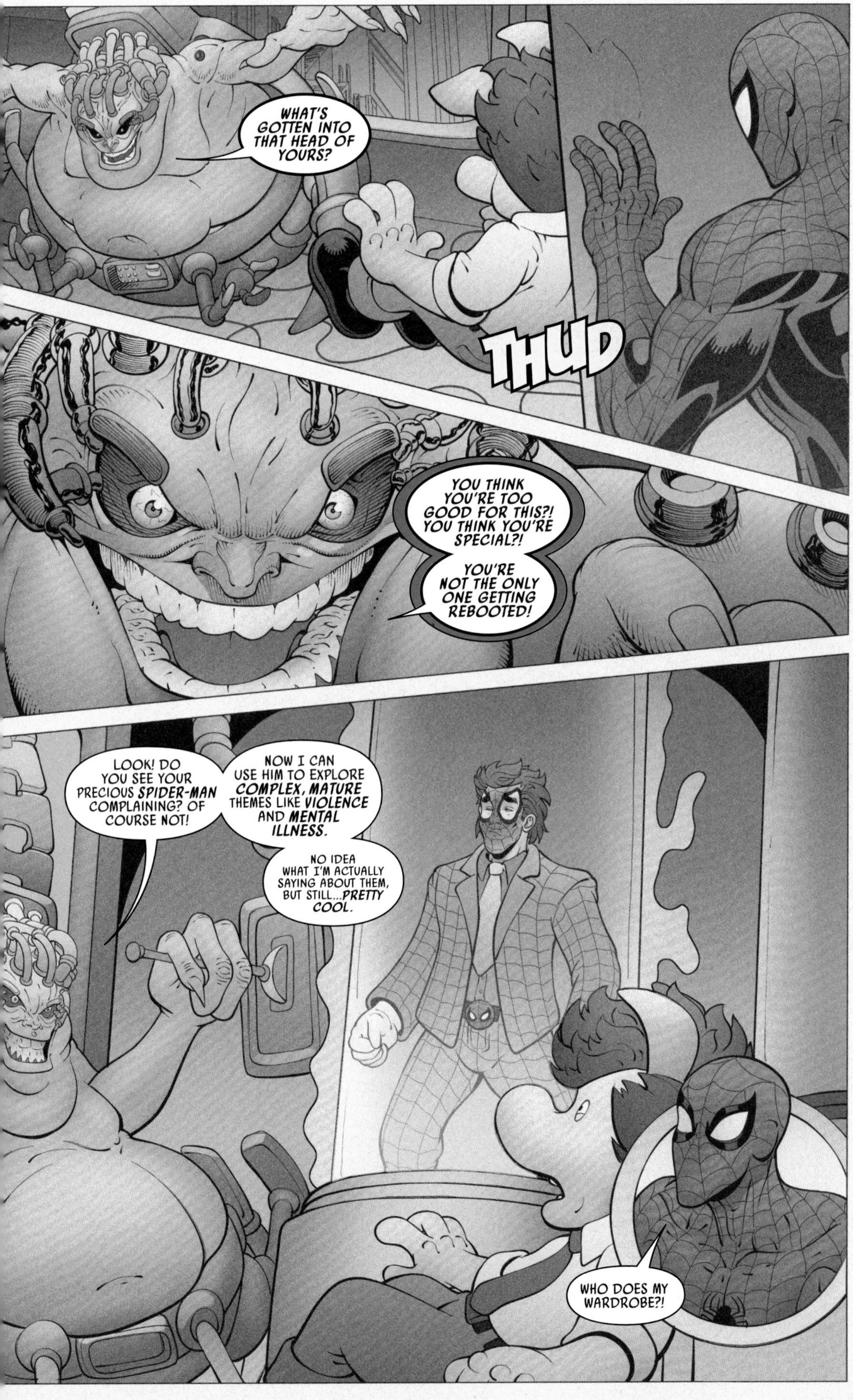
WHAT'S GOTTEN INTO THAT HEAD OF YOURS?
THUD
YOU THINK YOU'RE TOO GOOD FOR THIS?! YOU THINK YOU'RE SPECIAL?!
YOU'RE NOT THE ONLY ONE GETTING REBOOTED!
LOOK! DO YOU SEE YOUR PRECIOUS SPIDER-MAN COMPLAINING? OF COURSE NOT!
NOW I CAN USE HIM TO EXPLORE COMPLEX, MATURE THEMES LIKE VIOLENCE AND MENTAL ILLNESS.
NO IDEA WHAT I'M ACTUALLY SAYING ABOUT THEM, BUT STILL...PRETTY COOL.
WHO DOES MY WARDROBE?!

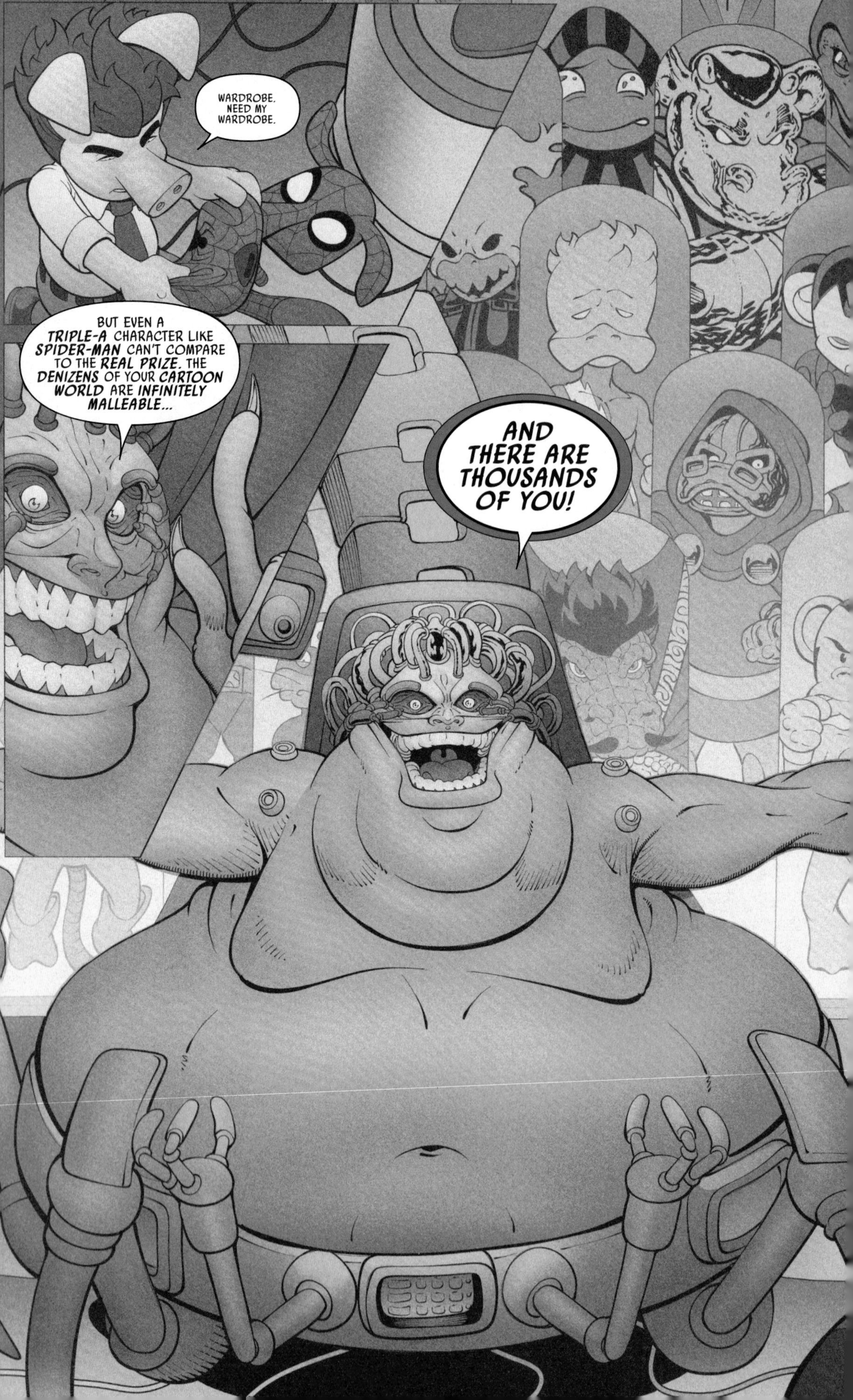
WARDROBE. NEED MY WARDROBE.
BUT EVEN A TRIPLE-A CHARACTER LIKE SPIDER-MAN CAN'T COMPARE TO THE REAL PRIZE. THE DENIZENS OF YOUR CARTOON WORLD ARE INFINITELY MALLEABLE...
AND THERE ARE THOUSANDS OF YOU!

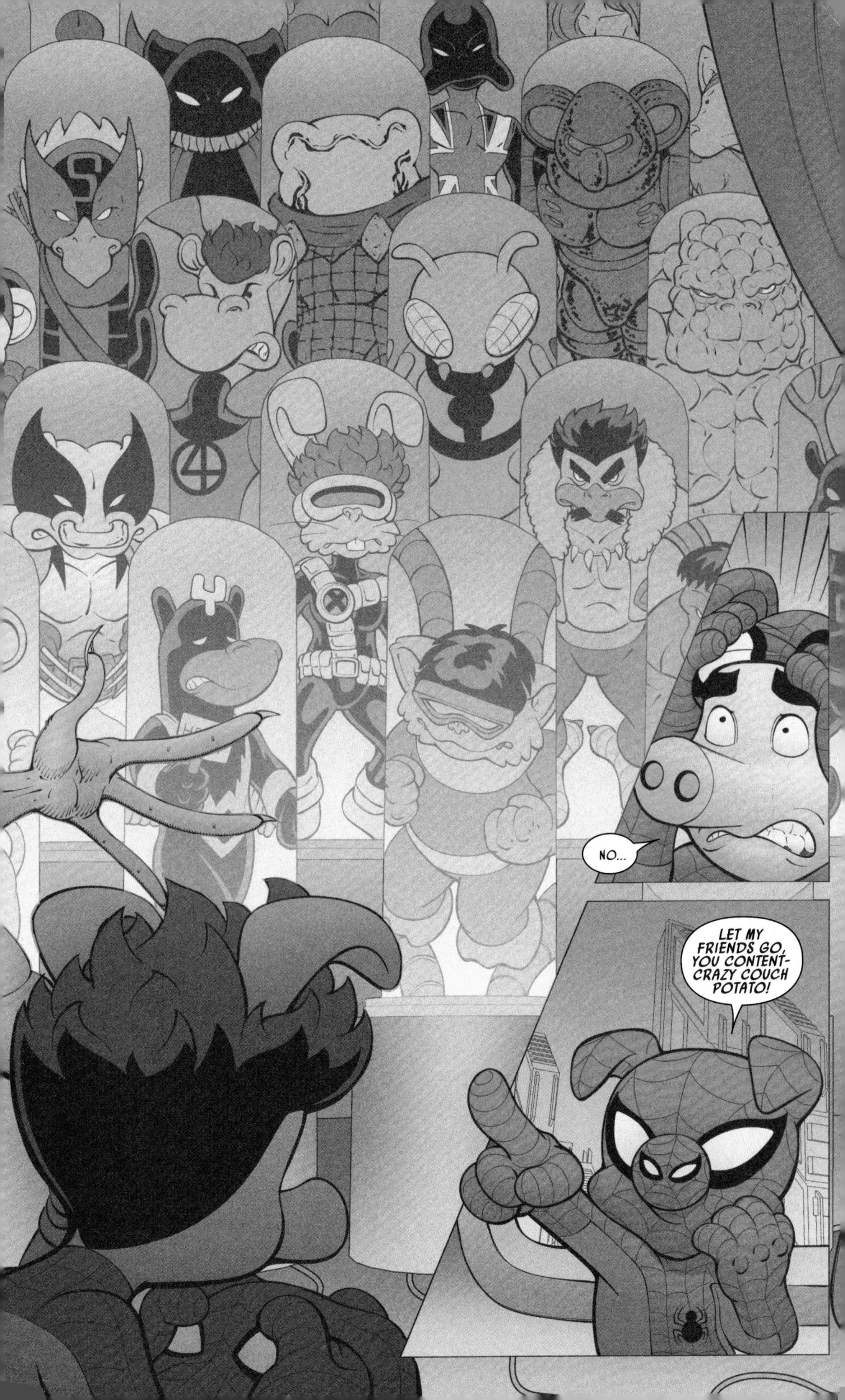
NO...
LET MY FRIENDS GO, YOU CONTENT-CRAZY COUCH POTATO!

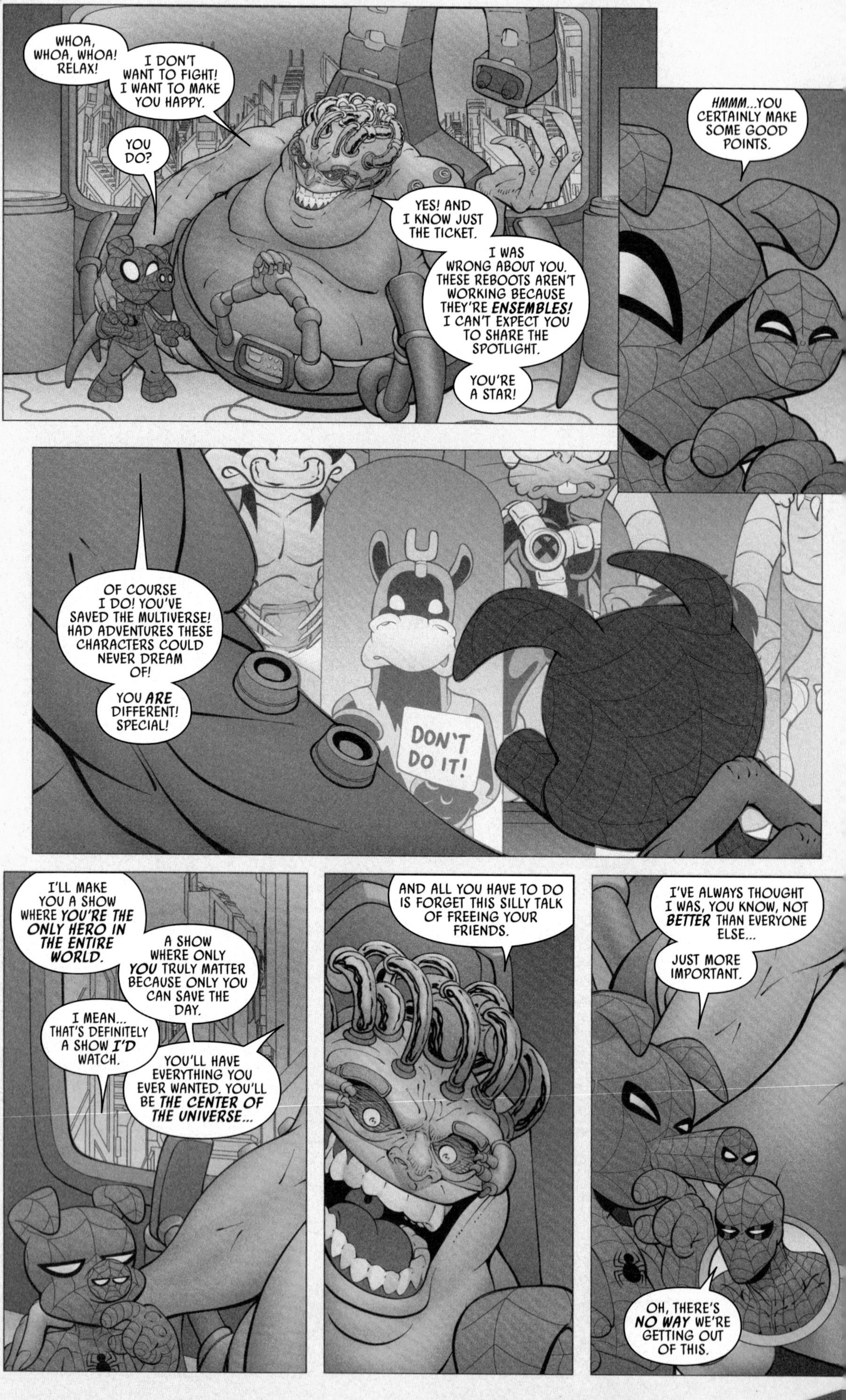
WHOA, WHOA, WHOA! RELAX!
I DON'T WANT TO FIGHT! I WANT TO MAKE YOU HAPPY.
YOU DO?
YES! AND I KNOW JUST THE TICKET.
I WAS WRONG ABOUT YOU. THESE REBOOTS AREN'T WORKING BECAUSE THEY'RE ENSEMBLES! I CAN'T EXPECT YOU TO SHARE THE SPOTLIGHT.
YOU'RE A STAR!
HMMM...YOU CERTAINLY MAKE SOME GOOD POINTS.
OF COURSE I DO! YOU'VE SAVED THE MULTIVERSE! HAD ADVENTURES THESE CHARACTERS COULD NEVER DREAM OF!
YOU ARE DIFFERENT! SPECIAL!
DON'T DO IT!
I'LL MAKE YOU A SHOW WHERE YOU'RE THE ONLY HERO IN THE ENTIRE WORLD.
A SHOW WHERE ONLY YOU TRULY MATTER BECAUSE ONLY YOU CAN SAVE THE DAY.
I MEAN... THAT'S DEFINITELY A SHOW I'D WATCH.
YOU'LL HAVE EVERYTHING YOU EVER WANTED. YOU'LL BE THE CENTER OF THE UNIVERSE...
AND ALL YOU HAVE TO DO IS FORGET THIS SILLY TALK OF FREEING YOUR FRIENDS.
I'VE ALWAYS THOUGHT I WAS, YOU KNOW, NOT BETTER THAN EVERYONE ELSE...
JUST MORE IMPORTANT.
OH, THERE'S NO WAY WE'RE GETTING OUT OF THIS.

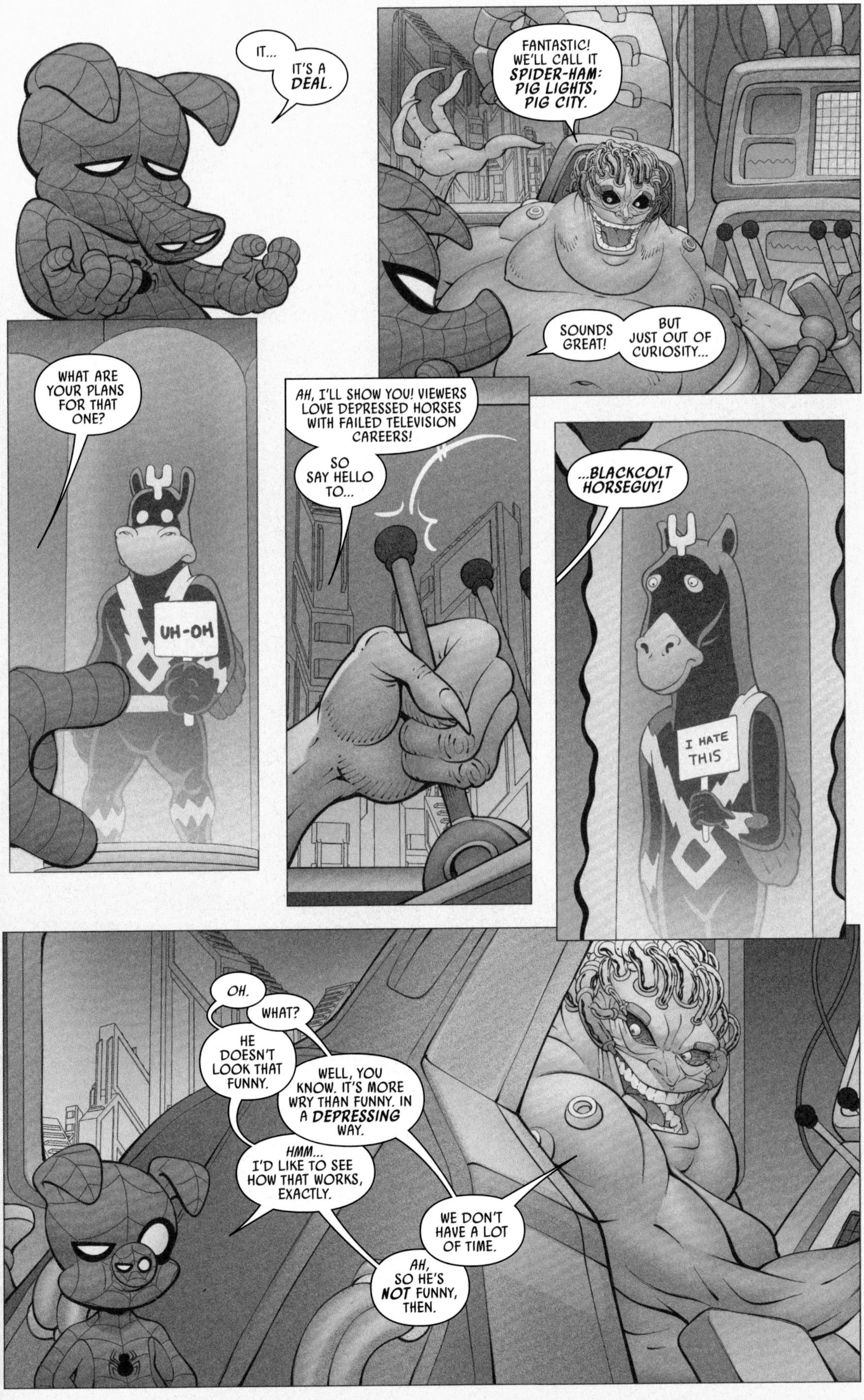
IT... IT'S A DEAL.
FANTASTIC! WE'LL CALL IT SPIDER-HAM: PIG LIGHTS, PIG CITY.
SOUNDS GREAT!
BUT JUST OUT OF CURIOSITY...
WHAT ARE YOUR PLANS FOR THAT ONE?
UH-OH
AH, I'LL SHOW YOU! VIEWERS LOVE DEPRESSED HORSES WITH FAILED TELEVISION CAREERS!
SO SAY HELLO TO...
...BLACKCOLT HORSEGUY!
I HATE THIS
OH.
WHAT?
HE DOESN'T LOOK THAT FUNNY.
WELL, YOU KNOW. IT'S MORE WRY THAN FUNNY. IN A DEPRESSING WAY.
HMM... I'D LIKE TO SEE HOW THAT WORKS, EXACTLY.
WE DON'T HAVE A LOT OF TIME.
AH, SO HE'S NOT FUNNY, THEN.

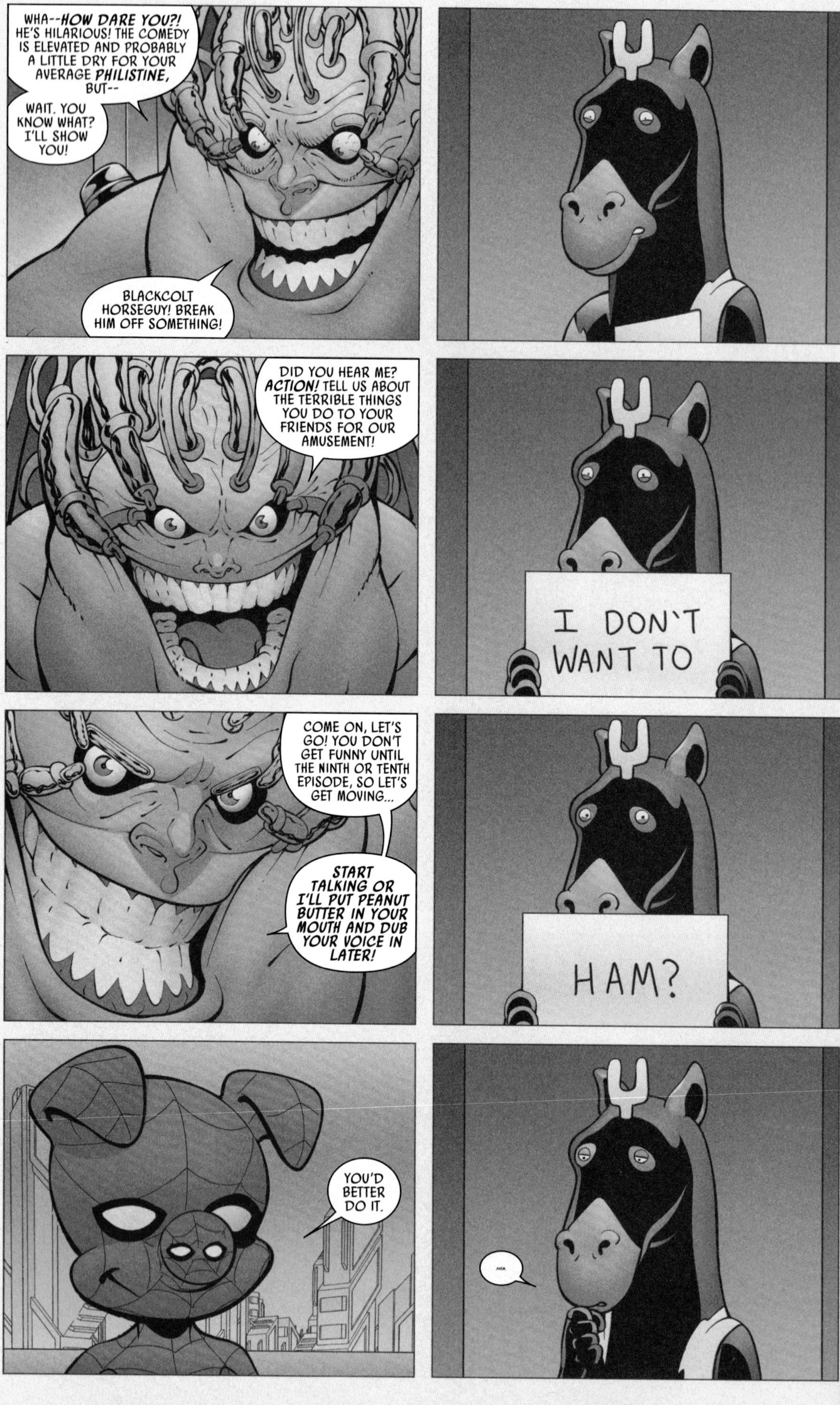
WHA--HOW DARE YOU?! HE'S HILARIOUS! THE COMEDY IS ELEVATED AND PROBABLY A LITTLE DRY FOR YOUR AVERAGE PHILISTINE, BUT--
WAIT. YOU KNOW WHAT? I'LL SHOW YOU!
BLACKCOLT HORSEGUY! BREAK HIM OFF SOMETHING!
DID YOU HEAR ME? ACTION! TELL US ABOUT THE TERRIBLE THINGS YOU DO TO YOUR FRIENDS FOR OUR AMUSEMENT!
I DON'T WANT TO
COME ON, LET'S GO! YOU DON'T GET FUNNY UNTIL THE NINTH OR TENTH EPISODE, SO LET'S GET MOVING...
START TALKING OR I'LL PUT PEANUT BUTTER IN YOUR MOUTH AND DUB YOUR VOICE IN LATER!
HAM?
YOU'D BETTER DO IT.
AHEM.

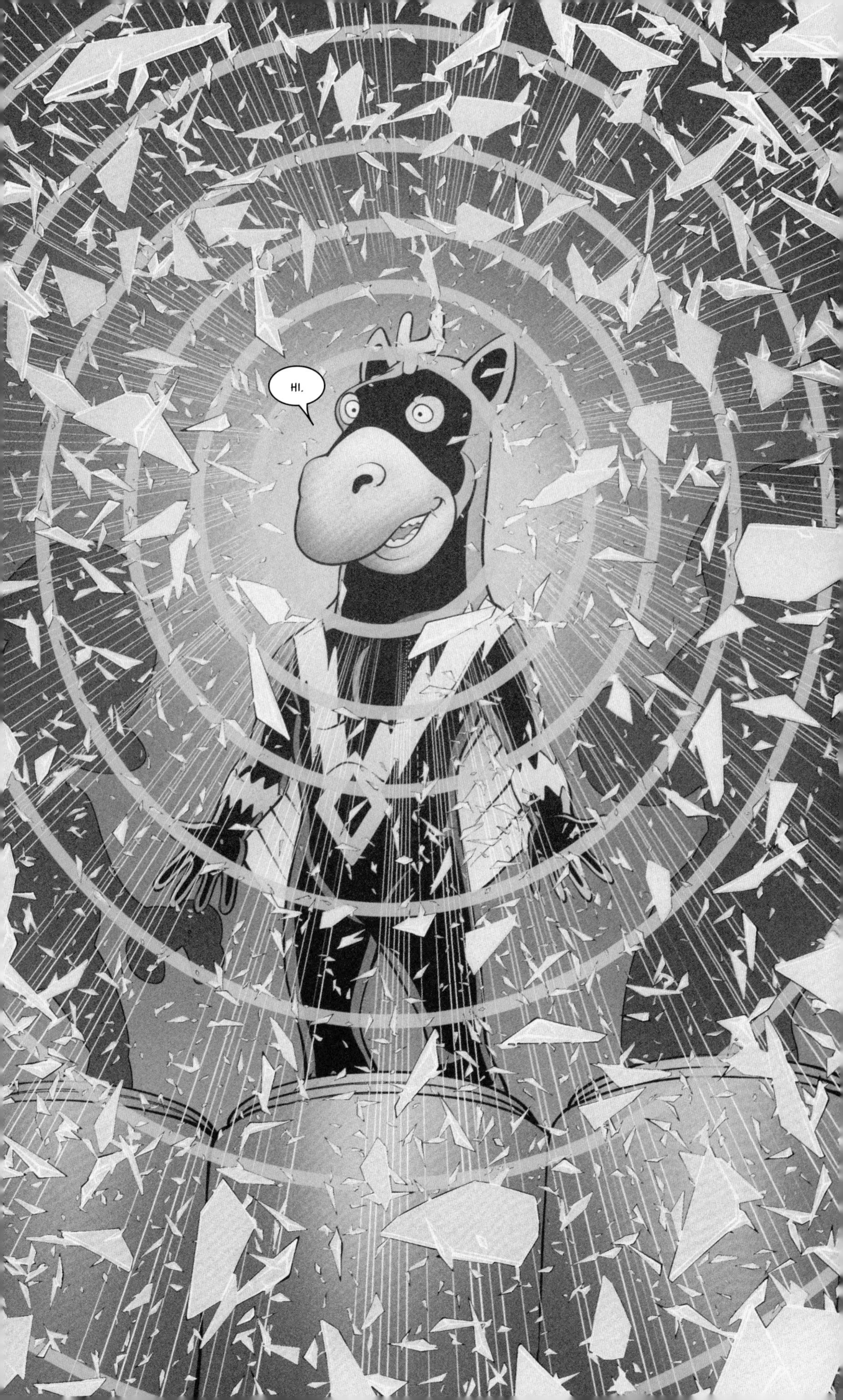
HI.

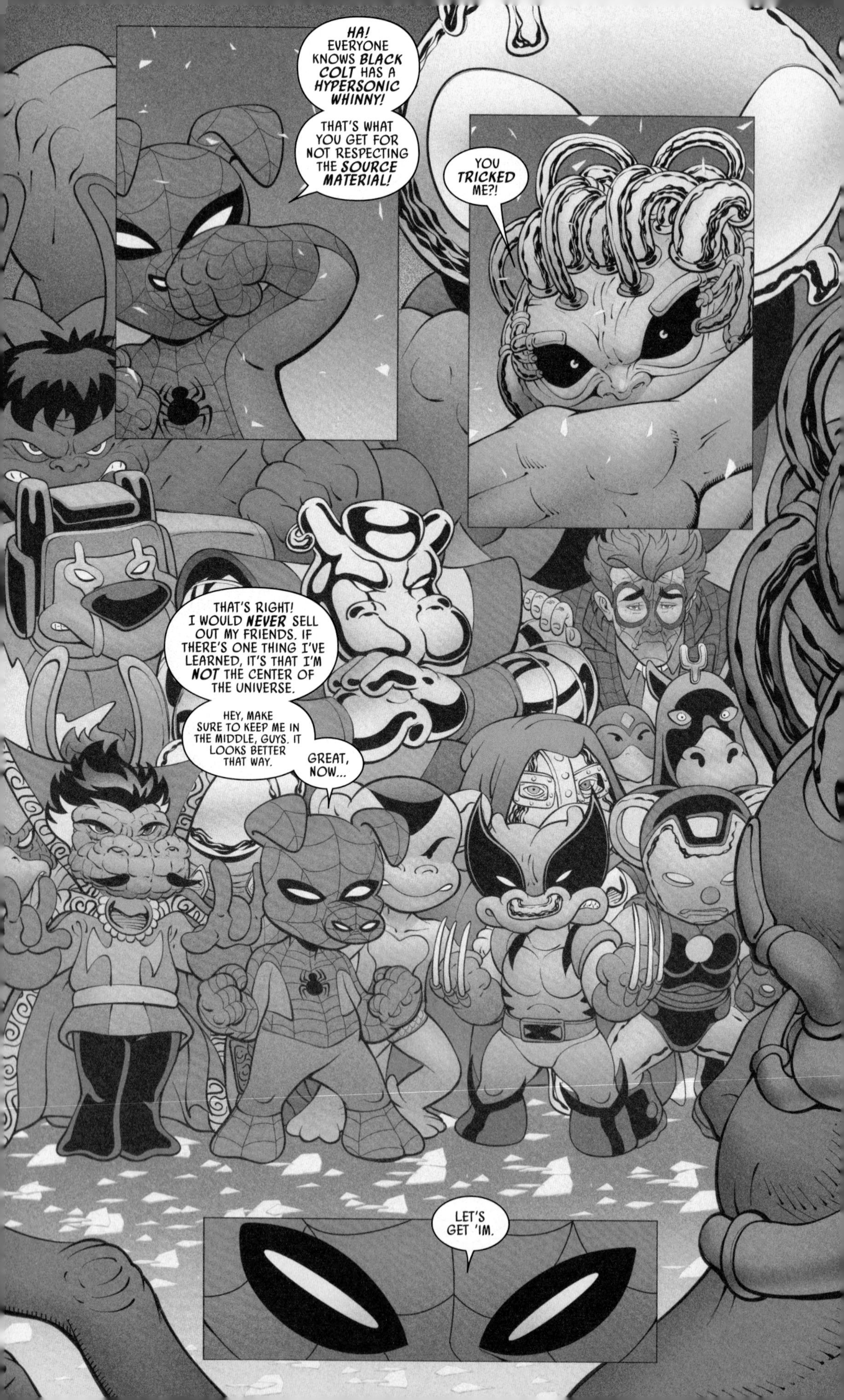
HA! EVERYONE KNOWS BLACK COLT HAS A HYPERSONIC WHINNY!
THAT'S WHAT YOU GET FOR NOT RESPECTING THE SOURCE MATERIAL!
YOU TRICKED ME?!
THAT'S RIGHT! I WOULD NEVER SELL OUT MY FRIENDS. IF THERE'S ONE THING I'VE LEARNED, IT'S THAT I'M NOT THE CENTER OF THE UNIVERSE.
HEY, MAKE SURE TO KEEP ME IN THE MIDDLE, GUYS. IT LOOKS BETTER THAT WAY.
GREAT, NOW...
LET'S GET 'IM.

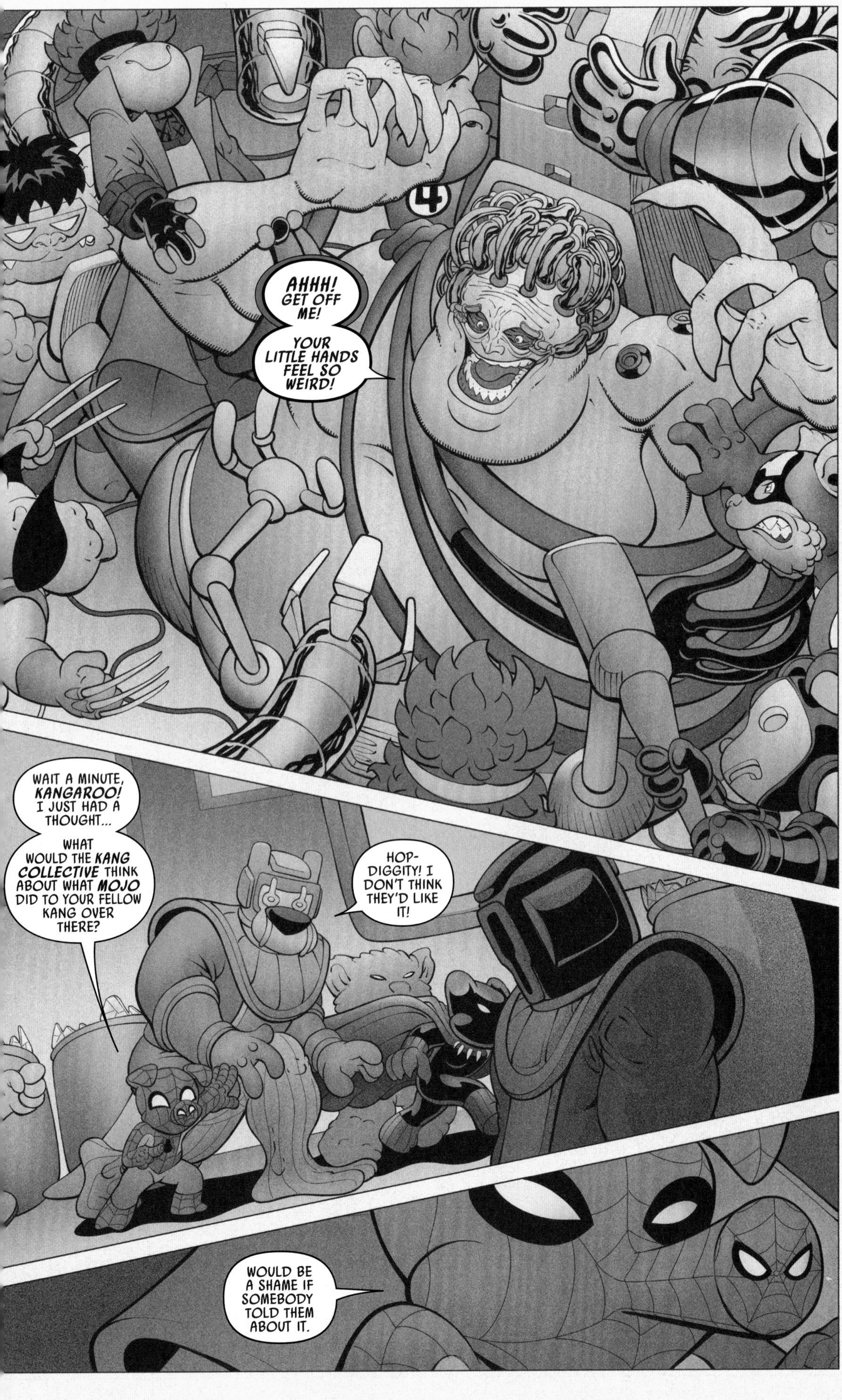
AHHH! GET OFF ME!
YOUR LITTLE HANDS FEEL SO WEIRD!
WAIT A MINUTE, KANGAROO! I JUST HAD A THOUGHT...
WHAT WOULD THE KANG COLLECTIVE THINK ABOUT WHAT MOJO DID TO YOUR FELLOW KANG OVER THERE?
HOP-DIGGITY! I DON'T THINK THEY'D LIKE IT!
WOULD BE A SHAME IF SOMEBODY TOLD THEM ABOUT IT.

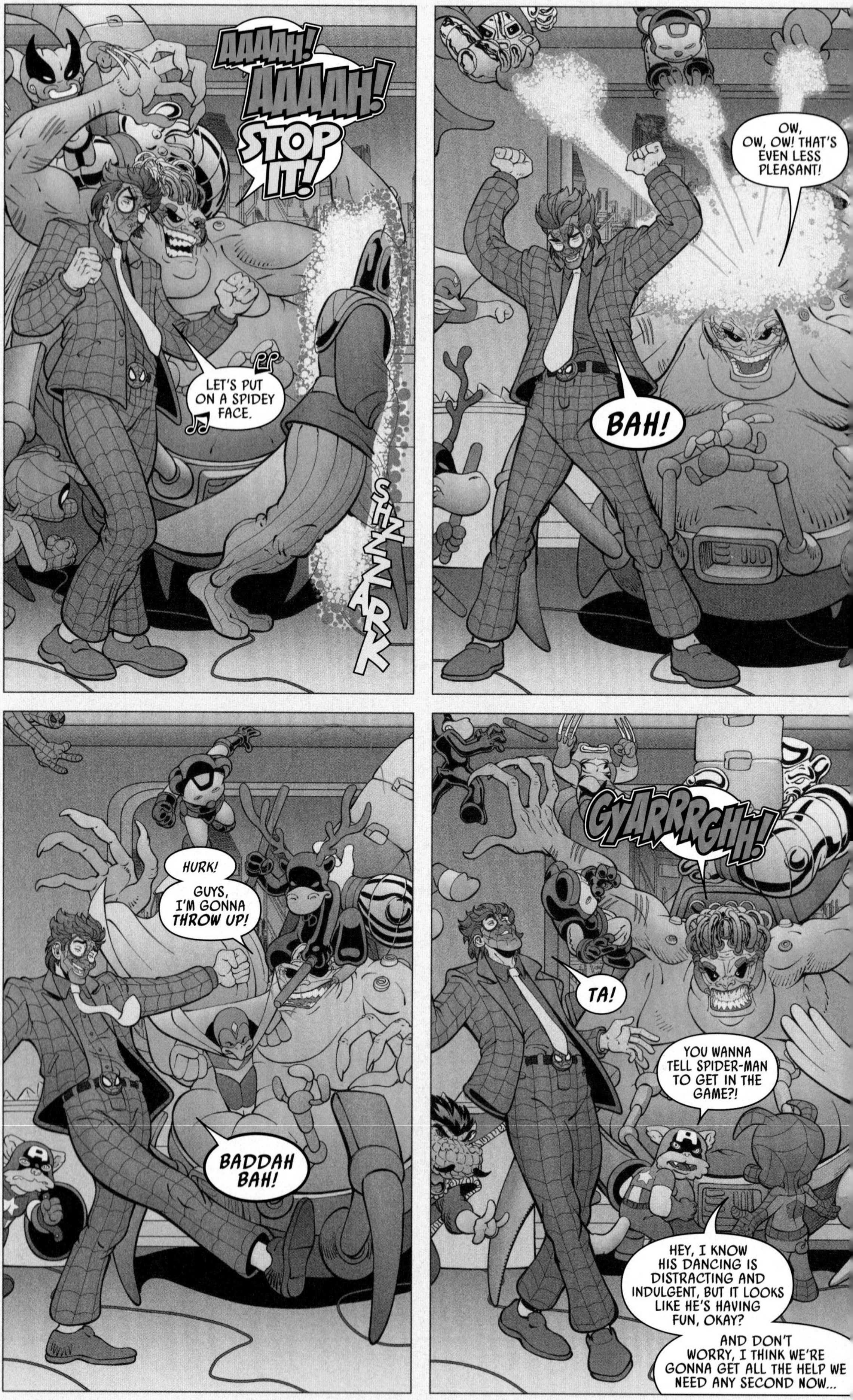
AAAAH! AAAAH! STOP IT!
LET'S PUT ON A SPIDEY FACE.
SHZZZARK
OW, OW, OW! THAT'S EVEN LESS PLEASANT!
BAH!
HURK!
GUYS, I'M GONNA THROW UP!
BADDAH BAH!
GYARRRGHH!
TA!
YOU WANNA TELL SPIDER-MAN TO GET IN THE GAME?!
HEY, I KNOW HIS DANCING IS DISTRACTING AND INDULGENT, BUT IT LOOKS LIKE HE'S HAVING FUN, OKAY?
AND DON'T WORRY, I THINK WE'RE GONNA GET ALL THE HELP WE NEED ANY SECOND NOW...

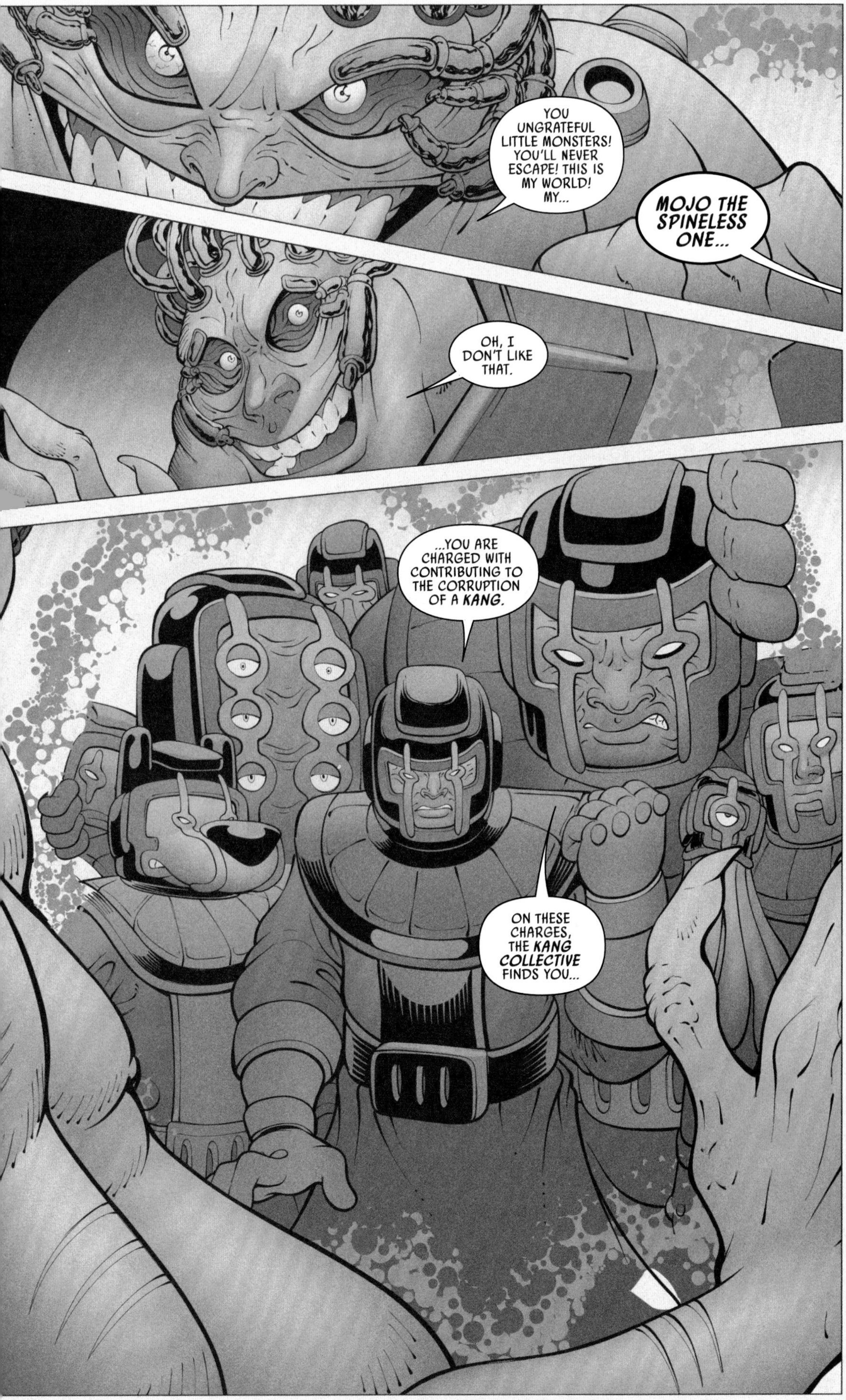
YOU UNGRATEFUL LITTLE MONSTERS! YOU'LL NEVER ESCAPE! THIS IS MY WORLD! MY...
MOJO THE SPINELESS ONE...
OH, I DON'T LIKE THAT.
...YOU ARE CHARGED WITH CONTRIBUTING TO THE CORRUPTION OF A KANG.
ON THESE CHARGES, THE KANG COLLECTIVE FINDS YOU...

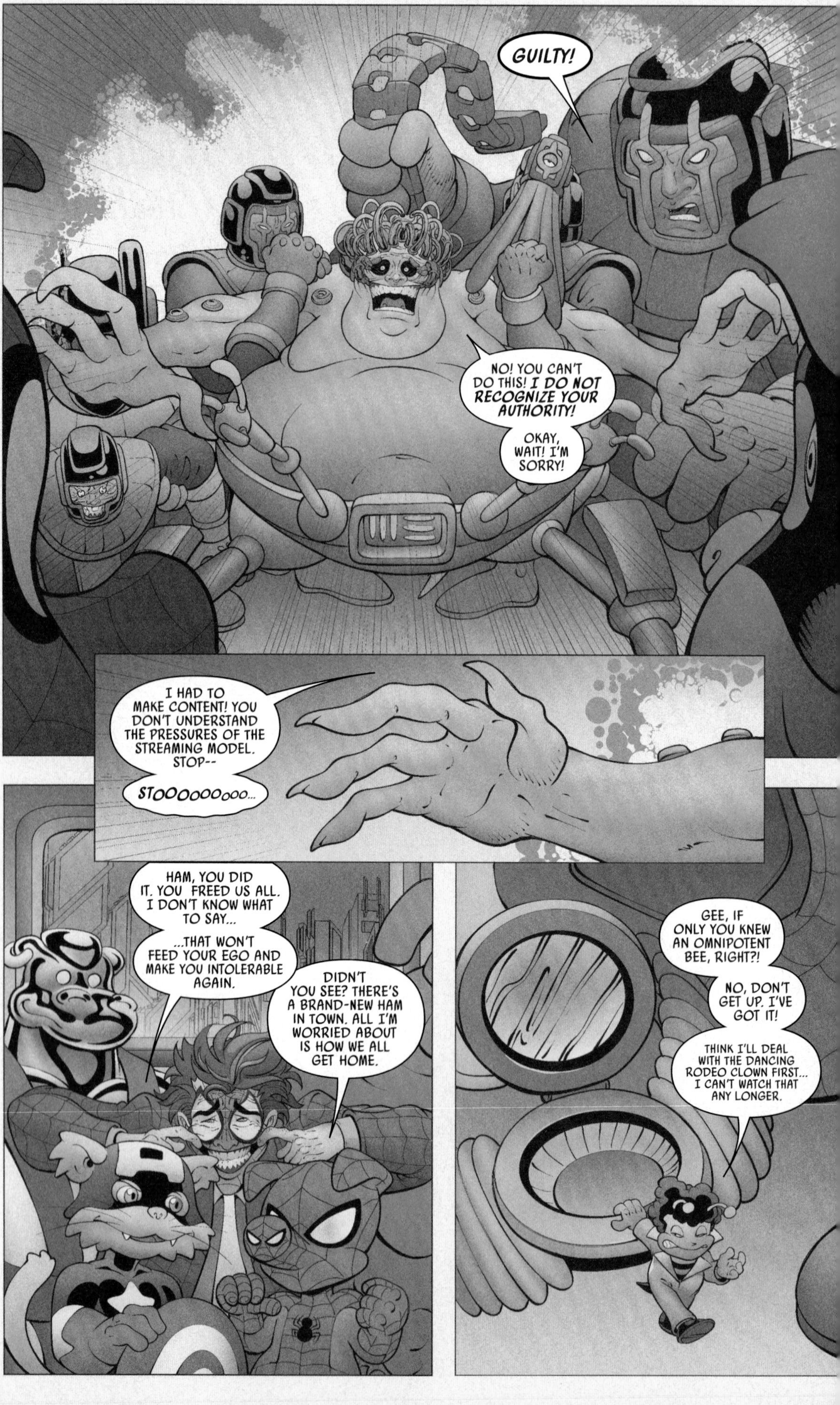
GUILTY!
NO! YOU CAN'T DO THIS! I DO NOT RECOGNIZE YOUR AUTHORITY!
OKAY, WAIT! I'M SORRY!
I HAD TO MAKE CONTENT! YOU DON'T UNDERSTAND THE PRESSURES OF THE STREAMING MODEL. STOP--
STOOOOOOOOO...
HAM, YOU DID IT. YOU FREED US ALL. I DON'T KNOW WHAT TO SAY...
...THAT WON'T FEED YOUR EGO AND MAKE YOU INTOLERABLE AGAIN.
DIDN'T YOU SEE? THERE'S A BRAND-NEW HAM IN TOWN. ALL I'M WORRIED ABOUT IS HOW WE ALL GET HOME.
GEE, IF ONLY YOU KNEW AN OMNIPOTENT BEE, RIGHT?!
NO, DON'T GET UP. I'VE GOT IT!
THINK I'LL DEAL WITH THE DANCING RODEO CLOWN FIRST... I CAN'T WATCH THAT ANY LONGER.

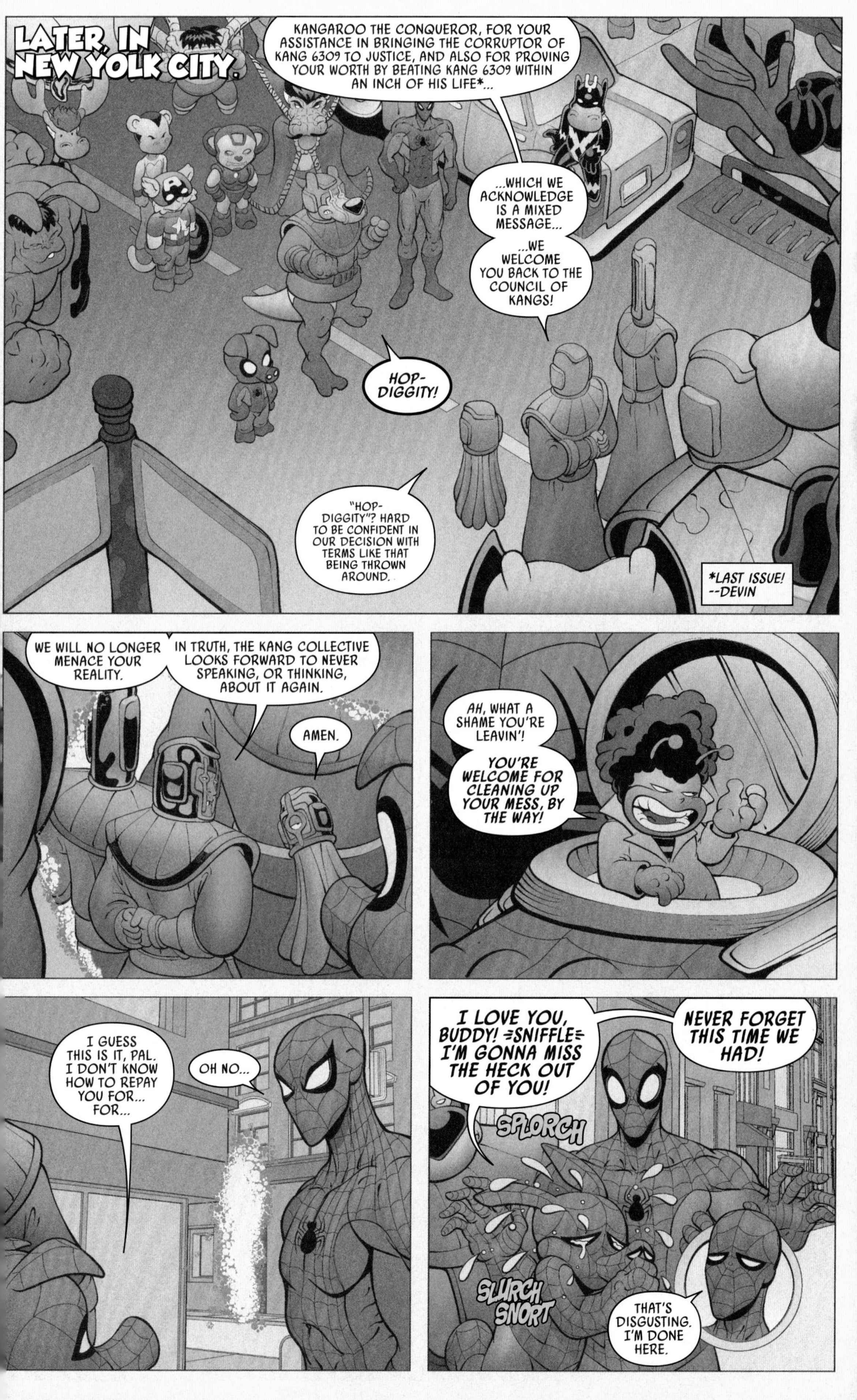

LATER, IN NEW YOLK CITY.
KANGAROO THE CONQUEROR, FOR YOUR ASSISTANCE IN BRINGING THE CORRUPTOR OF KANG 6309 TO JUSTICE, AND ALSO FOR PROVING YOUR WORTH BY BEATING KANG 6309 WITHIN AN INCH OF HIS LIFE*...
...WHICH WE ACKNOWLEDGE IS A MIXED MESSAGE...
...WE WELCOME YOU BACK TO THE COUNCIL OF KANGS!
HOP-DIGGITY!
"HOP-DIGGITY"? HARD TO BE CONFIDENT IN OUR DECISION WITH TERMS LIKE THAT BEING THROWN AROUND.
*LAST ISSUE! --DEVIN
WE WILL NO LONGER MENACE YOUR REALITY.
IN TRUTH, THE KANG COLLECTIVE LOOKS FORWARD TO NEVER SPEAKING, OR THINKING, ABOUT IT AGAIN.
AMEN.
AH, WHAT A SHAME YOU'RE LEAVIN'!
YOU'RE WELCOME FOR CLEANING UP YOUR MESS, BY THE WAY!
I GUESS THIS IS IT, PAL. I DON'T KNOW HOW TO REPAY YOU FOR... FOR...
OH NO...
I LOVE YOU, BUDDY! =SNIFFLE= I'M GONNA MISS THE HECK OUT OF YOU!
NEVER FORGET THIS TIME WE HAD!
SPLORCH
SLURCH
SNORT
THAT'S DISGUSTING. I'M DONE HERE.

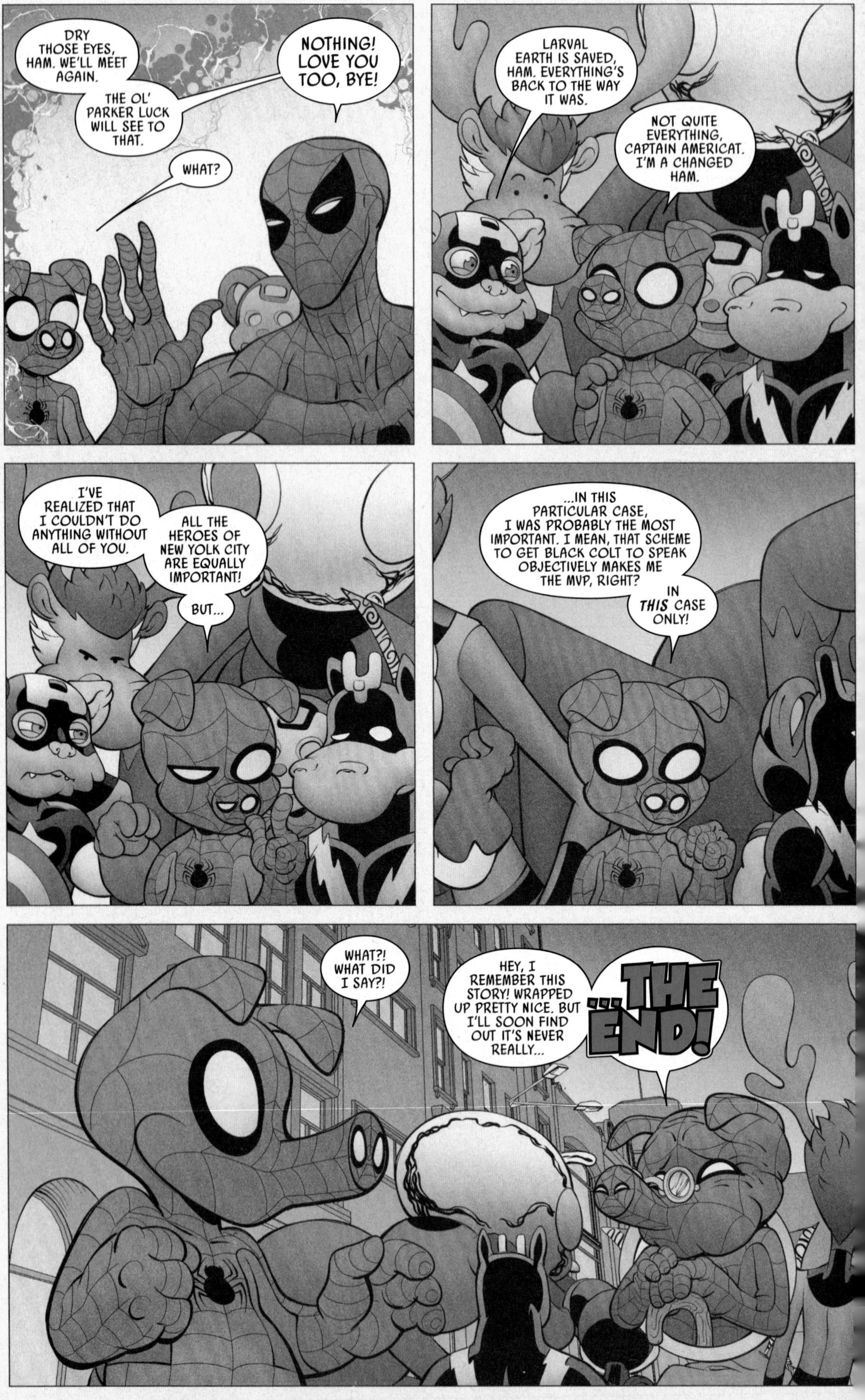
DRY THOSE EYES, HAM. WE'LL MEET AGAIN.
THE OL' PARKER LUCK WILL SEE TO THAT.
WHAT?
NOTHING! LOVE YOU TOO, BYE!
LARVAL EARTH IS SAVED, HAM. EVERYTHING'S BACK TO THE WAY IT WAS.
NOT QUITE EVERYTHING, CAPTAIN AMERICAT. I'M A CHANGED HAM.
I'VE REALIZED THAT I COULDN'T DO ANYTHING WITHOUT ALL OF YOU.
ALL THE HEROES OF NEW YOLK CITY ARE EQUALLY IMPORTANT!
BUT...
...IN THIS PARTICULAR CASE, I WAS PROBABLY THE MOST IMPORTANT. I MEAN, THAT SCHEME TO GET BLACK COLT TO SPEAK OBJECTIVELY MAKES ME THE MVP, RIGHT?
IN THIS CASE ONLY!
WHAT?! WHAT DID I SAY?!
HEY, I REMEMBER THIS STORY! WRAPPED UP PRETTY NICE. BUT I'LL SOON FIND OUT IT'S NEVER REALLY...
...THE END!

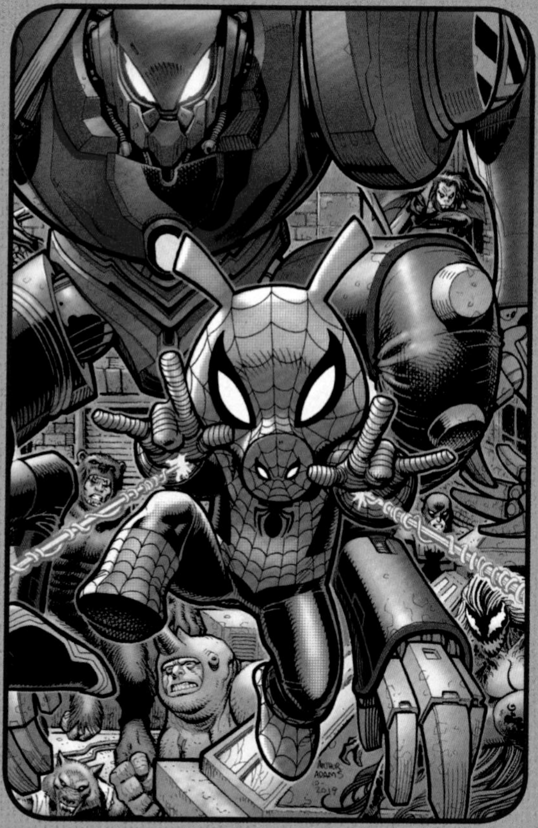

#1 CONNECTING VARIANT BY
ARTHUR ADAMS & EDGAR DELGADO

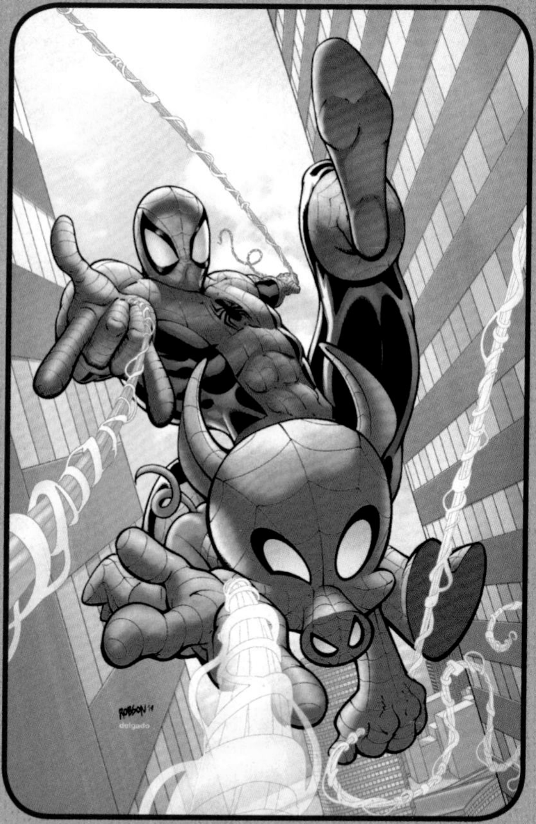

#1 VARIANT BY
WILL ROBSON & EDGAR DELGADO

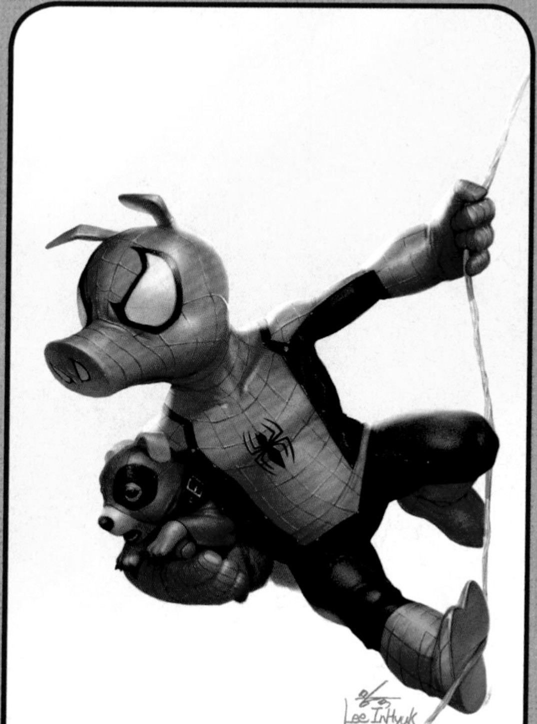

#1 VARIANT BY
INHYUK LEE

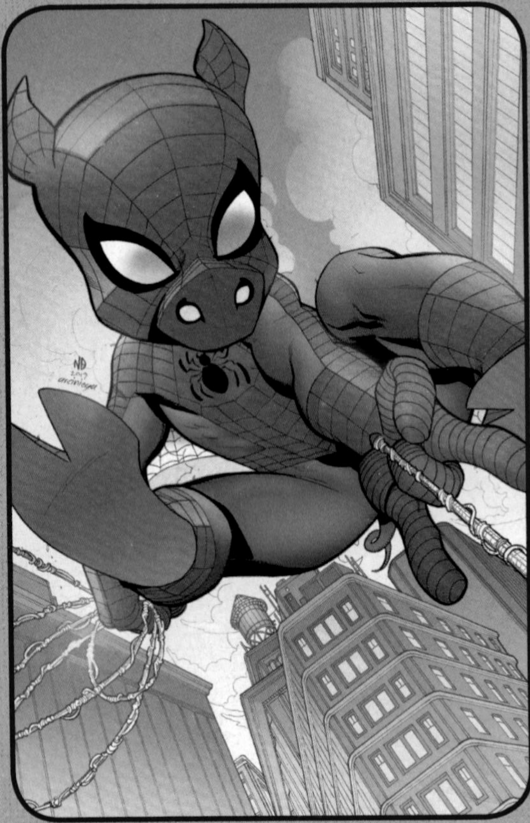

#2 VARIANT BY
NICK BRADSHAW & ERICK ARCINIEGA

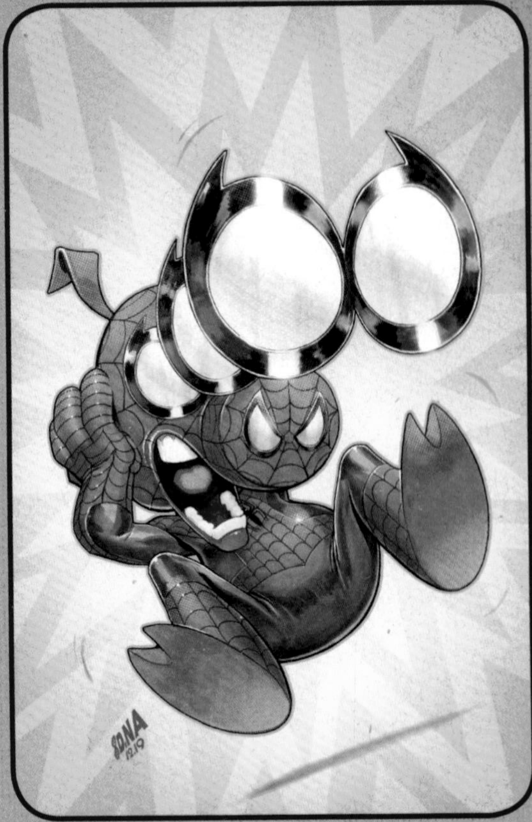

#3 VARIANT BY
DAVID NAKAYAMA

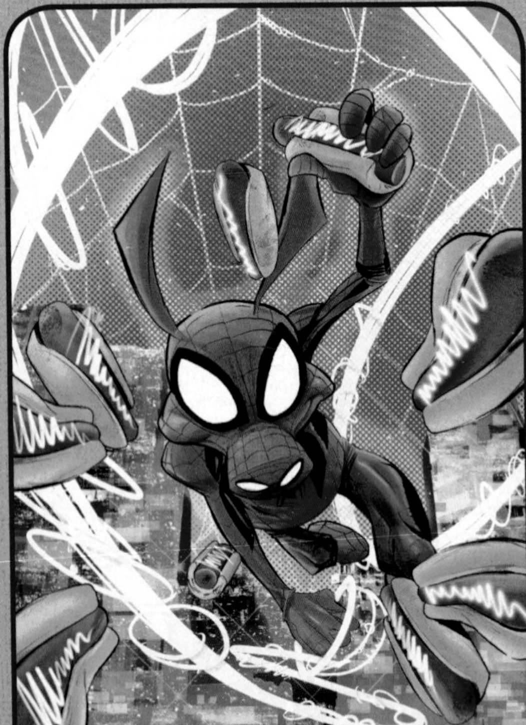

#4 VARIANT BY
ROBBI RODRIGUEZ

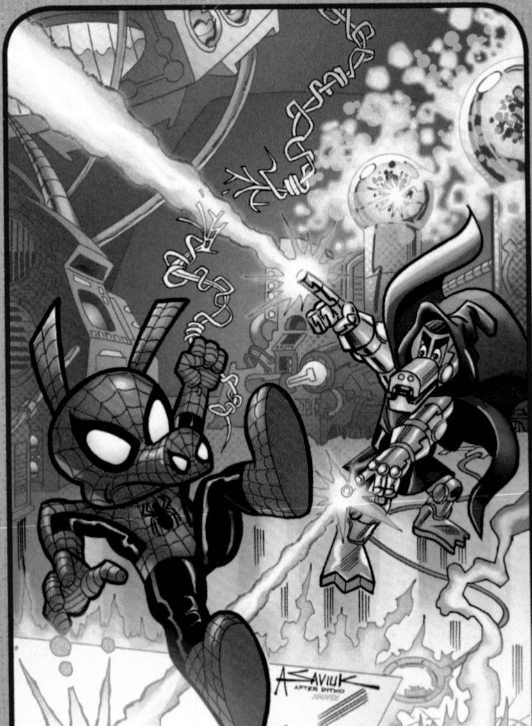

#5 VARIANT BY
ALEX SAVIUK & CHRIS SOTOMAYOR